THE
STATE OF

THE REAL
STATE OF
THE UNION

From the Best Minds in America,
Bold Solutions to the Problems
Politicians Dare Not Address

TED HALSTEAD

NEW
AMERICA
BOOKS

A New America Book, Published by Basic Books
A Member of the Perseus Books Group
New York

Books published by Basic Books are available at special discounts for bulk purchases in
the United States by corporations, institutions, and other organizations. For more
information, please contact the Special Markets Department at the Perseus Books
Group, 11 Cambridge Center, Cambridge MA 02142, or call (617) 252–5298, (800)
255–1514 or e-mail special.markets@perseusbooks.com.

Designed by Bookcomp, Inc.

Library of Congress Cataloging-in-Publication Data

The Real State of the Union / [edited by] Ted Halstead.
        p. cm.
    Includes bibliographical references and index.
    ISBN 0-465-05052-2 (alk. paper)
    1. United States—Social conditions—1980–   2. United States—Economic
conditions—2001–   3. United States—Politics and government—2001–
I. Halstead, Ted.   II. Title.

    HN59.2.R433 2004
    306'.0973—dc22   2003028163

04 05 06 / 10 9 8 7 6 5 4 3 2 1

Contents

CONCLUSION

PREFACE

Ted Halstead

Let all of us pause now, think back, consider carefully the meaning of our national experience. Let us draw comfort from it and faith and confidence in our future as Americans.

The Nation's business is never finished. The basic questions we have been dealing with . . . present themselves anew. That is the way of our society. Circumstances change and current questions take on different forms, new complications, year by year. But underneath the great issues remain the same—prosperity, welfare, human rights, effective democracy, and, above all, peace.

—Harry S. Truman, State of the Union Address,
January 7, 1953

ONE OF THE OLDEST traditions in American politics—spanning from George Washington to George W. Bush—is the yearly delivery by the President of what used to be known as the "Annual Message." Renamed the "State of the Union" address in 1945, it provides a precious opportunity for the President to shape the national debate by presenting his assessment of the health of our republic and advancing specific recommendations for reform. The history of the United States—as seen through the eyes of each President—is told in these addresses.

In recent decades, unfortunately, the State of the Union address has become both shallower and more partisan. It is now largely an exercise in self-congratulatory rhetoric and showmanship, loaded with snappy sound bites and made-for-television tributes to special guests planted in the audience. It wasn't always this way. If you go back and read the annual addresses of Washington, Lincoln, Theodore Roosevelt, Franklin Delano Roosevelt, Truman, or Eisenhower—to name just a few—they are remarkably candid and substantive by today's standards.

The words quoted above from Harry Truman's final address reflect this seriousness of spirit.

The trivialization of the State of the Union address is all the more troubling in light of the challenges that America faces today. This is a moment of consequence in American history. When Al Gore faced off with George W. Bush in the 2000 election, most Americans could be forgiven for thinking that there was not that much at stake: after all, we were basking in the afterglow of our nation's longest economic expansion and considered ourselves largely immune to the dangers plaguing the rest of the world. All of that suddenly changed, of course, as the result of the tragedy of 9/11, the implosion of the Nasdaq bubble, a stream of corporate scandals, the erosion of jobs at home, and two costly foreign wars in rapid succession.

In contrast to the election of 2000, then, it seems clear that a great deal will be at stake in the election of 2004. Yet for all the new and daunting challenges confronting America at home and abroad, neither Democrats nor Republicans have proven capable of offering a coherent, honest, or forward-looking agenda to guide our country. More concerned with petty partisanship than with pragmatic progress, our contemporary political leaders have shown themselves to be incapable of solving—and in some cases even acknowledging—the overarching dilemmas of our time.

One of those is the impending retirement of the baby boom generation, which given our low personal savings rate, will put tremendous strain on the public purse in years ahead. Instead of facing this challenge honestly, both parties recently colluded to make it worse by supporting a large-scale expansion of Medicare, the most insolvent of the entitlement programs. It is as if a fire truck pulled up to a burning house, only to spray gasoline on the flames instead of water. Their rationale is to pander to the elderly voting bloc while avoiding for as long as possible the unpleasantness of stating the obvious: The coming entitlement crunch will force us to cut benefits, raise taxes, or both.

Another challenge is how to maintain a broad-based middle-class in the face of increasing global competition that is driving down the cost of labor and capital while eroding our manufacturing base. Neither the supply-side tax-cuts, Keynesian spending binge and economic protectionism of the GOP, nor the Clintonian combination of financial liberalization, fiscal discipline, and mild redistributionism provide adequate formulas for ensuring that the new tide continues to rise and to lift all boats in the process. That America succeeded in building the world's first mass middle-class was not by accident; it owed a great deal to a series of public policy interventions that were as bold as they were enlightened. Preserving and expanding our middle class in the future will require no less.

Profound structural inefficiencies—especially in the ways we approach health care, education, and energy use—also threaten our collective well-being. Although America spends more per capita on health care and K-12 education than virtually any other nation, our return on these investments is uniquely low: spiraling health care costs alongside inadequate quality and coverage, and educational outcomes inferior to those of other advanced nations alongside vast disparities in school funding and student achievement within our own borders. Meanwhile, we consume far more energy inputs per unit of economic outputs than our closest competitors, placing us at a considerable economic and environmental disadvantage.

Just as the American economy is undergoing tectonic transformations in the post-industrial age, so is the American community. And just as our politicians are failing to respond adequately to the former, so too with the latter. The American family, in particular, has changed dramatically in recent decades as more women enter the workforce and as families with no stay-at-home parent become the new norm. Sadly, neither the workplace itself nor government policies have kept pace with these changes, making it ever more difficult for Americans to balance their work and family responsibilities. At the same time, the very identity of our nation is constantly evolving, largely as a result of population aging, increased immigration, and high levels of racial inter-marriage. These developments carry good news and bad: The coming of a post-minority America, for instance, is cause for celebration, while the growing alienation of Muslim Americans is cause for concern.

When it comes to foreign policy, both Republicans and Democrats seem equally convinced that countering terrorism is now the defining challenge to the world order and that preserving America's dominance in the world is the best grand strategy. Yet there is a strong case to be made that the greatest threat to the world order could come from a global economic collapse, and that we can best advance our national interest through pooled sovereignty and a multilateral division of labor. At the same time, neither party has set forth a convincing strategy to wean ourselves from an over-dependence on foreign capital, or to counter the proliferation of weapons of mass destruction without abandoning the internationalism and alliance-building that enabled us to safely pass the first nuclear age.

More broadly, both major parties lack a vision able to strengthen and unify the American people in the face of the fragmenting and destabilizing forces remaking America. The inevitable result is an erosion of trust, whether trust in our fellow citizens, in politicians, or in private or public institutions. Today, neither party is even able to articulate an updated vision of citizenship or patriotic responsibility, as became painfully obvious in the wake of 9/11 when the majority of Americans were more than willing to make sacrifices for the good of their nation, if only their leaders would point the way.

To judge from our political establishment, it would seem that America is a nation bitterly divided along partisan lines. Likewise, it would seem that we are beset by collective problems that are simply intractable. Neither assumption is accurate.

The American people are not nearly as polarized as their elected officials. To the contrary, polls consistently reveal that most Americans consider themselves to be "moderates" rather than "liberals" or "conservatives," and that more identify as "independents" than as Republicans or Democrats. Given the recent performance of both parties, it is hardly surprising that so many Americans feel alienated from politics. But alienation and polarization are two very different conditions, though the former will only worsen if politicians fail to cure the latter.

It would be no less of a mistake to assume that our nation's foremost problems are beyond remedy. They may be—if the range of potential solutions is limited by antiquated or partisan ideologies. But if we are willing to look at these problems anew, from an unbiased and practical perspective, there is reason for optimism. Many of these problems, in fact, suddenly seem much more solvable. That is the basic contention of these essays.

THIS BOOK WAS CONCEIVED through a unique partnership between the New America Foundation and *The Atlantic Monthly*— with the goal of renewing the great annual tradition of reflection on the true state of the American union. It invites the reader to ask two far-reaching questions: How are we really doing as a country? What practical steps could we take to improve our national condition?

What follows are 32 essays on many of the most important facets of our nation's well-being, written by some of the most talented and original minds of our day. What ties them together is a commitment to an honest search for innovative and non-partisan solutions. Most essays begin with the best empirical data in their subject area, and seek to uncover the root causes of the problem at hand. In many cases, the authors offer solutions that are simultaneously bold and practical. These solutions seldom fit comfortably in the familiar boxes of left and right. If there is a discernable ideological bent to them, its name is the radical center.

All authors—with the exception of Matthew Miller, Jonathan Rauch, and Paul Starobin—are directly affiliated with the New America Foundation, whether as Fellows, senior staff, or members of our Board of Directors. Two-thirds of the essays that appear in this book were first published in the January 2003 or 2004 issues of *The Atlantic Monthly*.

The Real State of the Union reflects the commitment of the New America Foundation to escaping the ideological orthodoxies of the twentieth century in order to do justice to the greatest challenges facing the United States at the beginning of the twenty-first. Only by embracing a new spirit of heterodoxy, creativity, and pragmatism can we learn what the actual state of the union is—and how much better it could be.

INTRODUCTION

1

The State of the Union Moment

James Fallows

It is startling how out-of-date and out-of-touch our official politics has become.

AT KABUKI PERFORMANCES in Japan audiences sometimes exclaim "*Matte mashita!*" during crucial points in the drama. In context this means something like "Here it comes!" or "This is what we've been waiting for!" and it greets the best-known lines in the play. If American theatergoers followed the same custom, people would yell "*Matte mashita!*" when they heard "To be or not to be . . ." in *Hamlet* or "I'll be back" in a Terminator movie.

In American political culture, which displays some of the same affection for formulaic stagecraft, the theatrical highlight of the year is the State of the Union address. Presidents have presented Congress with reports on the state of national affairs since the republic's beginning, as required by the Constitution. But since Woodrow Wilson established the modern custom of a President's delivering the report in person, in a speech to a special session of Congress, the State of the Union address has evolved into the main kabuki-like ceremony in our national politics.

Even more than the inauguration, the State of the Union has become a ritual celebration of the glory of the presidency. At an inauguration the excitement surrounding the President is often tempered by the pathos of an old President's being ushered off the scene. The State of the Union is all about the incumbent.

3

With live TV cameras on them, representatives and even proud senators fidget in a packed House chamber until the President arrives. Foreign diplomats troop in to pay the world's respects to America's leader. The military chiefs of staff, in their uniforms, are there; the justices of the Supreme Court, in their robes; the members of the Cabinet—minus one, who will take over the government in case of disaster. Honored guests, whose achievements will be praised in the speech, are seated near the President's spouse. With all the supporting cast in place, the sergeant at arms comes to the chamber's door—and the President makes his way toward the dais through a crowd of cheering politicians from both parties, many reaching to touch him as he moves by. He stands at the front of the chamber until the cheers finally die—and as soon as they do, the speaker of the House plays his role in the drama. He tells his colleagues that he has the "high privilege and the distinct honor in presenting to you the President of the United States." As he utters these words, another minutes-long standing ovation begins.

On it goes for most of the next hour: the President's backers cheering the partisan items in his list of proposals, the opposition sitting noticeably still at those moments. The Vice President and the speaker of the House, onstage props visible whenever the President is on camera, try to sit still at all times. Perhaps at the beginning of the speech, perhaps at the end, the President builds toward his *Matte mashita!* line. "The state of the union," he tells the crowd—which prepares to cheer, knowing that the expected sentence has arrived—"is *good.*"

Or perhaps it's not just "good." It was good "with room for improvement" according to Gerald Ford as he prepared to leave office in 1977; and it was "sound" according to Jimmy Carter the following year. For Bill Clinton in 1995, speaking after his party had been routed in midterm elections, the state of the union was merely "stronger than it was two years ago." By the end of his second term Clinton was ready to declare the state of the union "the strongest it has ever been." George W. Bush began his first State of the Union address, as bombs fell in Afghanistan, with the speech's punch line, an artful two-sentence version of the usual one-liner: "As we gather tonight, our nation is at war, our economy is in recession, and the civilized world faces unprecedented dangers. Yet the state of our union has never been stronger."

In its substance as in its procedural pomp, the State of the Union address has come to represent all that is ritualistic and insiderish about modern politics. It is the one major speech a President is sure to deliver each year. Therefore, the day after one address has been given, much of the government gears up to influence the content of the next year's. The impetus comes in the coded language of Washington: a sentence here about the "high priority" of some new education program, which can be used to defend an extra $100 million in budget requests; a mention there of a "strong new partnership" with a certain country, which can settle a dispute between the State Department and the Pentagon. Speechwriters dread this speech as they do no other assignment (or at least I did, when working for Jimmy Carter), because so many forces conspire to make it a clotted, committee-bred document whose hidden signals the ordinary listener will completely miss. The closest thing to a memorable line in recent addresses was Bill Clinton's declaration, in 1996, that "the era of big government is over."

THE ODDITY OF THIS SITUATION is that although the State of the Union in the Washington sense has become stylized and removed from everyday American concerns, the real state of the union is of enormous social and cultural interest. Pollsters have known for years that one question above all indicates Americans' satisfaction with public life and confidence in their leaders—the question that is typically phrased as "In general, do you feel that things in America are moving in the right direction or the wrong direction?" This is another way of asking whether the state of the union is sound—and when answering the question, people consider a wide range of concerns: How they and their family members are doing, materially and spiritually. What they observe or believe about others. What they think the future will bring. To what extent they feel in control of events, rather than feeling like objects or victims. Some components of this real state of the union are purely private matters, but many others are part of the environment that public life is supposed to help determine. The education system, the robustness of the national economic base, the physical safety of citizens, their pride in what the nation stands for—these and many other areas involve politics to some degree.

That the components of the real state of the union are complex and subjective doesn't mean they can't be discussed—and in many cases measured. An attempt to think broadly and originally about these elements of national well-being lies behind this special section. Some of the essays that follow offer specific action plans; others identify trends to watch. And although they are political in the broadest sense, most don't bother with comparisons of the Democratic and Republican positions on the subject at hand. The assumption is that in most of the areas under discussion the major-party platforms are essentially fundraising tools or ways to organize blocs of interest groups.

Lasting principles and clear, simple statements do rise above the specifics of any situation. But it is startling how out-of-date and out-of-touch each party's platform seems when compared with the details in the essays that follow. Indeed, if one theme emerges from these essays, it is how disconnected our official politics has become from the real-world, fast-changing, interesting-in-their-details elements that constitute our national welfare.

Americans have traditionally been vain about their pragmatism. Let the French have their *philosophes*, the British and the Germans their aristocrats who stand on ceremony. Ours would be the culture of the doer, the tinkerer, the keen observer who noticed what actually worked. In ideal form the American leader would be a Benjamin Franklin, with lofty interests but an unshakably realistic bent. Better, he would be a Lincoln: a true visionary who also recognized that the drunken General Grant was the best man for the job.

Lincoln, too, issued State of the Union messages, at a time when the existence of the union itself was in question. His second, in 1862, is the most memorable. "The dogmas of the quiet past, are inadequate to the stormy present," he said. "As our case is new, so we must think anew, and act anew." We offer these essays in that spirit.

2

The American Paradox

Ted Halstead

The richest and most powerful country is also the one with the highest levels of poverty, homicide, and infant mortality among modern democracies. A case for revising our social contract.

NOTHING ILLUSTRATES AMERICA'S profound contradictions more starkly than a comparison with other advanced democracies: among these the United States is either the very best or the very worst performer on a wide range of social and economic criteria. We are simultaneously the leader and the laggard among our peers—almost always exceptional, almost never in the middle.

Without question we are the richest, most powerful, and most creative nation on the planet. Our economic and military might stems from our embrace of a particularly high-octane brand of capitalism, supported by financial markets that are deeper and broader than any others, labor markets that are more flexible, and a culture of entrepreneurialism that is unparalleled. These attributes have turned America into the world's unrivaled engine of innovation and wealth creation. We boast more patent applications than the entire European Union; more Nobel Prizes, in recent decades, than the rest of the world combined; and more business start-ups per capita than almost every other advanced democracy. One in twelve Americans will start his or her own business, evincing another outstanding American trait—our great tolerance for risk. And our export of movies, television shows, music, and fast-food chains makes us, for better or worse, the dominant cultural force on the globe.

But like the Roman god Janus, America has two faces. Despite being the richest nation on the planet, we suffer from higher rates of poverty, infant mortality, homicide, and HIV infection, and from greater economic inequality, than other advanced democracies. We have far more uninsured citizens, and a lower life expectancy. On a per capita basis the United States emits considerably more greenhouse gases and produces more solid waste. We spend more per student on K-12 education than almost all other modern democracies, yet our students perform near the bottom on international tests. We have the highest rates of teen pregnancy and among the highest proportions of single parents, and American parents have the least amount of free time to spend with their children; indeed, the average American works nine weeks more each year than the average European. Our performance on many social indicators is so poor, in fact, that an outsider looking at these numbers alone might conclude that we were a developing nation.

How do we reconcile these two faces of America? To a remarkable degree the United States seems to have exchanged social cohesion and a broad-based middle class for economic dynamism and personal freedom. Have we abandoned what used to be referred to as the common good?

SOME BELIEVE THAT our bifurcated national condition represents a necessary and acceptable tradeoff; others believe it is a Faustian bargain. Even those who would tolerate a considerable amount of social fragmentation as the price of prosperity, however, must concede that this bargain is yielding ever diminishing returns. Our economic growth over the past decade has been weaker than it was in the 1950s and 1960s. Yet our levels of economic inequality and social breakdown have clearly worsened. In short, we are producing fewer of the goods and more of the bads, suggesting that our nation is increasingly out of balance. What is more, the very idea of a necessary tradeoff between our social and our economic well-being is un-American. It runs against the idealistic foundation on which our republic was built.

To improve the nation's social health and economic vitality at one and the same time will require a new social contract for America. Our current social contract is now as antiquated as it was once innovative. Its primary author, Franklin Delano Roosevelt, would be the first to tell

THE TWO FACES OF AMERICA

This list of "bests" and "worsts" is based on a variety
of sources—including statistics from the United
Nations and the Organization for Economic Cooperation
and Development, and a number of other groups and
experts—but the basic criteria are consistent. Among
advanced democracies, America had to rank in the top
three for a category to be listed under "bests," and in the
bottom three for a category to be listed under "worsts."
(Where applicable, all rankings were determined on
a rate basis or as a percentage of total population.)

BESTS	WORSTS
Gross domestic product	Poverty
Productivity	Economic inequality
Business start-ups	Carbon dioxide emissions
Long-term unemployment	Life expectancy
Expenditure on education	Infant mortality
University graduates	Homicide
R&D expenditure	Healthcare coverage
High-tech exports	HIV infection
Movies exported	Teen pregnancy
Breadth of stock ownership	Personal savings
Volunteerism	Voter participation
Charitable giving	Obesity

us so. "New conditions impose new requirements upon government
and those who conduct government," Roosevelt said in 1932. "Faith in
America, faith in our tradition of personal responsibility, faith in our
institutions, faith in ourselves, demand that we recognize the new terms
of the old social contract."

America has so far experimented with three social contracts, each of
which reflected the political forces of its time. The purpose of the first,

in the eighteenth century, was to found a nation. The goal of the second was to put it back together after the Civil War. The third—first articulated in FDR's New Deal and later expanded in Lyndon B. Johnson's Great Society—sought to build a mass middle-class society by relying on ambitious government programs and new economic regulation.

It is now time for a fourth American social contract. To fit the post-industrial age it must be able to reconcile the competing demands of flexibility and fairness. In a time characterized by constant job mobility, a proliferation of consumer choices, just-in-time production, and—perhaps most of all—increased uncertainty, individuals, firms, and governments all need unprecedented flexibility. Fairness, meanwhile, springs from the commitments to meritocracy and shared prosperity that have inspired our nation since its inception. A social contract that simultaneously enhances both flexibility and fairness will require new roles and responsibilities for all three parties to the contract: government, business, and the citizenry.

In the public sector our political leaders must stop imposing false choices on the American people. All too often our two-party system frames issues as if flexibility and fairness were mutually exclusive. Republicans are fond of advocating for school choice and Social Security privatization, on the grounds that these would confer more choices and flexibility on all citizens. Democrats, meanwhile, typically oppose such proposals, on the grounds that they would undermine fairness and the economic security of ordinary citizens. As the essays that follow suggest, however, there are elegant ways to square these circles: for instance, by pairing school choice with a national equalization of school funding.

Our elected officials must dare to think big once more. Major advances in our nation's well-being have usually resulted not from tinkering at the margins of existing institutions but, rather, from bold new programs—the Homestead Act, Social Security and Medicare, rural electrification, the race to space, the GI Bill. A modern equivalent of such big ideas would be to endow every American child with a $6,000 asset stake at birth, thus inaugurating a new era of more-equal opportunity.

The private sector is no less in need of reform. In the 1980s we began revising our social contract in at least one respect—through a wave of corporate deregulation. This experiment rested on the implicit promise that in exchange for less government regulation, companies would not only create more wealth but also act responsibly, often through self-regulation. But as the dramatic stock-market decline and the corporate scandals of the past couple years illustrate, this promise has been broken on both counts.

Not surprisingly, public trust in corporations is low. There are two ways out of this predicament: one is corporate re-regulation; the other is a more sincere effort by business to put its own house in order. The latter would render much of the former unnecessary, but at a minimum we need better accounting standards, stronger defenses against conflicts of interest and insider dealing, and greater restraint in executive compensation.

As part of this movement toward greater corporate accountability, it is also time to relieve employers of some of the administrative responsibilities with which society has burdened them. Now that the median job tenure is down to five years, it no longer makes sense to rely on employers to provide basic benefits such as health care and pensions. Our antiquated system of tying benefits to full-time jobs not only adds to the stress of losing one's job but also deprives parents of the flexibility they need to balance their work and family responsibilities. One way or another, we need to jettison this paternalistic model and replace it with universal citizen-based benefits that are fully portable from job to job.

Any new social contract ultimately hinges on a new conception of citizenship. Yet our collective expectations of one another have atrophied in recent years, to the point where even voting—the most basic act of citizenship—is done by only a minority of Americans. Ironically, this emaciation of the notion of citizenship is occurring at a time when ordinary Americans are becoming ever more sophisticated; the majority of Americans now have credit cards, own homes, and have money invested in financial markets. Surely our increasingly sophisticated citizens should be able to handle more civic responsibilities, not fewer. If every American is to be empowered with the right to choose his or her own health insurer, is it too much to ask that each citizen pay a manageable share of the cost? If better incentives are put in place to help all Americans save for their retirement, is it too much to ask that they actually do so?

Finally, as the definitive stakeholders in the social order, citizens must reclaim their collective power over both the body politic and the marketplace. The only way to free both major parties from the minoritarian groups that now wag the dog—whether teachers' unions or moral fundamentalists—is for Americans to re-enter the political process en masse. Similarly, if the increasing number of American stockholders began asserting their rights, corporate America would become more accountable. Like an unused muscle, collective power need only be exercised to regain its inherent strength.

How LIKELY IS IT that a new social contract, pairing flexibility with fairness, will emerge? Cynics will be quick to downplay the prospects of large-scale reform, so accustomed are we to incrementalism and tinkering. But what the cynics fail to appreciate is that something very powerful may be brewing—a near perfect political storm.

American history reveals that periods of fundamental reform are typically triggered by one or more of the following: a major war; a large-scale shift from one industrial era to another; extreme levels of economic inequality; a dramatic change in the composition of the political parties. On the rare occasions when these forces coincide, they fundamentally transform society. That is what happened when Reconstruction coincided with the dawn of the first industrial revolution; it is also what happened when the Roaring Twenties and the Great Depression coincided with the beginning of the second industrial revolution. All the requisite ingredients for change are now coming together again, at the onset of the post-industrial age. If patterns hold, our nation's next major reinvention cannot be far away.

BROADENING THE MIDDLE CLASS

3

Are We Still a Middle-Class Nation?

Michael Lind

It's no accident that the United States until recently has been a middle-class paradise. Government policy invented the middle class, and now needs to reinvent it—before it's too late.

IN 1909 HERBERT CROLY, the founding editor of *The New Republic* and one of the patron saints of the twentieth-century progressive-liberal tradition, published his manifesto, *The Promise of American Life.* "The Promise of America," he wrote, "has consisted largely in the opportunity which it offered of economic independence and prosperity." According to Croly,

> The native American, like the alien immigrant, conceives the better future which awaits himself and other men in America as fundamentally a future in which economic prosperity will be still more abundant and still more accessible than it has yet been either here or abroad . . . With all their professions of Christianity their national idea remains thoroughly worldly . . . The Promise, which bulks so large in their patriotic outlook, is a promise of comfort and prosperity for an ever increasing majority of good Americans.

The idea that the promise of American life lay in widespread material prosperity as much as in civil liberties or political democracy is an old one. As Croly pointed out, in 1782 Hector St. John de Crèvecoeur wrote in his *Letters From an American Farmer,*

> What, then is the American, this new man? . . . Wives and children, who before in vain demanded of him a morsel of bread, now, fat and

15

frolicsome, gladly help their father to clear those fields, whence exu-
berant crops are to arise to feed and to clothe them all; without any
part being claimed, either by a despotic prince, a rich abbot, or a
mighty lord . . . From involuntary idleness, servile dependence,
penury, and useless labor, he has passed to toils of a very different
nature, rewarded by ample subsistence. This is an American.

The equation of America with widespread middle-class prosperity persists today. Of the millions of people who came to the United States
following the resumption of large-scale immigration in the last third of
the twentieth century, a few were refugees from political or religious
persecution. Most, however, wanted what previous generations of
European immigrants had sought: "America has been peopled by Europeans primarily because they expected in that country to make more
money more easily," Herbert Croly wrote.

America, then, is not simply the land of political liberty. It has always
also been an economic paradise for the middle class—at least until now.

WHAT EXACTLY DOES IT MEAN to say that the United States is a
middle-class society?

In the pre-modern societies of Europe the terms "burgher" (Ger-
man) and "bourgeois" (French) referred to the minority of largely
urban merchants and professionals who were above the peasant majority and below the minority of landholding aristocrats. But when Americans talk about the middle class, they are not talking about burghers
or the bourgeoisie. What makes the United States and similar societies
middle-class is the economic predominance of the middling sort, no
matter what their major source of employment happens to be.

Thus the American middle class has migrated from sector to sector over the past two centuries. The "fat and frolicsome" yeoman farmers of Crèvecoeur and Jefferson became the well-paid factory workers
of William McKinley and Henry Ford, and then moved to the suburbs
to become white-collar "organization men" (or, less frequently,
women) after World War II. Over the years the social prestige of various economic sectors rose as the middle-class center of gravity passed
through them. In medieval England "clown" and "villain" were words
for the farmer who later became the symbol of middle-class rural Amer-

ica. In the eighteenth century yeoman farmers and aristocrats alike despised the "greasy mechanic," who by the early twentieth century had been promoted to middle-class factory worker. In the fiction of Victorian Britain and Gilded Age America the office worker was a miserable, stunted figure—Scrooge's assistant Bob Cratchit, or Bartleby the scrivener. But after World War II the cringing, bleary-eyed clerk became the confident professional who left his suburban home armed with a briefcase—Ward Cleaver, of *Leave It to Beaver.*

To most of us, the transition from farmer to industrial worker to service worker—sometimes within three generations of one family—appears in retrospect to have been inevitable, like some geological process. Indeed, many conservatives and libertarians seem to believe that a mass middle class is an inevitable by-product of capitalism. The truth is that each of America's successive middle classes has been artificially created by government-sponsored social engineering—a fact that is profoundly important for us to admit as we think about the future of middle-class America.

Consider the first American middle class, composed of yeoman farmers. There could never have been a mass agricultural middle class in the United States without vast quantities of cheap farmland, divided up into small farms.

From 1800 to 1848 the U.S. government acquired more than two million square miles of territory, much of it arable, by purchase or negotiation (the Louisiana Territory from France in 1803; Florida from Spain in 1819; Oregon from Britain in 1846), by annexation (Texas, 1845), or by conquest (the Mexican Cession in 1848). Populists sought to ensure that this land went to small farmers rather than large landowners or speculators. The danger of European-style feudalism in the United States was neutralized by the land ordinance of 1785, which guaranteed that the federal domain would be broken up into "fee simple" properties, with no complex web of multiple ownership. And the Homestead Act of 1862 provided 160 acres of free public land to settlers who would live on it and improve it for at least five years. Meanwhile, the federal government subsidized continent-crossing railroads, and the Army Corps of Engineers built much of the country's rural infrastructure. This was social engineering on a colossal scale.

The story was similar for the second American middle class, made up of prosperous urban industrial workers. From Abraham Lincoln to Herbert Hoover, American politics was dominated by a bargain between capitalists and workers; high tariffs on imports served the interests of both, by protecting goods from foreign competition. In addition, the dominant industrial labor force successfully lobbied the government to protect it from competition with other groups. In the late nineteenth century Congress cut off "Oriental" immigration, and after World War I—with the support of organized labor—it cut large-scale European immigration. Before World War I informal discrimination prevented southern black Americans from moving to the Northeast and the Midwest to compete for industrial jobs. Finally, child-labor laws removed children from the work force, and "family wage" or "breadwinner" systems—which paid married fathers more than unmarried, childless men—encouraged married women to become homemakers. Today nostalgic conservatives attribute the prosperity of the 1920s to free enterprise. In reality the market was rigged.

A product of the early industrial era, the second American middle class was largely limited to the industrial states of the Northeast and the Midwest. Unlike the factory workers in those states, the rural majority in the South and the West did not share in the income gains from industrialization; tariffs were, in effect, a tax imposed on them to subsidize urban workers and capitalists. The protectionist system also hurt the professional elite, because it raised prices on high-end consumer goods. Economics goes a long way toward explaining why elite progressives from the North teamed up with southern and western populists in the New Deal coalition that lasted from 1932 until the 1960s. The New Dealers created the third American middle class.

Whereas the second American middle class was founded on high wages for workers in the industrial sector, the third American middle class was founded on the supplementation of wage income by government benefits that collectively constituted a "social wage." The social wage included not only private-sector benefits encouraged by the tax code, such as employer-provided health insurance, but also subsidies such as the home-mortgage-interest deduction and government entitlements such as Social Security and Medicare (which freed many middle-class families from the bankrupting burden of caring for elderly parents), the GI Bill for higher education, and student loans. As the Yale political scientist Jacob Hacker has pointed out, when the hidden welfare state is counted along with the visible welfare state, the United States has a system of social provision as generous as those in Western Europe—though in this country much of that system extends only to the middle class and the professional elite.

The social-wage system had many flaws—for example, it failed to provide health insurance for tens of millions of Americans. Nevertheless, the third American middle class, the product of Franklin Roosevelt's New Deal, Harry Truman's Fair Deal, and Lyndon Johnson's Great Society, was larger and more inclusive than the earlier two. From the 1930s to the 1970s income inequality in America shrank dramatically, producing what the economic historians Claudia Goldin and Robert Margo have called the Great Compression.

BY THE BEGINNING of the twenty-first century, however, economic changes were threatening the third American middle class. In the 1970s an increasing number of U.S. corporations started to transfer production jobs and certain service jobs to low-wage workers abroad. This process accelerated through the 1980s and 1990s, as the demise of communism and the rise in many Third World countries of export-oriented development strategies greatly enlarged the global market for both skilled and unskilled labor. Although globalization helped the middle class in some ways, reducing the cost of such imports as toys from China and shoes from Indonesia, it destroyed the jobs—and undermined the bargaining power—of workers in sectors from automobile production to back-office services. Even if the United States had used protectionism to shield workers in every sector from foreign competition, an ever growing number of manufacturing and service jobs would still have been eliminated by technological innovations—a trend that will probably prove even more important than globalization over time.

Nevertheless, thanks to technologically driven increases in productivity, life has steadily gotten better for the majority of Americans. Advances in manufacturing and automation have slashed the prices of consumer appliances such as televisions and personal computers. At the same time, however, this kind of productivity growth threatens the middle class in three ways: by raising the costs of certain labor-intensive services necessary for a middle-class lifestyle; by changing the occupational structure; and by increasing inequality.

The disparity between rapid productivity growth in mechanized sectors and slow productivity growth in human service jobs produces Baumol's disease—named after the economist William J. Baumol. According to Baumol, in a technological economy falling prices for manufactured goods and automated services eventually increase the relative cost of labor-intensive services such as nursing and teaching. Baumol has predicted that the share of gross domestic product spent on health care will rise from 11.6 percent in 1990 to 35 percent in 2040, while the share spent on education will rise from 6.7 percent to 29 percent.

The shifting of relative costs need not in itself be a problem. If Americans in 2050 or 2100 pay far more (as a percentage of their spending) for health care and education than they did in 1900, they may still be better off—if they pay correspondingly less for other goods and services. The problem is that as the relative cost of services like education and health care rises, more and more Americans will find themselves in service-sector jobs that, unlike the professions, have historically been low-wage.

Technology is changing the job market by shoving people out of sectors that can be mechanized or automated—factory production, data processing, clerical work—and into sectors requiring a human touch, from nursing to law. As the twenty-first century began, most jobs created were in non-unionized service sectors where wages were low because of a glut of labor and where the prospects for long-term productivity gains were minimal. According to the Bureau of Labor Statistics, the following are among the occupations with the largest projected job growth from 2000 to 2010: combined food-preparation and serving, including fast food; customer-service representative; registered nurse; retail salesperson; computer support specialist; cashier, except gaming; office clerk; security guard; computer-software engineer, applications; waiter; general or operations manager; truck driver, heavy and tractor-trailer; nursing aide, orderly, or attendant; janitor or cleaner, except maid or housekeeping cleaner; postsecondary teacher;

teacher assistant; home health aide; laborer or freight, stock, and material mover, hand; computer-software engineer, systems software; landscaping or groundskeeping.

Some economists assert that increases in productivity will inevitably translate into higher wages throughout the economy. But this is a matter of faith, not fact. Baumol's analysis tends to undermine such easy optimism. Most productivity advances occur in mechanized and automated sectors, which employ a shrinking number of Americans; so how will the growing number of Americans in service jobs share the gains of high productivity growth?

In the absence of some system of private or public redistribution, then, there is no guarantee that rising national productivity will spontaneously and inevitably produce rising incomes and wealth for most Americans, rather than just windfalls for the fortunate few.

Since the 1970s inequality of both income and wealth in the United States has increased dramatically. As Paul Krugman has observed in *The New York Times*, a Congressional Budget Office report shows that from 1979 to 1997 the after-tax income of the top one percent of families climbed 157 percent, while middle-income Americans gained only 10 percent, and many of the poor actually lost ground. The share of after-tax income that goes to the top one percent of Americans has doubled in the past three decades; at 14 percent, it roughly equals the share of after-tax income that goes to the bottom 40 percent. The concentration of wealth at the upper levels of the population has been even more extreme.

To some degree, the explosion of inequality in both income and wealth has resulted from private and public policy, such as lavish compensation for CEOs, the reduction of taxes on the rich, and the immigration laws that permit a large influx of poor and unskilled workers. But more to the point, the productivity gains in heavily automated, capital-intensive sectors such as manufacturing, agriculture, banking, and other routine services have gone almost entirely to the investors who own the machines and the software, not to the workers who remain, and certainly not to the workers displaced into other sectors. Such an outcome would be likely even if all CEOs and wealthy investors were generous and public-spirited.

This is where economics turns into politics. It is doubtful that in any society with universal suffrage the majority is going to sit on the sidelines and watch, generation after generation, while a handful of investors and corporate managers reap almost all the benefits of technological and economic progress.

One way to prevent this is through labor protectionism—restricting immigration and restricting imports. Neither is likely to be politically feasible. Protectionism would raise the price of goods for working Americans. Restricting immigration, while raising the wages of those who compete with immigrants for jobs, would also make nursing and many other personal services prohibitively expensive for all but the affluent. Higher wages produced by a much higher minimum wage or by the unionization of the service sector (politically unlikely as these scenarios are) might backfire by encouraging a black market in goods and services.

WHAT OUR CHILDREN MIGHT DO FOR A LIVING...

Occupations with the largest projected job growth

OCCUPATION	PROJECTED INCREASE 2000–2010	MEDIAN ANNUAL WAGE 2002
Combined food preparation and serving, including fast food	+673,000	$14,500
Customer-service rep	+631,000	$26,240
Registered nurse	+561,000	$48,090
Retail salesperson	+510,000	$17,710
Computer support specialist	+490,000	$39,100
Cashier, except gaming	+474,000	$15,420
Office clerk, general	+430,000	$22,280
Security guard	+391,000	$19,140
Computer software engineer, applications	+380,000	$70,900
Waiter and waitress	+364,000	$14,150

...AND WHAT THEY PROBABLY WON'T

Occupations with the largest projected decline

OCCUPATION	PROJECTED DECREASE 2000–2010	MEDIAN ANNUAL WAGE 2002
Farmer and rancher	–328,000	$17,090
Order clerk	–71,000	$24,810
Teller	–59,000	$20,400
Insurance-claim and policy-processing clerk	–58,000	$28,870
Word processor and typist	–57,000	$26,730
Sewing-machine operator	–51,000	$17,440
Dishwasher	–42,000	$14,860
Switchboard operator, including answering service	–41,000	$21,190
Loan interviewer and clerk	–38,000	$27,830
Computer operator	–33,000	$29,650

IF WE REJECT BOTH a new feudalism (under which most Americans provide personal services for the rich few) and a regime of protectionism and immigration restriction (which would benefit some workers at the expense of others), then some system of redistribution will be necessary to ensure that the middle-class majority benefits from long-term productivity growth. This can take two forms: redistributing income and encouraging the widespread ownership of income-producing assets.

The most obvious way to share the gains from technological progress is to tax the owners of high-productivity industries at high levels and spend the proceeds on the rest of the population. To varying degrees in different countries—more so in Sweden, less so in the United States—this is the system that now exists.

This "social wage" can take different forms. Some Americans prefer that the government provide universal services such as public schools and public health care. Others prefer voucher systems that permit a degree of individual choice. The social wage can likewise be either a supplement to incomes or a subsidy for goods. The earned-income tax credit, which has bipartisan support, supplements the incomes of low-wage workers to lift them out of poverty, and provides an alternative to raising the minimum wage. But there is also bipartisan support for tax breaks for homeowners, and for other subsidies on middle-class consumption.

In their groundbreaking book *The Two-Income Trap: Why Middle-Class Mothers and Fathers Are Going Broke*, Elizabeth Warren, of Harvard Law School, and her daughter Amelia Warren Tyagi demonstrate that fixed costs for the typical American middle-class family—home-mortgage payments, car payments, health insurance, child care, education, and taxes—have risen more rapidly than income over the past thirty years, eating up many of the gains from having two parents in the work force. According to the authors' analysis of government data, even when a two-earner family today brings in almost twice the income of a one-earner family in the 1970s (in inflation-adjusted constant dollars), the 1970s family had more discretionary income than today's.

If middle-class income does not grow as rapidly as middle-class costs, then one option is to further subsidize the rising relative costs of labor-intensive goods and services that are necessary to a middle-class lifestyle, such as education, child care, and health care. And the government will certainly be pressured to provide such subsidies. But taxing fewer and fewer rich people to subsidize more and more middle-class people would increase incentives for the rich to avoid taxation or even to leave the country. An alternative is to increase the number of people who own income-producing assets.

"Universal capitalism," the idea that everyone should own income-producing financial assets, was originally championed by Thomas Paine, in the eighteenth century, and variants of the idea have been proposed in more recent years by Louis Kelso, Mortimer Adler, Jeffrey Gates, and Bruce Ackerman. Today about half of American households, and roughly 70 percent of registered voters, own stock through pension funds and similar vehicles. But money set aside for retirement does no good during one's working life. Proposals for government-funded savings accounts for all children that would be restricted to a few purposes, such as college education or a first home purchase, have been made by the Washington University professor Michael Sherraden and the former IRS commissioner Fred T. Goldberg Jr. Ray Boshara, of the New America Foundation, has proposed a similar system of American Stakeholder Accounts. And last April, British Prime Minister Tony Blair announced the establishment of child trust funds in the United Kingdom.

Like retirement savings invested in the stock market, child trust funds would be earmarked for particular purposes. But it is possible to imagine a future in which middle-class Americans would receive part of the returns on their investments during their working lives (a small part at first, but more with each generation), which they would be free to save or to spend without any restrictions. Of course, a nation that confiscated private financial wealth and redistributed it among its citizens would wreck its economy and send not only capital but also capitalists fleeing across borders. Thus any plausible program of universal capitalism must start small, by planting seeds capable of growing along with the economy over time.

For example, one can imagine a means-tested program of private, regulated investment accounts in which the government matched the contributions of low-income workers. The seed money might come from spending cuts elsewhere, or from new taxes. Alternatively, citizens could all begin receiving modest amounts of money from the sale or lease of the airwaves and other public assets. In this way, even though most new middle-class jobs would not contribute to productivity growth in the way that farm and factory labor did in the past, universal capitalism could ensure that the fourth American middle class, like its predecessors, would be able to share directly in the long-term growth of the nation's economy.

This may seem a radical change. But only in recent generations have Americans begun to receive most of their income in the form of wages. The yeoman farmer didn't rely on wages. And only in the twentieth century did the New Deal add the social wage to the market wage. In the course of the twenty-first century what may be called the "capital wage" could be added to these, so that middle-class Americans—not merely an affluent minority—might derive income from three sources rather than just two.

In their own ways, with methods appropriate to their own times, Thomas Jefferson, Abraham Lincoln, Franklin Roosevelt, and their allies provided the institutional frameworks that permitted successive versions of middle-class America to grow and flourish. Their success set a high standard for the leaders of today. Every presidential candidate claims to want to help middle-class Americans. The challenge, though, is not to repair the current American middle class but to create a new one.

4

One-Dimensional Growth

David Friedman

Since 1998 the United States has lost 11 percent of its manufacturing jobs. We need an industrial policy that produces broad-based growth.

EVEN BEFORE THE COLLAPSE of the stock market and the recession of 2001 dispelled the illusion that we had escaped the business cycle, there were reasons to doubt that America was truly experiencing the miraculous rebirth that some people claimed it was. Although productivity, after years of stagnation, did increase during the boom years of the past decade, even at its late-1990s peak the economy did not produce jobs any faster or for a longer period than previous expansions had. In the ten years 1993 to 2002 the U.S. economy created barely more jobs than in the previous ten years, when the working-age population was smaller.

Moreover, job growth in the nineties was strikingly uneven across industries. Since 1998, in fact, America has shed nearly three million, or 16 percent, of its relatively well-paying manufacturing jobs, the second worst rate of job loss in the past 50 years. And more job losses may be on the horizon. Hostile land use and other policies biased against "messy," "old-economy" production, and strikingly unbalanced trade relationships, threaten to continue to decimate U.S. manufacturing and reduce the nation's industrial diversity.

The U.S. manufacturing decline is often downplayed as natural. Not to worry, we are told. As countries mature, they shift from making widgets to designing software. Moreover, the loss of manufacturing jobs is not a phenomenon restricted to the most advanced industrialized countries but a global trend. According to this view, manufacturing employment declines reflect a global rise in productivity that is reducing the need for workers everywhere. A widely-cited analysis by an Alliance Capital in October, 2003, for example, contended that since 1995 over 31 million industrial jobs have been lost worldwide, including millions in China. Commentators such as former Labor Secretary Robert Reich and *Wall Street Journal* editorialists seized on this data for evidence that, as with agriculture in the past, American industrial cutbacks are an unavoidable, and, in fact, a desirable outcome. The sooner blue-collar workers are displaced from outmoded factories and shift into the industries of the future, the better.

There are two problems with this position. First, it misreads what is actually happening with manufacturing. To begin with, the analytical time frame of the study in question, which extends from 1995 to 2002, is heavily influenced by the Asian financial crisis of 1997 and 1998, an event that obscures counter trends in the region's manufacturing employment. Since the crisis abated in 1998 and 1999, for example, half of the reported job losses Asia sustained have been recovered, a significant improvement at the very time that U.S. employment took a big hit downward. And reported manufacturing job losses are quite uneven. According to the report, Europe, an advanced industrial region that should be shedding manufacturing as rapidly as it can, has lost only 2 percent of its industrial workforce, a far slower cutback than is occurring in the United States.

More fundamentally, the claimed productivity gains in manufacturing remain highly suspect. The data has not still been adequately reviewed to account for the prevalence of imports, foreign pricing, internal corporate outsourcing, and potential inaccuracies caused by so-called "hedonic" modeling of output in key sectors like computers, which tend to inflate productivity gains. Take, for example, the distorting effect that the increased reliance on cheap imported component parts can have on the measure of productivity. When imported products are available at very low prices, as they were from cash-strapped Asian manufacturers in the late 1990s, U.S. productivity can artificially appear high. Production-related imports, such as semiconductors and engines, accounted for 50 percent of the value of American manufactured goods in 2000, up from 24 percent in 1987. U.S. productivity sky-rocketed, as domestic assemblers relied on bargain-basement parts from abroad to generate high-value finished goods for the U.S. market with less and less labor—which means that apparent domestic-output gains may owe more to foreign producers' ingenuity than to our own. A slight statistical adjustment in import values would erase almost all of the reported productivity gains. As this example illustrates, a number of factors can dramatically overstate U.S. manufacturing output in particular and distort the extent to which industrial employment declines are related to productivity.

The decline in American manufacturing jobs, then, is not necessarily the result of a surge in productivity. Indeed, there is a reason to believe that is more the product of a policy environment that has been strongly skewed against factories and blue-collar employment. Remember that in the early 1990s U.S. manufacturing enjoyed a considerable, and unexpected resurgence. Producers were enhancing skills, breaking up mass markets to appeal to more specialized, sophisticated tastes, and organizing more flexibly to redirect their production as fast as possible. Despite technological and automation advances, employment rose. Unlike agriculture, a quintessential commodity market, making diversified, constantly changing products increases demand for human flexibility and creativity.

But then this positive restructuring of American manufacturing was overwhelmed by a flood of cheap imports, especially from Asia in the late 1990s, and the seductive, seemingly effortless wealth generated by the "new economy" boom. Manufacturing costs rose, and profits declined. Trade agreements allowed U.S. firms to readily import whatever they needed or shift factories to lower wage areas. Almost overnight, American manufacturing was transformed into a commodity enterprise. And the nation's industrial employment went into a tailspin.

This brings us to the second problem with the argument that we should not be bothered by the loss of jobs in the manufacturing sector, because it is the inevitable result of much larger transition to a more prosperous, post-industrial economy. This change may inconvenience workers in the doomed sectors, so the argument goes, but over time, they will find more rewarding jobs and benefit from cheap, high quality imports or products churned out by automated factories. But, this part of the argument is also proving to be wrong.

Such beliefs were plausible in 1994–98, when business-service employment was booming. As millions of jobs in technically demanding work—programming computers, setting up communications systems, for example—were created, business services offset slower growth of job losses in manufacturing. Economists even debated whether such services should be reclassified to reflect their productive role in the economy.

But when manufacturing took a dive beginning in the late 1990s, the business-service growth that powered the healthiest phases of the decade's boom slowed too. Rather than supplant manufacturing, business-service enterprises depended upon on healthy factories, which, after all, were among their biggest clients. Worse still, service-sector expansion began shifting from the private to the public sector. In 1994–98, engineering, management, film and business services, all of which are private-sector wealth-producing activities, accounted for more than half of the growth in U.S. service employment. During the next four years, however, they generated just one-third of total service growth. Personal services, such as cutting hair, grow more rapidly instead. It's hard to imagine how service-sector expansion can play a role in wealth creation if growth in, say, manicurists, exceeds that of engineers. Currently, growth in service jobs appears to be increasingly dependent on government spending, a connection not normally correlated with sustainable wealth creation.

In retrospect, it is clear that we have been seduced by the fantasy that a handful of Wall Street whiz kids and their computer-savvy counterparts had somehow reinvented the economy—a fantasy that seemed to justify America's growing reluctance to foster traditional industrial development. As early as 1969, for example, New York City adopted a plan that explicitly called for the systematic displacement of the city's "low wage" industrial base by a subsidized "modern" office economy. (The city provided tax breaks and development assistance to businesses in the office economy while it zoned and regulated many businesses in the industrial economy out of existence.) Over the next three decades this policy stripped 600,000 well-paying manufacturing jobs from what was once America's largest and most diverse production center, replacing them with a small number of professional positions at one extreme and many more low-paying service jobs at the other.

Despite these consequences, most other U.S. industrial centers followed suit. Seattle and Portland—which not so long ago were hardscrabble lumber, aircraft, and shipping communities—have mutated into elite post-industrial enclaves over the past decade. Soaring property prices have driven out the working class. Increasingly anti-industrial policies have alienated even the regions' most coveted manufacturers, such as Boeing and a once world-class cluster of metals and machinery producers. Similar one-dimensional growth has long been apparent in deindustrialized Boston, San Francisco, and other cities. The drive to transform our cities seems in part to reflect an almost aesthetic or cultural distaste for blue-collar work among our political, economic, and media leaders.

The advent of the New Economy seemed to validate this strategy, at least for a while. If investing in appealing white-collar sectors such as Internet development, software, and finance spurred reasonably robust job growth, then why not tailor domestic and international policies to favor office parks at the expense of factories? But, as we have seen, many of the problems thought to have been vanquished by America's purported economic transformation have now returned. U.S. job growth is anemic. The 1990s expansion generated record disparities in wealth. U.S. trade deficits are at all-time highs. The economy is increasingly reliant on public sector and consumer spending—a big reason why public deficits and private debt are ballooning.

Although it became fashionable to imagine that America could flourish as a de-industrialized society, manufacturing remains crucial for prosperity. The average production-sector job creates three times as many additional employment opportunities as the average service job. Given that more than 60 percent of U.S. workers lack college degrees, and that manufacturing disproportionately employs the non-college-educated and pays wages roughly 20 percent higher than other sectors, it is not surprising to find that as manufacturing declines, economic inequality rises.

If our goal is to create jobs, boost productivity, reduce income inequality, and ensure our international competitiveness, then America needs an industrial policy that cultivates development across a broader spectrum. An effective industrial policy would have several key elements. One would be to have a more consistent dollar policy. It is not a coincidence that U.S. manufacturing took a big hit as the dollar surged in value over the past five years. A strong dollar, after all, hurts U.S. exports and undercuts the ability of domestic manufacturers to compete with foreign producers while benefiting the financial-services industry and affluent American consumers. But when the dollar falls again, as it has recently, it is not as easy for American producers to take advantage of their new price competitiveness for the damage has already been done.

A second element would be to exercise a more balanced trade policy. Over the past decade the U.S. government has gone to great lengths to force other economies to open up their financial markets and to protect intellectual property for the sake of New Economy companies worried about copyright infringement or MP3 downloads. But it has largely turned a blind eye to the unfair trade practices in the goods-producing sectors of those economies. When it has acted, as the Bush administration did in imposing steel tariffs in 2002, it has been in such a half-hearted and politically calculating way that it has often done more harm than good.

For a while, the administration's "safeguard" steel tariffs appeared to work, as American steel companies, even bankrupt behemoths like Bethlehem Steel, regained market share and moved toward profitability. Yet, the politics behind the protection doomed the whole enterprise. The tariffs were selectively imposed to benefit firms in electoral swing states. Politically favored steel exporters—Canada, Mexico, Israel, and Jordan—were exempted from the measures. Other economic sectors deserving of protection—aircraft, plastics, film production—were ignored. Such a haphazard, self-interested approach to trade made it impossible to build widespread support for the tariffs, at home and abroad. And thus it was not surprising that the administration reversed course in the face of an unfavorable ruling by the World Trade Organization.

If we are to maintain a healthy and diverse economy, we are going to need a more coherent approach to trade policy. Above all, an effective trade policy means making other countries play by the same rules we do. And in turn that means we need to do a better job of protecting U.S companies and workers, not just against surges in imports but against persistent price competition from countries that are unwilling to assure their citizens a reasonable wage, protect their environments, abide by global currency rules, or allow reciprocal access to their markets.

Finally, the most important part of an effective industrial policy would be to abolish the discriminatory state and local business incentives, including land-use rules, that have over the past decade increasingly favored information-age jobs over working- and middle-class jobs. The growing political influence of New Economy corporations transformed tax, land-use, and development policies throughout much of the country. As a result it became virtually impossible for an "old economy" business, such as a factory or a shipping company, to secure permits in a timely manner in many communities. Meanwhile, broadband and fiber-optic companies received billions of dollars in tax and other subsidies, leading to the misallocation of some $3 to $4 trillion in investment capital. Today those regions that excessively favored New Economy interests are bleeding jobs and revenues, while those few that did not are experiencing sustained growth and development.

A more balanced industrial policy might temporarily lower our production numbers (from the artificially inflated to the genuine), but it would maximize the diversity of our economy, generate the widest range of employment opportunities for all our citizens, and stimulate real advances in our collective skill and creativity.

5

Spendthrift Nation

Michael Calabrese and Maya MacGuineas

It's a precarious situation: U.S. consumer spending is sustaining the economy—but we need to save more to prepare for the surge in retirements. Here's how to boost personal saving without undermining the economic recovery.

AMONG THE WORLD'S advanced industrialized nations, the United States stands out for its high level of consumption. Robust consumer spending can be an indicator of a healthy economy if it is the product of rising incomes and ever improving productivity. But it can also be a worrying sign of future trouble if it is the result of a falling saving rate and increased borrowing. Judging from the savings and spending patterns over the last decade, there is reason to worry about America's economic future.

At well over $8 trillion, household debt in the United States now exceeds Americans' annual disposable income. Debt-service burdens for both mortgages and consumer credit are at near record levels—a striking fact, considering that interest rates are close to a forty-year low. Both personal bankruptcies and home foreclosures hit all time highs in 2002. And despite the fact that Baby Boomers should be in their prime saving years, the household saving rate for Americans plummeted during the 1990s, dropping almost to zero in the fall of 2001—a level not seen since the Great Depression. Even though the personal saving rate has risen slightly since 2001, Americans are still saving at a rate that is less than half the post-World War II annual average of 8.5 percent of after-tax income.

The fact is that for the past decade we have been living well beyond our means. Americans have done so by borrowing from abroad—to the tune of more than 5 percent of GDP in 2003. In the process, we have accumulated an international debt of more than two trillion dollars, a sizeable and growing burden that will be borne by the next generation.

Consumption may help to fuel the economy in the short term, but it is saving, not spending, that provides the capital for productive investment and long-term growth. This point is particularly important in light of the impending retirement of the Boomer generation. For it is only by creating a more productive economy that we will be able to increase output while relying on fewer workers.

How then can we reduce the economy's dependence on consumers spending beyond their means? The first step is to recognize that the fiscal policy of neither the Clinton nor the Bush administration is appropriate for the economic conditions facing the country today. In the 1990s, Clinton used swelling budget surpluses to pay down the national debt, providing a counterbalance to low personal saving. Bush, by contrast, cut taxes and relied on consumer spending to help lift the economy from its first economic downturn of the new millennium. But neither practice provides a sustainable answer to America's savings problem: politicians cannot be counted on to save surpluses over an extended period as seen by how quickly the commitment to fiscal discipline degenerated into deficits; and individuals cannot keep borrowing money and liquidating home equity forever. What our national policy should do, then, is in fact the reverse of the Clinton and Bush policies: encourage individuals to save while allowing the government to run budget deficits, if necessary, but only when the economy needs a boost.

An economic expansion provides an ideal opportunity to encourage higher levels of consumer saving. But in order to take advantage of this opportunity, the emphasis of fiscal policy needs to shift away from providing tax relief and stimulus toward encouraging higher levels of individual saving on a permanent basis. By reorienting President Bush's ten-year tax cuts, and by changing how some of the saving incentives in the current tax code work, it would be possible both to give money back to a majority of Americans (in the form of subsidies to boost personal saving) and to hold government savings constant (because these subsidies would be drawn from funds that otherwise would have been spent on tax cuts). Indeed, this solution might finally allow the major political parties to break through the protracted stalemate over Social Security and tax cuts while at the same time addressing the serious shortcomings of the two federal programs—private pensions and Social Security—that have the biggest effect on personal saving.

As currently structured, neither of the pillars of our nation's retirement system effectively encourages a sufficient level of savings among all Americans. Our private pension system perversely provides the strongest savings incentives to those who need them least, while failing to cover more than half of the workforce. Meanwhile, attempts to increase national saving by running large Social Security surpluses have for the most part failed because politicians have seen the intended savings as theirs to spend. It is time to take a fresh look at making both our private and public pension systems more effective in increasing national savings.

WE'LL ADDRESS THE PENSION problem first. In many respects America's private pension system is the envy of the world. Pensions are how America saves. With nearly $7 trillion in assets, traditional pension and 401(k)-style saving plans account for the vast majority of financial assets accumulated by households in recent years and are a major underpin-

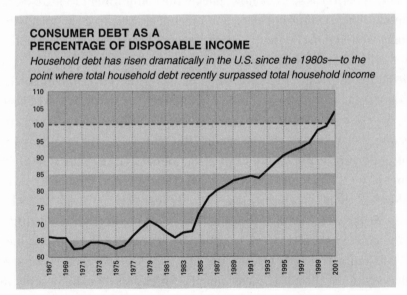

CONSUMER DEBT AS A PERCENTAGE OF DISPOSABLE INCOME

Household debt has risen dramatically in the U.S. since the 1980s—to the point where total household debt recently surpassed total household income

ning of the world's most sophisticated market for patient capital. One reason the system works as well as it does is that powerful incentives—in the form of tax breaks and employer matching contributions—encourage individuals to contribute a portion of their income to an employer-sponsored saving plan. Additional reasons include the convenience and discipline provided by automatic payroll deductions, and the tax penalties that deter early withdrawals.

But our private pension system is perverse: it provides the strongest saving incentives to the affluent, who need them least, while covering fewer than half of all workers. More than 70 million Americans have no access to a tax-subsidized payroll-deduction saving plan, and therefore tend to save very little for retirement. As a result, fewer than 60 percent of today's workers aged forty-seven to sixty-four are likely to receive benefits equal to even half their pre-retirement income when they stop working.

The U.S. General Accounting Office found that 85 percent of the adults without access to a saving plan at work are young, low-income, work part-time or work at a small firm. One in four U.S. workers are in non-standard work arrangements (part-time, temporary and contract workers) that rarely include pension coverage. Coverage among private sector workers under age 30 has fallen dramatically over the past 20 years—to 30 percent in the 1999 Census data. Of course, the later workers begin saving, the more difficult it becomes to achieve the savings needed for an adequate retirement income by the normal retirement age. And at small firms (fewer than 100 employees) three of four workers at small firms remain on their own. Without access to a tax-subsidized and payroll-deducted saving plan, these workers tend to save very little on their own.

Even when less well-off workers are able to participate in an employer-sponsored plan, the tax incentives for saving are upside down: income-tax deductions are worth the most to high-bracket taxpayers who need little incentive to save—whereas the lowest-paid third of workers, whose tax burden consists primarily of the Social Security payroll tax (and who have no income-tax liability), receive no subsidy at all. Federal tax subsidies for retirement saving exceed $120 billion a year, but two thirds of that money benefits the most affluent 20 percent of Americans. This is no way to structure a pension system—and certainly not an efficient way to encourage national savings.

The solution is to give every individual access to a tax-subsidized savings account, regardless of whether his employer sponsors a pension plan. Think of it as a government-facilitated 401(k): just as employers match contributions by eligible employees, the government would match voluntary saving by providing a refundable tax credit that would be deposited directly in workers' accounts. As a tax cut targeted to encourage and reward saving, this fundamental reform of our private pension system has the twin virtue of adding directly to national saving (since low earners save next to nothing now) and giving strong incentives to those who find it most difficult to save. (Regular tax credits are simply dollar-for-dollar reductions in the total amount an individual owes in income taxes; a "refundable" tax credit is one that pays money directly to individuals even when they have no income tax liability to offset. So even the poorest workers, who owe nothing in income tax, would automatically get direct matching contributions to their accounts from the government.)

To create an even stronger incentive for saving among those who currently save least, the government should provide proportionately larger matches for saving by the bottom half of wage earners. Refundable tax credits to subsidize saving would give employers a greater incentive to contribute on behalf of low-wage and part-time workers, because even the employer's contributions would be eligible for federal matching. In this sense a refundable pension tax credit is analogous to the Earned Income Tax Credit: rather than make low-wage job creation more expensive for employers, more of the burden of ensuring basic benefits to all should instead be paid for on a progressive basis by society as a whole.

Creating a universal and portable system of accounts would not be hard. Employers are already required to withhold and remit workers' income and payroll taxes. Workers could simply specify a monthly saving deduction, which employers would forward (along with other tax deductions) to an IRS clearinghouse. The Federal Thrift Savings Plan, which already manages 401(k)-style accounts for three million military and civilian federal personnel, could manage these small accounts, or the administration could be contracted out to a private investment firm. Either way, individuals would always have the option of transferring their account balances to a private financial institution of their choice, or to a future employer's 401(k).

The greater flexibility and portability of citizen-based savings accounts would benefit employers and employees alike: companies could choose to avoid the burden of administering pension plans without denying their employees valuable tax breaks for saving. And by simply requiring all but perhaps the smallest employers to withhold and remit the voluntary saving of workers lacking access to a company pension plan, we can achieve a more universal, portable and equitable system of private pension saving.

THE OTHER PART of the retirement-saving equation—Social Security—is more challenging to fix. Given the multi-trillion-dollar shortfall the program is facing, the nation's retirement system is clearly in need of shoring up (it would take an immediate infusion of $3.5 trillion for the program to make good on all promised benefits over the next seventy-five years). But efforts to prepare for the future by having the government accumulate Social Security reserves before they are needed have had only minimal success. The program's actual surpluses, built up over the past decades, have been tapped to pay for other government programs, and their mere presence has reduced budgetary discipline by causing federal budget revenues to appear larger than they otherwise would. This in turn has provided legislators with more money for tax cuts and new spending while doing little to prefund Social Security in a way that would help the economy. Moving the Social Security program off-budget didn't effectively wall it off, nor did hiding the surpluses in a government lock-box to which Congress holds the key.

The solution is to insulate the savings that Social Security accrues by introducing a system of individually owned investment accounts. The accounts would serve the dual purpose of walling off the money intended for Social Security from the rest of government—creating a far more effective lockbox than the government ever could—while also providing a second revenue stream for participants to augment the Social Security benefits paid out by the current system.

Though there is a closing window of opportunity to implement proactive and balanced reforms, little progress has been made in addressing Social Security's problems because of the overwhelming gridlock between the two political parties surrounding this issue. The major disagreement is not so much whether individual accounts could be beneficial but how they would work with the rest of the system. Liberals, for the most part, fearing that private accounts would lead to large benefit cuts in traditional benefits for their low-income constituencies, have chosen to oppose accounts even though they hold the best hope of prefunding the system in an economically meaningful way. Perhaps to their own detriment, they ignore that the tax increases they tend to favor as a way to shore up the system will inevitably squeeze out other spending programs—including everything from low-income healthcare benefits, to the environment, to education.

Conservatives, on the other hand, continue to ignore the important redistributive properties of the current Social Security system that help to keep many seniors out of poverty. Under many of their plans, the private accounts, which would replace a portion of traditional benefits, would undermine the system's overall progressivity. Furthermore, most private account plans ignore the large transition costs—costs that have become significantly harder to cover with the disappearance of budget surpluses. Whatever money is channeled into the accounts will not be available to cover benefits for today's older workers, and that money will have to be made up from somewhere else. Simply borrowing the funds—or the "free lunch" approach favored by many politicians because it appears relatively painless—would undermine the purpose of using the accounts to build up national savings. (Personal saving would be increased, but government saving would be decreased by the same amount.) It would also unfairly shift huge costs to future generations, which would be burdened with repaying the borrowed funds.

In order to meet the multiple objectives of truly saving the program's surpluses, ensuring broad economic security and rebalancing the out of whack Social Security program, a universal system of "Progressive Private Accounts" should be created as a part of Social Security. The important question of how to fund the accounts would be addressed through the ultimate fiscal compromise. Since entering office, the President has been trapped between two campaign promises: his massive tax cuts and strengthening Social Security. Thus far, the first has come at the expense of the second. But by diverting the remainder of the tax cut into private investments accounts, he could actually achieve both. Using the tax cut to fund the accounts would provide hundreds of billions in seed capital to jump-start the accounts while the other necessary changes to the traditional Social Security system, such as slowing the growth of benefits and increasing the retirement age, were gradually phased in. As important, by diverting funds into personal investment accounts, the President could actually achieve both the effect of tax cuts (since he would still be returning money to citizens) *and* Social Security reform.

Secondly, the redistributive aspects of the current system could be preserved by making the funding of these private accounts progressive. Under such a system, all participants would build up savings in their Social Security accounts, but the saving of low-income workers—including additional voluntary contributions—would be augmented with progressive matches, enabling them to amass a significant nest egg for retirement, while more than compensating for the reduction in their traditional benefits.

For instance, the government could contribute two dollars for every dollar saved by the lowest-income workers, one dollar for every dollar saved by workers who make slightly more, and so forth, with government subsidies phasing out at fifty cents per dollar for workers earning around the national median income. The accounts would be folded into the existing Social Security system and the accounts would be used in part to replace promised traditional benefits that the system will not be able to afford in the future. Moreover, workers would also be guaranteed a minimum benefit that would keep them out of poverty—a guarantee that Social Security does not offer at present.

In short, these accounts would not only help to shore up Social Security for the long term and provide workers with an additional source of retirement income, but they would also maintain the program's fundamental commitment to a progressive design. While there are clearly many benefits to structuring the accounts in a progressive manner, one of the most important is that they would be more effective in boosting national saving than other types of accounts since those who received the progressive matches would be the least likely to substitute lower saving elsewhere.

Shifting our economic priorities from consumption to saving will not be easy. But whether created separately or together, government-subsidized universal 401(k) accounts and progressive private accounts for Social Security would help individuals to prepare for retirement and would set our economy on a course for long-term prosperity.

Fortunately this is an instance where good policy makes for good politics. For one thing, a major reform and expansion of the private pension system could appeal equally to workers and employers. For another, Democrats and Republicans are locked in bitter fights over Social Security reform and the tax cut. Linking the two issues would allow Republicans to claim a major victory by establishing personal accounts while ensuring that the trillion dollars earmarked for the tax cut remains the property of individual citizens. Democrats, meanwhile, could also claim victory by redirecting a tax cut from the wealthy to the average worker while shoring up Social Security in a manner that protects the interests of the most vulnerable Americans. In any event, with the American consumer sinking further into debt and the retirement of the Baby Boomers fast approaching, we need to restructure the nation's two primary saving programs soon.

6

America's "Suez Moment"

Sherle R. Schwenninger

The growing trade deficit threatens U.S. living standards and makes the country dangerously vulnerable to economic extortion. The way out is to make foreigners act more like us.

DESPITE ITS UNCHALLENGED military might, the United States has an Achilles' heel: its economy depends on foreign capital. Though hardly anyone acknowledges this publicly, China and Japan already hold so much American debt that, theoretically, each could exert enormous leverage on American foreign policy. So far, the economic dependence of these countries on American consumers has kept them from exercising such power. But what would happen if, for instance, Washington changed its one-China policy and officially recognized Taiwan? Or if the Bush Administration threatened to invade North Korea? Simply by dumping U.S. Treasury bills and other dollar-denominated assets, China—which holds more federal U.S. debt than any other country—could cause the value of the dollar to plummet, leading to a major crisis for the U.S. economy.

China and Japan wouldn't have to be consciously hostile to wreak havoc; they could create a currency crisis by accident, through either bad policy decisions or instability in their own economies. Both countries have weak banking systems that are burdened by bad loans that will never be repaid. Economists have long warned that the collapse of Japan's banking system could devastate the United States. A Chinese banking crisis could cause equally severe problems.

America is like no other dominant great power in modern history—because it depends on other countries for capital to sustain its military and economic dominance. In comparison, consider the British Empire. At the height of its imperial reign, in 1913, Britain was a net exporter, or investor, of capital; it invested the equivalent of nine percent of its gross domestic product in foreign countries that year, helping to finance the infrastructures of the United States, Canada, Australia, and Argentina. Even long afterward Britain was able to retain a prominent international role in large part because it earned interest and dividends on the enormous investments it had made during its heyday. In contrast, the United States today is a net importer, or borrower, of capital—not only from China and Japan but also from Europe and emerging economies, at a rate of more than $500 billion a year, or approximately five percent of our GDP.

The British Empire eventually declined, of course, and in 1956 it endured the humiliating demise of its great-power status in a clash over the Suez Canal. U.S. policymakers should take note: Britain was brought to its knees not by a military defeat but by an economic one—specifically, America's refusal to support the British pound, which created a monetary crisis for the British government, forcing it to call off its ill-advised campaign with France and Israel to recapture the Suez Canal after nationalization by Egypt. As its international debt grows, the United States becomes ever more vulnerable to its own Suez moment.

The United States has so far been able to slow its relative global economic decline because of its unique role in the international economic system as the consumer of first and last resort. Other countries have been willing to lend us money (generally by buying U.S. assets and Treasury bills) not because investing in America has been so profitable but because we provide a market for the goods produced by their industrializing economies.

America is the world's only consumption superpower. As such, it deserves a great deal of credit for the recovery of European economies in the 1950s and 1960s, the Asian export miracle of the 1980s and 1990s, and the recent commercial rise of China. American consumers have powered the Keynesian engine that lifted the world economy out of its past three recessions, in 1982–1983, 1991–1992, and 2001–2002. The problem, however, is that with each turn of the global economic cycle, America has gone deeper into debt to the rest of the world. Today we owe almost $3 trillion—close to 30 percent of annual GDP—in international debt.

This problem is largely a result of our propensity to live beyond our means; Americans save too little and consume too much. But it is exacerbated by the behavior of our closest trading partners in Asia and (to a lesser degree) Europe, who are our fiscal mirror opposites: they save too much and consume too little. America and its trading partners are locked in co-dependency. In the short term this co-dependency has actually worked reasonably well: our principal trading partners lend us money to buy their cheaper goods with a strong dollar. In return they have access to a stable market for their products, enabling their economies to grow at an impressive rate.

But for the United States this relationship has significant costs that are only now beginning to be felt. For one thing, the availability of cheap foreign goods and services has led to the erosion of America's productive capacity. More important, now that the United States depends as heavily as many developing nations on borrowing from abroad, our standard of living and our dominant position in the world are at risk.

American policymakers have been slow to grasp this, however, because the initial effects of our growing debt burden have been more positive than negative. But eventually our growing international debt will produce more painful consequences. If foreign investors become reluctant to lend to us, as they will if they foresee that we can't keep up with our mounting obligations, the dollar will fall, driving up interest rates and increasing the cost of living for most Americans. The modest decline in the value of the dollar over the past six months may be a harbinger of much steeper declines to come.

Some "new economy" theorists argue that in today's borderless world economy, the current-account deficit—the broadest measure of our negative balance of payments with the rest of the world—no longer matters, because we can endlessly borrow and attract capital from outside the United States. But current-account deficits and international debt do matter; they represent real claims on U.S. assets by foreign individuals and corporations—claims that will eventually need to be repaid. If China, Japan, and Europe are today subsidizing our national standard of living at a rate of more than five percent of GDP a year, then at some point we will need to subsidize theirs—and we will need to do so by an even larger amount, because of interest on the debt (and dividends on the assets) they own. Moreover, if the dollar declines, we will have to pay other countries more for their goods. This will lead to declining standards of living for most Americans.

The U.S. standard of living may at first seem to have little direct connection to our country's global military standing. But will taxpaying American voters be willing to spend ever larger sums of money to sustain our military position and assume responsibility for nation-building in dangerous parts of the world even as their standard of living is falling? The current debate over the growing price tag of the occupation and reconstruction of Iraq, which cuts across party lines, suggests not.

How to escape this predicament? The United States cannot, of course, undo its debtor position overnight. But there are steps that it can take to keep the current-account deficit from getting worse, and to begin to wean our economy from its unhealthy relationship with Asian exporters. Essentially, we must begin to reverse the pattern of overconsumption by Americans and underconsumption by Asians that now characterizes the U.S.-Asian relationship. The first step, if we want to stop accumulating international debt, is to begin producing more than we consume—and to do that we must increase our national levels of saving and investment.

But that in itself could cause a global economic crisis: if American consumers stop buying, the world economy might sputter and collapse. Thus we must also encourage other societies to consume more, particularly more U.S. goods and services. There are inherent limits to how much the aging societies of Europe and Japan will be able to absorb from American producers, so the fastest route to decreasing the current-account deficit while growing the global economy lies in building a middle class of consumers in the emerging economies of Asia, Eastern Europe, and Latin America. The way to do this is to encourage Europe and Japan to invest their surplus savings in countries such as South Korea, China, Taiwan, Brazil, Malaysia, Turkey, and Mexico. Such an influx of investment would allow those emerging economies to both consume more and invest more, helping to produce what might be called middle-class-oriented development.

How would middle-class-oriented development work? The American experience in creating mass affluence in the twentieth century offers a model. The United States grew rich not by exporting its wares to Britain and France but by creating a large domestic market for American-made goods and services. This market was created in part by establishing a system of credit that allowed millions of Americans to get thirty-year mortgages to buy or build their own homes; by establishing a municipal and state bond market that allowed local governments to build new schools and roads and to finance modern electricity and water systems; and by developing loan programs that allowed entrepreneurs to provide needed services to new homeowners and growing businesses. All these activities helped to create millions of jobs for architects, engineers, plumbers, electricians, bricklayers, and others— along with enough demand to encourage ever more investment. Even today homeownership remains one of the cornerstones of American prosperity; and the home-mortgage market is one of the pillars of the U.S. financial system. To promote middle-class development in their emerging economies, therefore, governments should aim not simply at boosting manufactured exports but also at expanding domestic consumption, homeownership, and public infrastructure. They could begin to do so (with the help of the international financial community) by creating the equivalent of Fannie Mae and Freddie Mac, two quasi-governmental institutions that have helped make homeownership possible for millions of working Americans, and by creating local and state bond markets to finance new roads, schools, and water systems.

Unfortunately, over the past several decades the United States has all but ignored the success of its own middle-class-oriented development in formulating international economic policy, choosing instead to push developing countries to export in a way that has served the interests of neither its middle class nor aspiring middle classes in emerging economies. If the United States is to regain long-term international solvency without provoking a global economic crisis, it will only be by urgently promoting middle-class-oriented development worldwide.

RETHINKING TAXES
AND GOVERNANCE

7

Radical Tax Reform

Maya MacGuineas

The tax system is unfair and inefficient, and fails to generate enough revenue to cover government expenditures. Here's how to fix that.

WE HAVE BECOME accustomed to thinking that taxes, like hemlines, can only go up or down. This isn't true. Over the centuries changes in the *form* of U.S. taxes have been at least as dramatic as changes in the *rate* of taxation.

For instance, most federal revenues now come from personal and corporate income taxes, and from the payroll taxes that fund Social Security and Medicare. But most government revenues originally came from excise taxes on luxury items such as tobacco, spirits, and sugar, and throughout much of the nineteenth century the bulk of federal revenues came from tariffs on imported manufactured goods. In fact, the federal income tax, which we tend to think of as an eternal fixture, was introduced as an emergency measure during the Civil War, and did not become permanent until the Sixteenth Amendment was ratified, in 1913. Even then income taxes were levied on only the richest Americans. Not until World War II did the income tax metamorphose into something we would easily recognize today: a mass tax that reached the middle class.

Our tax system has continued to evolve in the postwar era. The second half of the twentieth century witnessed a decreased reliance on progressive taxes (those that, like the income tax, charge higher earners at a steeper rate) and an increased reliance on regressive taxes, such as payroll and sales taxes.

In analyzing the tax system we need to look not just at rates but at the forms that taxes take. There are three basic questions to consider: Is the system fair? Does it encourage efficiency? Does it raise enough to pay for government spending? Let's take each question in turn.

ARE TODAY'S TAXES FAIR? In some ways this is the hardest of the questions to answer, because it requires a definition of "fairness." This could be rephrased as: To what extent is one's overall tax burden commensurate with one's ability to meet it? In this regard taxes are much less fair than they were a generation ago, because over the past several decades tax reformers have focused on reducing the federal income tax while ignoring the explosive growth of other, more regressive taxes.

In a sense the federal income tax remains one of the most progressive taxes there is: half of all the revenue it generates comes from workers earning more than $200,000 a year. But income-tax rates are actually not nearly as progressive as they were several decades ago: the top marginal income-tax rate has declined since the Kennedy Administration, from 91 percent in 1960 to 35 percent in President George W. Bush's plan. Meanwhile, the corporate income tax—whose effects are felt more directly by shareholders than workers—has contributed less and less to overall federal revenues, as changes in the tax code have allowed corporations to shield more and more of their income. At the beginning of World War II the corporate income tax provided almost 50 percent of federal revenues; today it accounts for only 10 percent.

Decreasing the progressivity of certain taxes, and relying more on regressive taxes, shifts the tax burden down the income scale from the rich to the middle class and the working poor. This is exactly what has happened over the past several decades. Since the end of World War II state and local taxes—which are far less progressive than federal taxes— have more than doubled as a share of the American economy, while total federal tax revenues have slightly decreased as a percentage of GDP.

Social Security and Medicare payroll taxes, also regressive, have grown to the point where they are the largest federal taxes that most American families pay. Though the basic structure of the federal payroll tax has hardly changed in fifty years, its rate has been raised repeatedly. Today it is 15.3 percent, and all earners, whether they make

$25,000 a year or $250,000, pay it on the very first dollar of earnings. But the 12.4 percent Social Security tax applies only to wage earnings below $87,900—meaning that the $25,000-a-year earner (every dollar of whose income is taxed at 15.3 percent) pays a higher effective tax rate than the $250,000-a-year earner (most of whose income is exempt). And investment income and employer benefits—which accrue dispro- portionately to high-income earners—go completely untaxed, making the system still more regressive. People who live entirely off inherited wealth pay no payroll taxes at all.

Of course, reasonable people—and even reasonable economists— can disagree about how the tax burden should be distributed; a tax sys- tem's relative progressivity can affect how efficiently an economy functions and how quickly it grows. (More on this in a moment.) But current economic realities suggest that we should be making taxes *more* progressive, not less. For instance, the benefits of recent productivity growth—the result of rapid technological advances—have not spread evenly through American society; most of the gains have flowed to investors and high-income professionals. The result? A degree of economic inequality not seen in this country since before the Depres- sion. If fairness means taxing people in accordance with their ability to pay, it is unfair to shift taxes away from the few who have benefited most from the New Economy and toward the many who have benefited much less (or even been hurt). But that is exactly what many of the tax reforms of the past several decades have done.

IS TODAY'S TAX SYSTEM EFFICIENT? In other words, does it send the right signals to individuals and businesses, and promote economic growth? Not really.

The dominant economic themes of our time have been globaliza- tion and technological change. Both these forces have intensified inter- national competition, particularly in the manufacturing sector—a fact that has enormous implications for our tax system. Globalization has made it easier for multinational corporations to follow the lowest labor costs and tax rates around the world; countries that can keep their tax burdens low have a competitive advantage over those that can't. Dur- ing the past two decades efforts to reduce taxes on dividends and capital

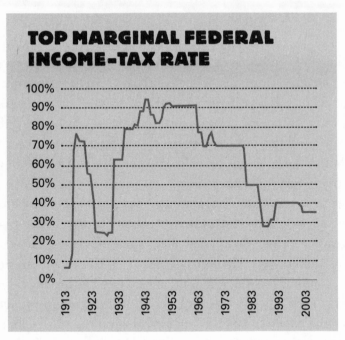

TOP MARGINAL FEDERAL INCOME-TAX RATE

gains have all been aimed at lowering the cost of capital—and thereby encouraging investment and boosting competitiveness—in the United States. This is a sensible strategy as far as it goes—but its application has been only piecemeal, and has produced uneven effects.

Furthermore, the number of elderly people as a percentage of the overall U.S. population will rapidly increase in the decades ahead. Common sense dictates that our tax system encourage saving—both to boost the economy and to help pay for the Baby Boomers' retirement. The current system, however, favors consumption, which is one reason why we have one of the lowest saving rates among advanced industrialized countries. As a consequence, we are staring at not only trillions of dollars' worth of payments we cannot afford to make to future Social Security and Medicare recipients but also a growing international debt. At some point we will finally have to finance the retirement of millions of Americans and pay off the foreign investors who have lent us money over the years—a task that will be made much easier if we start saving now.

Given increased global competition and our graying population, it is very important that our tax system not only encourage saving but also

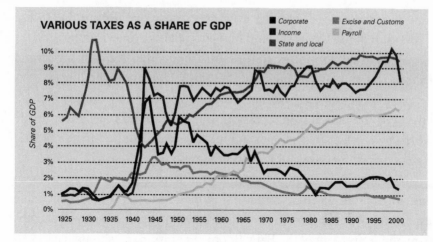

discourage harmful consumption. Too many behaviors that impose "negative externalities"—social costs that are not factored into the direct accounting figures—go untaxed. For instance, Humvee owners don't have to pay taxes for the environmental destruction wrought by their vehicles. Moreover, many of the indirect costs of the country's dependence on oil—such as the expense of shipping it from the Middle East (and the additional national-security expenses that generates), along with the damage it does to the environment—go untaxed. A more efficient tax system would discourage this waste, and provide incentives for more productive investment.

ARE OUR TAXES SUFFICIENT? The fundamental requirement of any tax system is that it raise enough revenue to pay for government expenditures. Although it's defensible—and even desirable, given the stimulus effect—to run short-term budget deficits during an economic downturn, this borrowing should be offset by surpluses during the boom period that follows.

By this standard our tax system is a failure. Last year, in large part because of recent tax cuts, federal tax revenues as a percentage of GDP were lower than they have been at any time since the Eisenhower Administration, falling for the third straight year—an unprecedented occurrence when the economy is coming out of a recession and we are at war. Meanwhile, spending on government programs grew by nearly nine percent—more than the average growth rate during the 1990s. The result is the largest federal budget deficit in American history.

Meanwhile, the states are in a fiscal mess that stems from several factors: state tax cuts throughout the 1990s, increased spending on government programs, escalating health-care costs, and the dampening effects of the nationwide recession. But state deficits have been made worse by the fact that many state income taxes are tied to the federal tax code and thus rise and fall with federal taxes.

Neither the federal government nor state governments are doing enough to redress these structural deficits. In light of the inevitable expansion of public pension and health-care programs that will accompany the retirement of the Baby Boom generation, we should have been building up either government reserves or individual savings. Instead we have been allowing our personal savings to fall and have been cutting taxes and increasing spending, thereby locking ourselves into deficits for decades to come. This is like kicking a live grenade down the road—and then walking up to it and kicking it again.

WHAT IF WE DECIDED to fix the tax system, to make it fairer, more efficient, and sufficient to pay for government outlays?

Only four basic things can be taxed: total income (including earnings from investment and other sources), wages, consumption, and wealth. Currently the federal government heavily taxes earnings, both wages and total income, while state and local governments rely more on taxing spending and wealth (mainly in the form of real estate). Roughly three quarters of all taxes are raised from what people earn, and only 15 percent comes from what they spend.

With these facts as our starting point, what reforms should we make? Let's start with how to make the system fairer. There are two options. We could make already progressive taxes even more progressive—for instance, by boosting marginal rates on the highest income brackets. Or we could eliminate the payroll tax and replace it with a more progressive tax. In recent years most left-leaning reformers have promoted the first option. That's the wrong choice. The purpose of the tax code should not be to punish rising incomes or wealth creation; besides, there are limits to how much we can tax income and capital gains without undermining our competitive position in the world. A better approach, therefore, would be the second. To begin with, we should reduce taxes on wages by eliminating the regressive payroll tax that currently funds Social Security and Medicare. A payroll tax might make sense as a way to fund *individual* medical-savings or Social Security accounts—that is, an individual's payroll deductions would go directly into that same individual's retirement account. But as a means of financing a redistributive universal social program, the payroll tax too often ends up funneling the wages of middle- and working-class Americans to affluent retirees.

Eliminating the payroll tax would have other advantages as well. For example, it would free employers from matching employees' Social Security contributions, which would encourage them to create new jobs. It would also effectively increase wages, making it easier for workers to save their own money for retirement. And it would produce a

A TAX PLAN *(the author's proposal)*	
Taxes to cut	
Payroll taxes	$720 billion
Estate taxes	$30 billion
Total	– $750 billion
Spending reductions	
Ending corporate welfare	$70 billion
Means-testing entitlements	$60 billion
Total	+ $130 billion
New sources of revenue	
Progressive consumption tax	$500 billion
Closing loopholes	$150 billion
Tradable carbon permits	$80 billion
Taxing inheritances	$60 billion
Spectrum-use fees	$30 billion
Total	+ $820 billion
Grand Total	**+ $200 billion**

substantial political benefit, one that would make it easier to solve long-term problems with Social Security and Medicare. Currently the payroll tax creates the misconception that people have a "right" to their Social Security and Medicare benefits. Not only is this false as a matter of law, but it makes it extremely difficult to reform these struggling programs—for example, by subjecting benefits for affluent retirees to a means test.

ELIMINATING PAYROLL TAXES could make the system much fairer at a stroke. But absent the payroll tax, how would Social Security and Medicare get funded? The ideal replacement would be a tax that boosted the saving rate, helping to increase productivity and build the capital to fuel the long-term growth we need. There are two approaches that might be effective in encouraging a higher saving rate. The first is to increase incentives for saving by reducing taxes on income and capital gains, while creating targeted tax breaks for saving, such as tax-sheltered IRAs. The second is to punish consumption more heavily—especially unnecessary consumption. We have already gone about as far as we can with the first approach; further reducing taxes on income and capital gains would further compromise the fairness of the system. But we have not ventured far at all with the second approach, which would allow us to discourage consumption without impairing the economy or making the system less fair.

It is true that state and local governments, which rely heavily on sales taxes, already do levy taxes on consumption. But these taxes tend to be highly regressive: proportionally, they take the biggest bite out of the smallest paychecks. There is an even bigger problem, too, in that sales taxes do not apply to most services. Not only does this penalize the manufacturing sector (because its products are taxed), but as the service sector becomes a larger share of the overall economy, the tax base shrinks. Furthermore, Congress has thus far exempted Internet commerce from taxation, thereby depriving states of substantial potential revenues. Simply increasing existing consumption taxes, in short, would not make the economy more efficient or the tax system more fair.

But what about a different kind of consumption tax—one that is both efficient and fair? Imagine a "progressive consumption tax" levied not on individual purchases but on total spending, as measured by the difference between what you earn and what you save. It might work like this: no tax at all on the first $25,000 you spent, a 10 percent tax on spending from $25,000 to $100,000, and a 15 percent tax on all spending above $100,000. In effect, basic necessities would not be taxed, and luxuries would be taxed at higher rates. This plan would be simple to execute. Each year taxpayers would calculate their total income from wages, investment income, and other sources, just as they do now. But then they would take a second step, subtracting the value of all their savings that year—such as savings accrued in a bank account, through a 401(k) plan, or through an investment fund (all of which are easily tracked, meaning that it would be hard for cheats to escape detection)— from their total income. The resulting figure would be the base amount to which the consumption tax would apply, at progressive rates. The less you spent, the lower your tax rate would be. Low-income earners would for the most part be taxed less onerously, since they spend less; and middle- and high-income earners would have an incentive to save their money, preparing for retirement and bolstering the country's long-term economic prospects. A national progressive consumption tax would go a long way toward recouping revenues lost from the elimination of the payroll tax, and it would make the system fairer, too.

LAST WE COME to the question of how to ensure that tax revenues are sufficient to pay for government expenditures. Even if the economy continues to recover from recession, the recent tax cuts and spending increases almost guarantee that the federal government will be deep in red ink for decades to come.

Once again we have two broad choices: we can increase the rates on what we already tax, or we can broaden the revenue base by taxing new things. The latter approach will yield both greater fairness and greater efficiency.

We can begin by eliminating a lot of "tax expenditures"—better known as tax loopholes. Many forms of income—including government entitlements and employer-provided health benefits—are sheltered from taxation by exemptions, deductions, or credits. For every one of these dollars we don't tax, we have to impose higher rates on the

THE REAL STATE OF THE BUDGET

The conventional view of the U.S. federal budget is that it totals $2 trillion, with roughly one third going to pay for discretionary programs (such as military planes or health-care research) and the other two thirds going to pay for entitlement programs (such as Social Security and Medicare) and interest on the national debt.

But tax expenditures—subsidies that run through the tax code and which the government pays for, in effect, through forgone tax revenues—account for another $800 billion, resulting in a "hidden budget."

The five largest federal tax expenditures are (in billions):

Exclusion for pension contributions and earnings for employer-sponsored plans	$88
Exclusion for employer contributions for health care	$69
Deduction for home-mortgage interest	$67
Reduced tax rates for capital gains	$65
Deduction for state and local income and personal-property taxes	$45

Share of tax expenditures going directly to corporations	11%

How is the hidden budget spent? Of the money included in the five largest tax expenditures, more than 50 percent is spent on households making above $100,000 a year—and only 15 percent is spent on those with incomes below $50,000 a year. In short, most of the hidden money in the budget benefits upper-middle-class Americans.

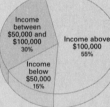

BUDGET FACTS
Percentage of real budget ($2.8 trillion) spent in various areas

Retirement	24%
Health care	20%
Defense	12%
Low-income families	12%
Education	2%

Ratio of dollars spent per senior to dollars spent per child	8:1

—*MAYA MACGuineas*

dollars we *do* tax in order to raise the same amount of money. This can be both inefficient (since higher marginal tax rates discourage work) and unfair (since two people earning the same amount of income through different kinds of compensation—or spending the same income in different ways—can pay dramatically different amounts in taxes).

We should turn next to slashing corporate welfare. Most industry-specific tax benefits insulate certain companies from competition that would force them to be more productive. If we stopped treating farming—to take just one example—as a favored industry, we would save $20 billion annually.

Next we should rethink the estate tax. Despite outcries over the "death tax," transfers of wealth through bequests largely escape taxation. But the estate tax in its current form may not be the fairest way to derive revenue from such transfers. Consider two families—one in which a wealthy patriarch leaves $10 million to a single heir, the other in which the same amount is divided among twenty-five heirs. Under current law all the heirs' inheritances would be taxed at the same rate, no matter the amount received—whether $10 million or a small fraction thereof.

A fair approach would be to repeal the existing estate tax and treat inheritance income and wage income the same way. This would simultaneously broaden the federal revenue base and lower the top rates at which heirs can be taxed.

Even if we subjected entitlements to a means test, closed tax loopholes, cut corporate welfare, and made all inheritance transfers subject to income tax, the government would still face a long-term deficit. Thus we need to find some other sources of revenue. One possibility is to levy taxes on pollution and the use of nonrenewable resources—a perfect example of taxing what you don't want in order to avoid taxing the activities you want to encourage. Another possibility is spectrum user fees. Rights to the public airwaves, which are valued at hundreds of billions of dollars, are practically given away. We should charge annual fees for the right to use and profit from publicly owned airwaves.

Radical tax reform won't happen overnight. In the past the impetus for major reform has almost always been dire need—either the need to pay for wars and other unplanned events or the need to shift tax burdens when growing income disparities have led to political discontent. So far the shifting of the tax burden from capital and the rich toward labor and the middle class has yet to produce the sort of populist rebellion the nation has witnessed in the past. But it may soon do so. Even if it doesn't, another strong incentive for reform—a fiscal crisis caused by mounting deficits—looms not far in the distance.

8

Up in the Air

Michael Calabrese and J. H. Snider

As the world goes wireless, the radio spectrum is emerging as the most valuable resource of the information age. Perhaps we should manage it accordingly.

EACH ECONOMIC ERA has a resource that drives wealth creation. In the agricultural era it was land; in the industrial era, it was energy. Today the American people collectively own the most valuable resource of the emerging information economy: the airwaves, also known as the radio frequency spectrum. Cell phone use is exploding and wireless Internet access already is available in urban "hotspots," on college campuses and in some rural areas. The rapid trend toward wireless communication has made access to the prime frequencies that pass easily through walls, trees and weather an increasingly valuable right. Economists estimate the commercial value of access to the airwaves in the United States alone at over $750 billion.

The fact that cell phone companies have been willing to pay tens of billions of dollars for spectrum licenses here and in Europe suggests that the airwaves are very scarce. But, in reality, the spectrum's capacity is hardly used at all. We recently measured the use of spectrum over downtown Washington, D.C., near the White House, and found that during peak hours between 60 and 80 percent of the prime frequencies are barely in use (frequencies used by local TV stations, cell phones and "unlicensed" consumer devices—such as cordless phones and wireless computer networks—are the notable exceptions).

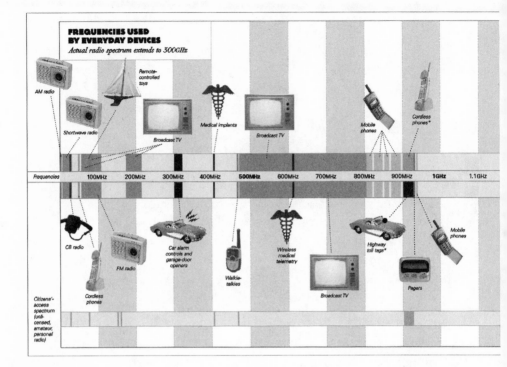

What's scarce is *access* to the airwaves. The prime low frequencies that allow signals to penetrate buildings and bad weather have all been allocated on an exclusive basis to broadcasting, the military and a host of industries and services—which, thanks to digital technologies, actually need only a fraction of the frequencies they license. Unless current users give up spectrum, the tremendous economic and social value of anywhere, anytime access to high-speed Internet connections may either be delayed or severely rationed by premium pricing.

The spectrum, once called *aether*, is nothing more tangible than the electromagnetic properties of the earth's atmosphere. It is the collection of frequencies useful for transmitting radio signals. Spectrum is divided into bands of frequencies, measured in hertz (Hz); the wider the band, the more information carrying capacity it has. The prime low-frequency bands are below 3 GHz (3 million hertz), where the most familiar consumer services such as broadcasting and cell phones are clustered (for a diagram of the spectrum, see New America Foundation's *Citizen's Guide to the Airwaves*, available free at www.spectrumpolicy.org).

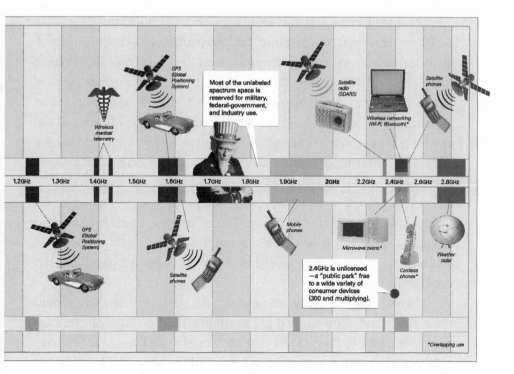

Citizens have access to only a small portion of the useable spectrum. Most of the white space along the "beachfront" bands depicted here are reserved for the military, federal agencies and various industries that use it as an input to production (examples include utility crews, taxi companies and TV reporters transmitting stories from the field). The federal government reserves for itself a majority of the bands below 3 GHz, most for military purposes, although its allocation by function is classified.

Like the atmosphere and navigable waterways, the spectrum is managed as a publicly owned asset—hence the moniker *"public"* airwaves. The Communications Act of 1934 plainly prohibits private ownership of spectrum and authorizes the Federal Communications Commission (FCC) to allocate frequencies to various services and to grant temporary licenses consistent with the "public interest, convenience, and necessity." For example, in 1945 the FCC allocated the frequencies between 174 and 216 MHz for TV channels 7 to 13 and more recently it reallocated frequencies between 824 and 849 MHz to mobile telephone companies.

The problem is that the FCC's 75-year-old allocation system—based on rigid spectrum "zoning" and perpetual, zero-cost licensing—gives incumbent users no incentive to give up spectrum or to use it more efficiently. Access to the airwaves is allocated service-by-service through elaborate rulemakings. Regulators rigidly define—and freeze in place, often for decades—the precise frequencies an industry can use and for what purpose. Although cell phone companies are desperate for additional spectrum, it is not available at any price. Congress mandated auctions in 1994 to assign new licenses, but it has not given the FCC authority to auction or charge rent for prime spectrum previously licensed. To the contrary, pressured by the broadcasting lobby, in 1996 Congress effectively *doubled* the share of the airwaves held by local TV stations—a giveaway then valued by the FCC at up to $70 billion, but now worth far more.

There is an emerging consensus that spectrum licenses should trade freely and allow users more flexibility, but no consensus on how to get from here to there. Deregulation would make licenses more valuable, but the vexing economic and political problem is: How can the public collect a fair return from politically powerful licensees who were given their spectrum for free?

One view, popular at the FCC, is that the most efficient solution is to simply grant incumbents complete and permanent control over the frequencies they now borrow. The FCC is already moving in this direction; in May, the Commission decided to facilitate secondary markets for spectrum by allowing firms, including those that never paid for licenses, to more easily sell or sublease underused spectrum. Another view, more prevalent in Congress, is that rather than give-away licenses, or "sell" spectrum at one-off auctions, the government should instead "rent" spectrum for a fixed period, allowing commercial users property-like flexibility during the term of the lease.

Technology is also changing the terms of the debate. The fastest growing service in telecommunications has been Wi-Fi (short for Wireless Fidelity), a technology that uses *un*licensed frequencies to create wireless local area networks. Thousands of coffee shops, hotels and campuses have set up "hotspots" that allow many users to share a high-speed Internet connection. On the spectrum, Wi-Fi is found at 2.4

GHz, where it shares a band—once derided as the "junk" band—with low-power in-home devices that include cordless phones, microwave ovens and baby monitors. Unlike licensed bands, where users have exclusive rights, unlicensed spectrum is managed like a public highway: subject to certain "rules of the road," access is open, free and shared. And while the Wi-Fi boom has been about short-range mobility, already roughly 1,500 wireless Internet service providers (WISPs) are offering high-speed wireless broadband connections up to 30 miles using relays over unlicensed spectrum at higher frequencies. This is particularly important for rural areas, where high-speed wireline connections are unavailable or unaffordable.

The engineers and Internet pioneers who advocate expanding unlicensed access to the airwaves argue that, in the near future, computer technology will usher in a new era of "smart" broadband devices that will make sharing the electromagnetic spectrum as practical as sharing the acoustic spectrum ("sound waves") at a cocktail party. In such a scenario, the government no more needs to regulate electromagnetic speech than acoustic speech. Whereas "dumb" analog receivers justified government grants of exclusive rights to narrow bands of frequencies, digital and "smart" technologies are making it feasible for any device to dynamically share wide ranges of underutilized spectrum without imposing harmful interference on other users.

But incumbent licensees are already lining up to oppose opening more prime spectrum for shared access, because it would increase competition and reduce the value of licenses. And while the FCC opened a substantial band of military spectrum in the high-frequency 5 GHz band to unlicensed citizen access on a shared "listen-before-talk" basis, it has so far refused to open unassigned broadcast channels and other more useful low-frequency bands for sharing by unlicensed broadband providers or individuals.

In recent months, through a series of rule changes, the FCC has begun to implement a radical shift in the nation's spectrum allocation policy that is contrary to both the policies codified in the Communications Act and to the obvious technological trend toward "smart" radio systems that can share spectrum more efficiently. In 2003, the Commission adopted rules to facilitate secondary markets for spectrum by allowing licensees—whether or not they paid the public for their license—to sell or rent unused capacity to other firms. It also put out for comment a proposed rule that would permit universities and other institutions that hold valuable free licenses for nonprofit educational purposes to sell their spectrum to private firms, encouraging these hard-pressed nonprofit institutions to abandon their educational use of the airwaves in return for a quick buck on the new private spectrum markets.

The blueprint for this ongoing privatization of the public airwaves is a pair of FCC staff reports released in November 2002. The FCC's Spectrum Policy Task Force proposed that incumbent licensees should be granted permanent, private property-like rights in the frequencies they currently borrow. The Task Force also recommended that future licenses grant firms "maximum possible autonomy" to decide what services to offer, what technical standards to adopt, or whether instead to sell or sublease their frequency assignments to other firms. If the Task Force's recommendations were to be adopted, access to the airwaves would become a commodity traded on secondary markets and free of all public interest obligations except to avoid harmful interference with other licensed services.

This is not all bad. The FCC's outdated command-and-control approach—based on rigidly zoning the airwaves by service and assigning exclusive licenses at zero cost—has exacerbated the scarcity of wireless bandwidth, stifling competition, slowing innovation and restricting citizen access to the airwaves. The problem is not the stated goals of the Task Force but its means of achieving them. The Commission's senior economists added a proposal that these new and valuable rights to sell and sublease frequencies be given away to incumbent licensees at no charge. The proposal is dressed up as an "auction," but one in which any incumbent opting to sell their license would be entitled to keep 100 percent of the revenue—money that under current law would flow into the public treasury. The logic of the proposal is that broadcasters and other spectrum incumbents have so much political clout that the only practical way to reduce scarcity is to bribe them to bring their spectrum to market.

There are three problems with this approach. First, it confers a massive and undeserved financial windfall—as much as $500 billion—

on a few lucky industries, taking revenues from the public during a time of ballooning deficits and shrinking revenues. Companies that never paid a nickel for scarce licenses will now be able to become absentee landlords and collect rents while paying nothing back to the public.

Second, freezing the old zoning system into permanent private property rights would forestall emerging "smart" radio technologies that can dynamically share today's underutilized spectrum space. Today the fastest-growing demand for telecommunications involves the inexpensive wireless networking made possible on unlicensed spectrum by Wi-Fi. Wi-Fi enables wireless home networks to link computers, audio/visual equipment, security systems, and cordless phones. It has also allowed WISP entrepreneurs and nonprofit Community Access Networks to offer high-speed wireless Internet access to homes, farms, schools and small businesses in low-income, rural and remote areas where wire-line service is unavailable or unaffordable. But this is merely the tip of the iceberg. Intel Corporation is planning for a world in which unlicensed devices could cost as little as pennies, with thousands of them scattered around houses in beehive-like wireless networks. Anticipated uses include monitoring electricity usage, temperature, bacteria, mold, appliance maintenance needs, food inventory, and potential crime. Unfortunately, if frequencies are privatized in the way the FCC proposes, it would turn such uses into "trespassing," allowing licensees to demand payment for access to *their* airwaves.

Finally, it would foreclose more sensible and fairer approaches to spectrum reform. Making spectrum allocation more market-based can be achieved without a massive giveaway. One approach would be to rent for fixed terms the flexible new licenses proposed by the FCC Task Force, with the rental revenues going to the public's coffers for the public interest. Such an approach would put all companies on a level playing field, permit property-like rights for limited periods, protect capital investment by incumbents, and internalize incentives to use spectrum efficiently, all while giving taxpayers something tangible in return for the use of a public resource.

A substantial share of any revenue from licensing the airwaves should be earmarked to fulfill the "public interest obligations" that justified giving broadcasters free monopoly access to the airwaves in the first place. There are many unmet public interest needs, including quality children's and educational programming, expanded civic discourse, and free media time for political candidates. Some of the revenue could also go into a "digital opportunity fund," which could invest in the educational content and innovative software needed to make meaningful the federal E-Rate program that has been wiring the nation's public schools and libraries to the Internet.

Getting spectrum policy right will require a new politics. Congress and the FCC have been able to give away tens of billions of dollars worth of spectrum rights without any discernible public outrage. They have also been able to favor incumbents at the expense of competition, innovation, and efficient spectrum use. The good news is that in June 2003 President Bush called for a comprehensive review of spectrum policy. And increasingly, important industries that lack FCC licenses—including the companies that make computer chips, software and wireless devices—are joining the effort to encourage a reallocation of prime spectrum frequencies for unlicensed citizen access.

One thing is for certain: as the Information Age goes wireless, getting spectrum policy right will have an enormous impact on our nation's economy—and on our democracy.

9

Taking Stock

Jonathan Rauch

The demands of our two politically mightiest generations—Boomers and retirees—have knocked the country's public-investment priorities out of whack.

I SOMETIMES THINK SOURLY of the Constitution's majestic call on the government to provide for the general welfare when my teeth are cracking together as I bounce over one of the District of Columbia's crater-sized potholes. Or when I forlornly watch bicyclists glide past my car as I wait, and wait, in the gridlocked morning traffic of northern Virginia. Government does grand things, but little of what it does is more important—or more noticeable when neglected—than the routine job of providing and maintaining public capital.

Markets, entrepreneurialism, and the miracle of compound interest are every bit as marvelous as their enthusiasts tell us, but private growth depends on public capital. Governments will often invest shortsightedly or inefficiently, as anybody knows who has spent ten minutes listening to Congress debate a highway or water bill. Still, public capital, even when less than ideally provided, often has the important benefit of stimulating private investment and thus economic growth. Build a road, and development follows. Invent a new method of encryption, and new forms of e-commerce flower. Much of what government does tends to crowd out private activity. Public capital, in sharp and important contrast, often crowds it in.

Two main categories of public capital are infrastructure (physical capital) and research and development. Public investment has gone through three distinct periods: a boom until the mid-1960s; a bust through the early 1980s; and then a moderate recovery, though not to pre-1970 levels. In response, the accumulated stock of public capital—relative to the size of the U.S. economy—climbed through the 1960s, leveled off, and then entered a long, gradual decline.

This is not as bad as it might seem. For one thing, the boom of the 1950s and the 1960s was occasioned largely by the postwar push to build the national highway system and by the need for new schools to accommodate the Baby Boomers. Now, of course, the highway system is finished and most of the schools we need are in place. Moreover, starting in the 1980s governments found themselves spending more of their capital budgets on computers, software, and other kinds of information technology that depreciate much faster than do bridges or buildings. That is probably why the capital stock continued to decline in value even after investment recovered in the 1980s: the lower figures reflect not so much a neglect of bricks and mortar as a shift toward bits and bytes. Roads and bridges, for example, are mostly in good shape, bone-rattling exceptions notwithstanding. Congress passed two large highway bills in the 1990s (politicians love nothing better than to pave the country), with the result that road conditions in the national highway system have steadily improved.

Even so, that classic example of how a public-capital bottleneck can restrict private-sector economic growth—to wit, the traffic jam—has grown more common. Recently the Texas Transportation Institute estimated that in 2000 alone, congestion cost the drivers of seventy-five urban areas a combined total of almost $70 billion in wasted fuel and time. Although the country's roads are not falling to pieces, more investment—especially in the better use of existing roads (through smart-highway technology and congestion pricing, for example)—would not go amiss.

From an economic point of view, then, the road system appears better than adequate but less than optimal. The same might be said of public infrastructure more generally. It turns out that periods of rising and

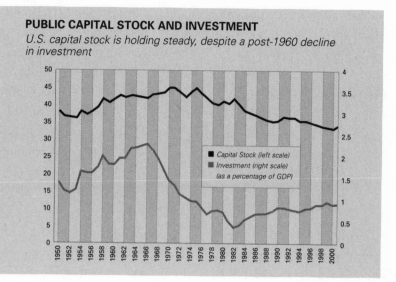

PUBLIC CAPITAL STOCK AND INVESTMENT
U.S. capital stock is holding steady, despite a post-1960 decline in investment

declining investment in infrastructure coincide rather nicely with periods of greater and lesser economic growth. That might be simply because the country has more to spend on public capital in boom times. But in 1989 an economist named David Alan Aschauer set the economics profession on its ear with a paper arguing that the causality ran at least as strongly the other way. Investment in public capital, he found, substantially increased productivity—"which implied," as he recalled in a recent phone interview from Bates College, in Maine, where he teaches, "that a substantial portion of the productivity slow-down we'd experienced could be connected to a slowdown in public investment."

Aschauer's findings set off a wave of research into the economic effects of public capital. The results came out all over the place, but the central tendency of various studies was to find that infrastructure investment does indeed spur productivity, though not as dramatically as Aschauer had initially found. In 1998 Aschauer revisited the subject in a paper called "How Big Should the Public Capital Stock Be?" He used data from forty-eight states to estimate the ratio of public to private capital that seemed to maximize economic growth. Various

methods all put that optimal ratio at roughly sixty cents of public capital for every dollar of private capital. Then he noted that the actual
ratio of public to private capital in those forty-eight states averaged only
about forty-five cents per dollar. "The public capital stock did not keep
pace with the private capital stock during the 1970s and 1980s," he
wrote. The implication was that the country might be considerably better off with more public capital. "Overall, we're doing pretty well,"
Aschauer told me, "but there's anecdotal and statistical evidence that
we could be doing better."

In his paper, however, Aschauer went on to make a point that
enthusiasts of government spending will find less congenial: most of the
benefit from increased investment in public infrastructure comes only
if the investment is funded by reducing other government spending.
The reason is that additional public investment financed by tax
increases or government borrowing comes partly at the expense of private investment. In fact, Aschauer says, his findings suggest that public
spending overall is too high from the point of view of economic efficiency, even as spending on public capital in particular is too low.

WHAT OF RESEARCH AND DEVELOPMENT? Here, by any measure, the
United States is the world's powerhouse. America alone accounts for
almost half of R&D expenditures among the thirty countries of the
Organization for Economic Cooperation and Development; indeed, America's R&D spending is more than double that of No. 2, Japan. Moreover, recently R&D spending has continued apace in the United States
even as it has slowed in many other places, so the gap has, if anything,
widened. America's university system is the envy of the world, and its
scientific establishment is unequaled in the history of civilization.
Today only a few countries spend more than the United States on R&D
as a percentage of their GDP, and with the important exception of
Japan, they are small economies—in 2000 Finland and Sweden—rather
than major competitors. All of that gives reason for pride and optimism.

However, the composition of America's public R&D has changed
dramatically in recent years, and perhaps excessively. Whereas most
R&D spending was roughly flat (in constant dollars) through the 1990s,

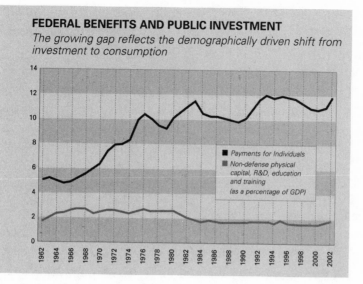

FEDERAL BENEFITS AND PUBLIC INVESTMENT
The growing gap reflects the demographically driven shift from investment to consumption

■ *Payments for Individuals*
■ *Non-defense physical capital, R&D, education and training*
(as a percentage of GDP)

health-related R&D went soaring into the stratosphere—almost literally, given that the level now nearly matches, and may soon exceed, spending on space research at its peak, in the moon-shot years. The extent of this change is hard to overstate. Medicine and biology accounted for almost half of the government's fiscal 2002 research budget. In fact, the National Institutes of Health alone has accounted for essentially all of the increase in Washington's non-defense research spending since the mid-1990s, and today more than half of all federal basic research is conducted under the NIH's auspices. It is as if the moon shot had become a health shot, with the NIH replacing NASA. Moreover, because the federal government is such an important sponsor of university research, the tilt in Washington's priorities is mirrored in academia.

"I think we're out of whack," Roger G. Noll, a Stanford University economist who studies R&D, told me recently. "Only about two thirds of the students who want to be physical-science and engineering majors can be, because of enrollment constraints." (Training scientists is expensive and heavily reliant on government support.) "We're right in the middle of the growth curve for information technology, and this is not a wise time to be cutting back on the basic research that supports those technologies," he says. "We really do know that the kinds of work people are doing in solid-state physics and algorithm design and other areas of information technology have a huge payoff."

Why, then, the lurch toward health? Here our two stories, one about infrastructure and the other about R&D, appear to converge. The U.S. population, as everyone knows, is aging. Baby Boomers are beginning to peer at mortality, and they don't like what they see. They want no expense spared in the search for new treatments for cancer and heart disease and Alzheimer's, and they are a large cohort that politicians are eager to please. Another influential constituency—possibly the most influential of them all—is retirees, and the aging of the population means that there are more and more of them. For more than thirty years Washington has been devoting steadily more resources, measured as a share of GDP, to writing benefits checks to individuals through entitlement programs like Social Security and Medicare, while the share devoted to public investment has remained the same.

IN SUM, THE DEMANDS of two politically mighty generations have shifted government's priorities toward consumption as a general matter and, within the R&D budget, toward the sort of research that most resembles consumption. Good health and long life are very important, but in economic terms they are not seed corn. That does not mean the future is being starved, but it probably does imply that opportunities for a still better future are being missed.

The hopeful news is that Washington has begun to notice, at least where R&D is concerned. A presidential advisory council on science and technology recently called for a better-balanced research portfolio to bring the physical sciences in line with the life sciences; and complementary efforts got under way in Congress to double the budget of the *National Science Foundation*—the NIH's counterpart in the physical sciences—over five years.

Infrastructure, however, is primarily in the hands of state and local governments, which at the moment are cutting back. What is true in flush times is doubly true in lean ones: the squeakiest wheel gets the grease, and long-term investment rarely squeaks the loudest. When public capital suffers relative to other priorities, that is generally because of thoughtlessness rather than hostility. Whether you are a state legislator crunching a budget or a voter losing your molars to a pothole, the remedy amounts to this: pay attention.

10

The Fuel Subsidy We Need

Ricardo Bayon

Oil dependence is still the Achilles' heel of the American empire. It doesn't have to be—and if we don't want to lose economic ground to Europe, it can't be.

TERRORISTS INTENT ON DAMAGING the United States need not fly planes into America's buildings; they need only do something to raise the price of oil. Far-off international crises—and relatively mild forms of extortion—have in the past brought the U.S. economy to its knees. The price spikes caused by the Arab oil embargo of the early 1970s and the Iranian revolution of 1979 each led to economic misery for the United States in the form of a deep recession, increased unemployment, and mile-long lines for gas. The Gulf War and its aftermath produced a milder version of the same phenomenon in the early 1990s. Every major U.S. recession of the past three decades has been preceded by a rise in the price of oil.

The United States remains acutely vulnerable to such price fluctuations today. The American economy is, after Canada's, the most energy-dependent in the advanced industrialized world, requiring the equivalent of a quarter ton of oil to produce $1,000 of gross domestic product. We require twice as much energy as Germany—and three times as much as Japan—to produce the same amount of GDP. Overall the United States consumes 25 percent of the oil produced in the world each year. This binds us to the Middle East, which still holds more than 65 percent of the world's proven oil reserves. Even if we were to buy all our oil from Venezuela, Canada, and Russia, or to find more oil here in the United States (which currently holds only 2.9 percent of proven reserves), Persian Gulf producers with excess capacity, such as Saudi Arabia and the United Arab Emirates, would still largely dictate the price we paid for it.

America's economic vulnerability to oil-price fluctuations has led Washington to strike a tacit bargain with Saudi Arabia and other Persian Gulf oil producers. In return for U.S. military protection and silence about the more unsavory aspects of their societies, these countries increase production when prices get too high and cut it when they get too low. In addition, they price their oil in dollars and recycle their petro-profits through U.S. financial institutions. But this has made the United States vulnerable not only to a sustained spike in oil prices but also to the possible fall of the dollar. In part because the dollar has been strong, we have been able to consume more than we produce and then to make up the difference by borrowing from abroad. As a result, our current net international debt has risen to $2.3 trillion, or 22.6 percent of GDP. What would happen if a war in Iraq went badly or if Islamic extremists gained ground in key oil-producing states? Oil prices could rise and the dollar could fall, inflicting a double blow to the U.S. economy from which it could not easily recover.

THE WAY TO ESCAPE this abiding insecurity is to wean the U.S. economy—and the world economy, too—off oil. And the way to do that is to encourage the commercial development of a technology called the hydrogen fuel cell. Solar power and windmills will surely be important parts of our energy future, but only the fuel cell can address our oil dependency by challenging the primacy of the internal-combustion engine.

Fuel cells are actually a relatively old technology (they were invented in 1839, Jules Verne wrote about them in the 1870s, and they were used by U.S. astronauts in the 1960s), and the concept underlying them is simple: by mixing hydrogen and oxygen, fuel cells generate both water and electricity. Not only do fuel cells turn two of nature's most abundant elements into enough energy to power a car, but they create no toxic emissions (drinkable water is their only by-product). And fuel cells are completely quiet, meaning that it is now realistic to imagine living in a world of silent cars and trucks.

The technology is not science fiction: fuel cells are on their way toward commercial viability. Fuel-cell-powered buses are running in Vancouver, Chicago, London, and parts of Germany. BMW has a prototype car powered solely by fuel cells. Honda, Toyota, and Daimler-Chrysler announced recently that they would begin shipping fuel-cell cars to retail customers around the world; General Motors and Ford are not far behind. Honda's car was shipped to its first major customer—the city of Los Angeles—at the beginning of December.

Geoffrey Ballard, the founder of the Canadian manufacturer *Ballard Power Systems* has said, "The internal-combustion engine will go the way of the horse. It will be a curiosity to my grandchildren." Even large oil companies believe that they must embrace hydrogen power. In a recent analysis of future energy scenarios Royal Dutch/Shell put forth the possibility that hydrogen could displace oil as the fuel of choice within the next thirty to fifty years.

WHY HAVEN'T FUEL CELLS moved into commercial use more quickly? There are two main reasons. First, the cells themselves are relatively expensive. Fuel cells capable of producing one kilowatt of electricity now cost more than $3,000—several times what it costs to produce a gas turbine or an internal-combustion engine that can deliver the same amount of power. That will not be a big problem for long, however, because with investment from car manufacturers and oil companies pouring in, the price of fuel cells is falling fast. (When oil was first introduced, in the early 1900s, it, too, was much more expensive than the alternatives—primarily coal—but it was soon overwhelmingly preferred, because of its cleanliness, efficiency, and ease of use.) Thus the real obstacle is the second one: we do not yet have the infrastructure necessary to deliver hydrogen cheaply and effectively to cars, trucks, and generators throughout the country. Such an infrastructure would include technologies capable of extracting hydrogen from natural gas or water, along with the means to transport that hydrogen to a network of "gas stations" nationwide.

How fast hydrogen enters the mainstream will be determined largely by how much support the government provides. Bear in mind that government choices and government subsidies account for much of our oil dependence in the first place: automobiles truly conquered America (helping oil to become the fuel of choice) only after the mid-1950s, when—partly as a way of promoting national security—Washington agreed to pay as much as 90 percent of the cost of building what was then called the National System of Interstate and Defense Highways. This program cost the federal government more than $1.2 trillion from 1958 to 1991. Some of this money came from taxes, license fees, and so forth, but David Roodman, an analyst at the *Center for Global Development*, estimates that the federal government still subsidizes automobiles at a rate of $111 billion a year above and beyond what it reaps in auto taxes and fees. (And that estimate does not include the associated environmental, health, and military costs of burning fossil fuels.) Other sources of energy and productivity—such as nuclear power, the national power grid, coal, and the Internet—have benefited from substantial government subsidies over the years. A similar federally sponsored project to build a hydrogen-distribution infrastructure would surely pay back the investment many times in the long run.

Even if the government did not actively subsidize a hydrogen infrastructure, it could point the nation toward a hydrogen future by ceasing to subsidize the burning of fossil fuels. Unfortunately, however, Washington is at the moment neither encouraging hydrogen development nor discouraging fossil-fuel use. President Bush's energy plan proposed considerably more in subsidies for fossil fuels and nuclear energy—$2 billion over ten years to support the development of oxymoronic "clean coal," and billions more for nuclear energy—than for hydrogen fuel cells, wind, or any other form of renewable energy. Currently the government is spending about $77 million a year on hydrogen fuel cells, or about a third of what the President has proposed for "clean coal."

Obviously, there would be short-term costs to building a hydrogen infrastructure—but the costs of inaction would be higher. If the United States does not take the lead in this industry, some other country will. It is no accident that the first fuel-cell-powered cars to hit the market will be European (DaimlerChrysler) and Japanese (Honda and Toyota). Consider that while the Bush Administration was proposing more support for coal and nuclear energy, the European Union was announcing that it would henceforth be obtaining 22 percent of its electricity (and 12 percent of all its energy) from renewable sources. The EU also announced that it would spend some $2 billion (twenty times previous amounts) on renewable-energy research over the next five years. A central focus of that money is expected to be hydrogen energy. Additionally, a number of European companies, including DaimlerChrysler, have pledged billions of dollars to the EU's work on fuel cells. Meanwhile, the Japanese government—which prior to the EU's announcement was widely believed to have the most ambitious hydrogen-energy program on the planet—is believed to have spent as much as $220 million on fuel-cell research in 2002. That is three times what the U.S. Department of Energy spent on such research, and 50 percent more than the Energy Department is requesting for all forms of hydrogen-related spending in 2003.

If the United States is left behind in adopting a promising new technology, it won't be the first time. In the 1970s America was the undisputed leader in both wind- and solar-energy technologies. By the early 1980s, however, federal support for these technologies had been drastically cut, falling far behind what both the Japanese and various European governments provided to develop them. Today—when wind is becoming cost-competitive with natural gas as a source of energy, and the solar-energy industry is growing by a remarkable 30 percent a year—the largest producers of wind energy are Danish (Vestas and NEG Micon), and the largest producers of solar energy are Japanese (Sharp and Kyocera) and European (BP Solar and Shell Solar).

History repeats itself: if current trends continue, the leaders of tomorrow's hydrogen economy will not be American. For the United States this will mean continuing vulnerability to oil-price shocks, increased insecurity, and diminishing economic competitiveness.

HELPING AMERICAN FAMILIES

11

The Insecure Family

Jacob S. Hacker

The American family is facing unprecedented new levels of economic insecurity. We must protect them against catastrophic drops in income.

SINCE 9/11, THE FEDERAL GOVERNMENT has become so concerned with risks to personal security that the Department of Homeland Security regularly issues new color-coded terrorist alerts—red for severe risk, green for low risk. Yet there is another collection of risks that is close to the red zone today, but about which our leaders are saying virtually nothing: risks to *economic* security. The financial consequences of common life events—losing a job, having a child, getting sick, separating from a partner or spouse—are increasingly devastating for America's families. But government and the private sector aren't just ignoring the problem; they are actually making it worse.

Consider, for example, fluctuations in family income. As illustrated by the accompanying chart, family finances have grown much more unstable since the 1970s. Families once could depend on relatively stable (and steadily rising) income sources. Over the past three decades, however, the volatility of family incomes has exploded. Indeed, at its peak in the 1990s, the fluctuation of family incomes *was approximately five times greater than in it was in 1972*. So dramatic is the rise, as the chart shows, that the growth in income instability has actually outpaced the much-discussed increase in income inequality. Put another way, while inequality *across* families did grow enormously over this period, changes in income *within* families *over time* rose even more.

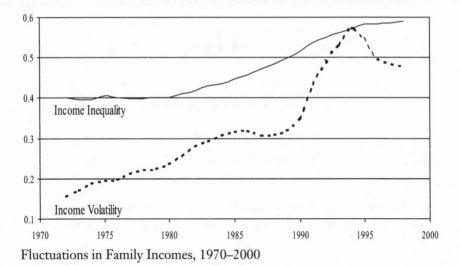

Fluctuations in Family Incomes, 1970–2000

The increased volatility in family incomes is not the only evidence of a new economic insecurity. Harvard Law Professor Elizabeth Warren and her colleagues, for instance, document a dramatic shift in personal bankruptcy filings. Over the past two decades, filings have increased fivefold to more than 1.5 million, and, even more worrying, a growing number of single moms and two-earner families are among the bankrupt. Indeed, the clearest predictor of bankruptcy is whether kids are in a family. And, revealingly, half of those filing for bankruptcy cite health problems, childbirth, or a similar family crisis as a prime reason for doing so, compared with just 11 percent of filers citing these reasons in 1964.

How can insecurity be on the rise during an era in which take-home pay has expanded? The most obvious reasons are changes in the American economy. True, incomes have risen, but for the vast middle class and the working poor, they have grown surprisingly little—even as wages have become increasingly unstable and the cost of things families need, from housing to education, has ballooned.

At the same time, the nature of employment and unemployment has changed. Increasingly, unemployment is structural, not cyclical: enduring, devastating, and giving way only when workers accept huge cuts in pay or in hours.

Just as important, families aren't what they used to be: a man at work and a wife at home. In theory, two-earner families enjoy a built-in financial cushion that single-earners don't. Yet the rise of two-earner families has not eliminated income volatility and potential hardship. To the contrary, two incomes are now necessary for maintaining a middle-class lifestyle, and in two-earner families, there's double the chance of one income being lost.

These trends are well known. What's not commonly recognized is how profoundly, and frequently, they affect Americans. Consider the following fact: Of Americans with income in the top half of the income distribution in 1983, nearly 18 percent saw their income fall below the poverty level in the next decade. This is the hidden side of the rags-to-riches story that Americans so love: many go from riches—or at least relative affluence—to rags.

Even less well recognized is that government and corporations have greatly exacerbated the problem. The generosity of welfare and a host of other programs for the poor has fallen precipitously. No less important, the biggest social insurance programs—Medicare, Social Security, unemployment insurance—have steadily eroded in the face of rising need. Medicare, for example, covers an ever smaller share of seniors' health care spending (although the recently enacted prescription drug benefit will remedy that slightly). And the proportion of pre-retirement income provided by Social Security has declined, and will continue to fall even without future cutbacks.

Yet the truly momentous changes are taking place in the private sector, and with even less discussion. Consider pensions. Once, workers lucky enough to have a pension—about half the workforce at the peak of coverage—enjoyed a guaranteed benefit in retirement. Now, thanks to so-called defined-contribution plans like 401(k)s, those same "lucky" workers have to put away their own wages—a real hardship for poorer workers, who tend not to participate even when 401(k)s are offered—and the returns of the plan depend entirely on their own investments. Some do well in this system, but others do not. The difference, in a word, is risk.

Or consider private health insurance—the first line of defense against medical costs for most Americans. For decades, coverage rose steadily. Since the early 1980s, it has fallen, especially among the working poor. Again, some have done well; some have not. But nearly everyone faces greater risk. Little wonder that personal bankruptcy and charity care have become America's de facto medical safety net.

It's tempting to think that these changes have little to do with public policy. Nothing could be further from the truth. Even as family income risks have dramatically intensified, America's leaders have largely—and, for the most part, deliberately—failed to renovate existing policies, while showering ever more expensive largesse on increasingly exclusionary and individualized private benefits.

This may be because rising insecurity doesn't truly fit into the storyline of either party. For Republicans, insecurity is basically good—a spur to work hard and accept responsibility for the choices one makes. Among Democrats, meanwhile, it has received much less notice than inequality and poverty, even though it's almost certainly an issue with far greater public resonance. Neither party has made protection against economic risks—rather than redistribution down (or, as with tax cuts, up) the income ladder—a central part of its economic and social policy agenda.

A focus on economic insecurity changes the subject completely. It says that what really matters is not whether some are rich and others are not, but whether Americans are protected against precipitous drops in their standard of living. And given that all of us face this possibility, risk protection doesn't have to be an us-versus-them issue. Instead, its goal is to cushion families against serious financial threats that can strike all of us, ensuring that these events do not so cripple family finances that they threaten normal, productive lives—and, indeed, risk-taking itself.

This is not a radical or new idea. It is already embedded in America's two most popular and successful social insurance programs: Social Security and Medicare. Together, these two programs have slashed poverty among the elderly and protected all Americans from the two major hazards of old age: inadequate income and exorbitant medical costs. But for the ideal of social insurance to be truly realized, it needs to be extended in two directions: *downward* to working-age Americans and their families, and *outward* to cover the new and newly intensified risks that threaten families' well-being.

The first priority is institutional, rather than programmatic: the unification of government responsibility for protecting economic security. In the 1940s, income security was the concern of the Federal Security Agency, which oversaw Social Security. But its eventual successor, the Department of Health and Human Services, is essentially a beleaguered overseer of a disparate set of programs, with little overarching rationale or independent capacity for planning. Just as we needed a new Department of Homeland Security to coordinate protection against terrorism, we need a new Department of Economic Security to coordinate protection against economic risk.

No less important are official measures of economic risk that would sensitize policymakers and families to the magnitude of the problem. The federal government compiles a wide range of economic statistics—gross domestic product, the consumer price index, unemployment, income inequality—but, strikingly, not a single one captures income variability. A standard government measure of income volatility like the one presented earlier would alert policymakers to the reality of income risk and help them track its change over time.

Not all indicators, however, have to be created by the government: The economist Robert Shiller has suggested, for example, that creating futures markets for volatile influences upon income, like median home prices and the long-term earnings of professions, would provide crucial information to families considering major life choices.

Ultimately, however, the best governance structures or information sources will not protect Americans when disasters strike. Nor will the market acting alone. Private insurance often works well, but it has inherent difficulties in the realm of social risks. Profit-making insurers simply will not offer affordable protection to higher-risk groups or ensure that insurance is affordable for less affluent citizens. Only government can.

The essential first step, then, is to shore up existing policies. As a start, we should ensure adequate and broad-based unemployment, pension, and health benefits to workers. We should also restore some measure of sanity to the tax code. A progressive tax system is a form of income insurance, requiring lower payments when income drops and higher payments when it rises. But our tax code is, in reality, only marginally progressive, and the tax cuts of 2001 and 2003 promise to shift it even farther from this goal.

Although these measures would help many Americans, simply protecting and improving existing programs will not do enough to help families during the working years. What is needed are policies, both public and private, that are robust enough to allow families to hedge against the most pervasive risks to their income, yet flexible enough to accommodate the ever changing nature of risks over time. Currently, the wealthy can hedge through private investments and through government-subsidized savings accounts, which are worth a considerable amount to people in the highest tax brackets (who gain the most from tax deductions and exemptions). The very poor often receive direct government assistance of some sort. Middle class families, however, have few comparable protections.

The last piece of the risk-protection puzzle, therefore, would be a new Universal Insurance program that protects families against catastrophic drops in income or budget-destroying expenses. Universal Insurance would serve as an umbrella insurance policy for family incomes. Premiums would be a small share of total income, and payouts would be based on the decline of income from its previous base, with the share of income replaced higher for lower-income families.

Universal Insurance, in turn, would be coupled with special tax-subsidized savings accounts that would help families to manage these expenses before they reached catastrophic levels. All contributions to and the interest income of the accounts would be tax-free up to a certain amount. Each year, and upon the birth of children, the government would contribute small amounts to each family's accounts. These contributions would vary inversely with income, offsetting the regressive distribution of the tax benefits.

Many details of universal insurance could be decided upon by political leaders, including the list of specific risks covered, the up-front deductible that families would pay before coverage kicked in, and the means by which the program would police fraud and protect against so-called moral hazard—the tendency for people with insurance to take more risks. The important principle is that Universal Insurance should provide general risk protection. Families should have access to more than the highly segmented programs that now characterize American social protection—programs that not only leave glaring gaps, but also lack the ability to respond to a rapidly changing world of risk.

Universal Insurance would protect Americans *before* they fell into poverty, lessening the burden on means-tested programs for the poor and protecting the dignity and well-being of its beneficiaries. In doing so, it would reduce the demand for regulatory and protectionist policies that stifle economic, technological, and social change. Its premise would be that rapid change is often good, but that it is only politically viable and morally defensible if families are protected from the most severe "hazards and vicissitudes of life," in FDR's famous and still-relevant words.

In the early twenty-first century, Americans face uncertainties of a scale not seen since the vast economic and family transitions of the early twentieth century. Today's great transformation—from an all-in-the-same-boat world of shared risk toward a go-it-alone world of personal responsibility—has taken decades to unfold and reflects a host of interlocking changes. Slowing, much less reversing, the tide will not occur overnight, and it will not be easy. But solutions exist, and the vital goal of expanding risk protection for the American family offers the best hope for reviving a constructive role for government—on bold new terms—in the next American century.

12

The Parent Trap

Karen Kornbluh

Working American parents have twenty-two fewer hours a week to spend with their kids than they did thirty years ago. Here's how to help the new "juggler family."

THE AMERICAN FAMILY changed dramatically over the last decades of the twentieth century. In the postwar years up to the early 1970s a single breadwinner—working forty hours a week, often for the same employer, until retirement—generally earned enough to support children and a spouse. Today fully 70 percent of families with children are headed by two working parents or by an unmarried working parent. The traditional family—one breadwinner and one homemaker—has been replaced by the "juggler family," and American parents have twenty-two fewer hours a week to spend with their kids than they did in 1969. As a result, millions of children are left in unlicensed day care or at home with the TV as a babysitter.

Yet the nation clings to the ideal of the 1950s family; many of our policies for and cultural attitudes toward families are relics of a time when Father worked and Mother was home to mind the children. Every time a working parent has to risk a job to take a sick child to the doctor, and every time parents have to leave their children home alone or entrust them to inadequate supervision, families are paying the price for our outdated policies.

The 1950s family is not coming back anytime soon, however, because the economic conditions that supported it no longer exist. Starting in the 1970s de-industrialization, corporate restructuring, and globalization led to stagnating wages and greater economic insecurity. Many women went to work to help make ends meet. Indeed, conservatives who lament that feminism undermined the traditional family model overlook the fact that the changing economic environment made that model financially impossible for most American families.

These days most women and men—across all income levels—expect to remain in the workplace after having children. Thus to be decent parents, workers now need greater flexibility than they once did. Yet good part-time or flextime jobs remain rare. Whereas companies have embraced flexibility in virtually every other aspect of their businesses (inventory control, production schedules, financing), fulltime workers' schedules remain inflexible. Employers often demand that high-level workers be available around the clock, and hourly workers can be fired for refusing overtime. Moreover, many employees have no right to a minimum number of sick or vacation days: more than a third of all working parents—and an even larger percentage of low-income parents—lack both sick and vacation leave. Though the Family and Medical Leave Act of 1993 finally guaranteed that workers at large companies could take a leave of absence for the birth or adoption of a baby, or for the illness of a family member, that leave is unpaid. This means that the United States is one of only two countries in the Organization for Economic Cooperation and Development without paid maternity leave—and the other country, Australia, is actively considering providing it.

Many parents who need flexibility find themselves shunted into part-time, temporary, on-call, or contract jobs with reduced wages and career opportunities and, often, no benefits. A full quarter of American workers are in these jobs. Only 15 percent of women and 12 percent of men in such jobs receive health insurance from their employers. In other developed countries health benefits are often government-provided, and therefore not contingent on full-time employment. The United States is the only advanced industrial nation that relies on a voluntary employer-based system to provide health insurance and retirement benefits to its citizens.

Our nation has also failed to respond to the need for affordable, high-quality childcare. Schools still operate on an agrarian schedule, closing at three every day and for more than two months in the summer.

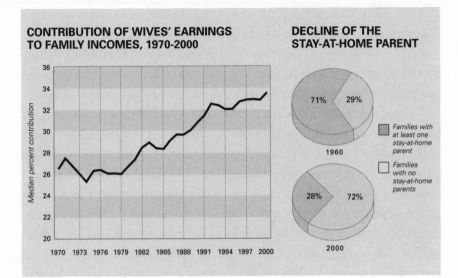

After-school-care programs are relatively scarce, and day-care standards are uneven. (Training requirements for hairdressers and manicurists are currently more stringent than those for child-care workers.) And the expense of day care—which is often more than the tuition at a state college—is borne almost entirely by parents alone. In stark contrast, most European nations view childcare as a national responsibility and publicly subsidize it. In France, for instance, day-care centers and preschools are heavily subsidized—and staffed by qualified child-care workers whose education is financed by the government.

A SENSIBLE MODERN FAMILY POLICY—that supports rather than undermines today's juggler family—would have three components. The first is paid leave. No American worker should have to fear losing a job or suffering a reduction in pay because he or she needs to care for a child or a parent. Every worker should be entitled to at least a minimum number of days of paid leave for personal illness or that of a family member, or to care for a new child. In September 2002, California adopted the first law in the country that provides workers with paid family and medical leave, up to six weeks' worth.

The second component of a smart family policy is high-quality childcare. The United States is practically alone among developed countries in leaving day care almost entirely to the private market. At a minimum, U.S. day-care facilities must be held to higher standards than they are now, and parents should be eligible for subsidies, so that they do not have to shoulder the cost of this care all on their own. In addition, preschool and after-school programs should be universally available.

The third and most important component is more fundamental: we should sever the link between employers and basic benefits. In today's labor market, when working parents need maximum flexibility and people move frequently from job to job, it no longer makes sense to rely on employers for the provision of health insurance and pensions. The link between them is an industrial-era relic that often denies benefits and tax subsidies to parents who require nonstandard working arrangements. We need a new approach to our social-insurance system, one in which control and responsibility lie with individuals, not their employers, and in which government subsidies are granted based on an individual's ability to pay, rather than on whether he or she works full time, part time, or flex time. Unlinking benefits from employment could do wonders for the American family: parents could have the flexibility of part-time work with the benefits that today accompany full-time work.

How to unlink pensions from employment—by providing universal 401(k) accounts that offer government subsidies to the poorest workers—is addressed elsewhere in this book (see "Spendthrift Nation"). Unlinking health care from employment could be accomplished in a number of ways. One way would be to expand Medicare to cover all citizens, not just the elderly, thus creating a single-payer system. But a better approach would be to create a system of mandatory self-insurance, with government subsidies for low-income workers and for people taking time off to care for family members. Creating such a system—one that ensures that everyone is covered while keeping costs low—could not be done easily or quickly, of course, but there are precedents. Switzerland, for instance, provides universal health-care coverage without relying on a single-payer system. Another model can be found closer to home: auto insurance, which almost all American states require car owners to have. In the health-care version of this model everyone would either choose a plan from a regional insurance exchange or be enrolled in a default plan by the government. Participating health insurance providers would be required to offer a "basic" plan—with a minimum level of coverage—and to cover anyone who applied. Federal subsidies would ensure that no one spent more than a fixed percentage of income on basic health insurance.

Though the government would have to subsidize those who cannot afford to pay for a basic plan on their own, this cost could be largely offset by redirecting both the funds currently spent on Medicaid and the nearly $100 billion that workers get in tax breaks through their employer-provided health insurance. Employers should welcome the change, because although they would likely continue to provide employees with the same level of total compensation they do now (for instance, by increasing wages), they would be relieved of the administrative burdens and the restrictions on flexibility imposed by the current social insurance system.

For the past few decades both Democrats and Republicans have tried to lay claim to the "pro-family" mantle. Neither party, however, has offered a coherent plan for giving American parents the security and the flexibility they need. A plan that offers both would appeal powerfully to the many voters who are having such difficulty balancing their work and family obligations.

13

The $6,000 Solution

Ray Boshara

The United States is more unequal than at any other time since the dawn of the New Deal—indeed, it's the most unequal society in the advanced democratic world. Here's how to fix that.

THROUGHOUT OUR HISTORY, periods of unbounded market exuberance, like the one we recently experienced, have been followed by periods of far-reaching social and economic reform. The Gilded Age of the late nineteenth century gave way to the Populist and Progressive reforms of the early twentieth century, the Roaring Twenties to the New Deal, and the Eisenhower-Kennedy Nifty-Fifty bull market to the Great Society and the War on Poverty. From this cycle of great wealth creation (and abuse) followed by great reform has emerged a social contract that has smoothed out the rougher edges of American capitalism while making us a more prosperous society.

Like the Gilded Age and the Roaring Twenties, the Roaring Nineties (which had its roots in the early 1980s) brought worrying new levels of inequality. Those who owned stock, homes, and other assets enjoyed substantial gains each year—and those with privileged access to initial public offerings often doubled their money in a day. Meanwhile, global competition and the ruthless restructuring of the economy put a lid on wages and benefits for the great majority of Americans, especially those without college degrees. While the rich monitored the gains on their monthly brokerage statements, Americans without financial assets struggled each month to pay the interest on their credit-card bills.

By the close of the 1990s the United States had become more unequal than at any other time since the dawn of the New Deal—indeed, it was the most unequal society in the advanced democratic world. The top 20 percent of households earned 56 percent of the nation's income and commanded an astonishing 83 percent of the nation's wealth. Even more striking, the top one percent earned about 17 percent of national income and owned 38 percent of national wealth. In nearly two decades the number of millionaires had doubled, to 4.8 million, and the number of "deca-millionaires"—those worth at least $10 million—had more than tripled, from 66,500 to 239,400.

In contrast, the bottom 40 percent of Americans earned just 10 percent of the nation's income and owned less than one percent of the nation's wealth. The bottom 60 percent did only marginally better, accounting for about 23 percent of income and less than five percent of wealth. The racial gaps are even more disheartening. The typical African-American household had fifty-four cents of income and twelve cents of wealth for every corresponding dollar in the typical white American household. Hispanics had sixty-two cents of income and four cents of wealth.

The wealth gap dwarfs the more oft noted income gap not only in size but also in significance, for several reasons. First, ownership of assets—a home, land, a business, savings and investments—provides the kind of security that permits planning for the future and the future of one's children. Second, although a job and an income are obviously important, they cannot be bequeathed to future generations, whereas wealth—and the status and opportunities it confers—can be. Finally, with wealth comes political influence. Many politicians spend more time raising money from the wealthy than they do speaking with their own constituents. As Kevin Phillips, the author of *Wealth and Democracy* (2002), recently observed, the intense concentration of the nation's wealth in a small sliver of society has raised the specter of plutocracy.

One way the rich use their influence, of course, is to protect and increase their wealth. But the political privileges enjoyed by the rich over the past decade cannot alone explain the size of the wealth gap. Clean up all the corruption on Wall Street and K Street, and we would still have huge inequalities of wealth. Deeper forces are at work, among them the introduction of labor-saving technologies that have benefited the owners of capital at the expense of workers; the downward pressure that globalization has exerted on wages; and changes that have made the tax code less progressive and more friendly to the better-off.

There is also the fact that wealth, like debt, is self-replicating. Compound interest turns wealth into more wealth and debt into more debt. Other things being equal, those with interest-bearing savings accounts will end up richer after a year, and those who must pay interest on credit card or consumer household debt will end up poorer. Thus even a neutral government policy toward wealth and asset building will end up exacerbating the wealth gap. But over the past several decades policy has hardly been neutral. The federal government currently has two distinct policies: asset-building incentives for better-off Americans (in the form of more than $300 billion in tax benefits each year for such things as home ownership, business development, college education, and retirement saving)—and income support for the rest.

Tax breaks that encourage asset building are smart policy—except that more than 90 percent of the benefits of the two largest programs (which support home ownership and retirement saving) go to the wealthiest 55 percent of taxpayers. This enormously regressive policy thus excludes people who don't earn enough to enjoy the benefits built into the tax code. In addition, many poorer Americans face limits on the assets they can own if they want to continue receiving necessary food, health, and other income-support assistance.

IF ASSET-BUILDING POLICIES are good for better-off Americans, shouldn't such policies be good for *all* Americans? Actually, broad-based asset-building programs have a long and successful history in America. The Homestead Act of 1862, for example, offered 160 acres of land to every American—rich or poor—who was willing to occupy and cultivate it for five years. And the GI Bill of 1944 helped millions of Americans get a college education or buy a first home. These programs greatly equalized the distribution of wealth in America—not by punishing the rich but by expanding opportunities and the ownership of assets.

In the effort to shrink the huge wealth gap that has developed over the past decade or two, the first step is straightforward: we should extend the same opportunities that better-off Americans now have to everyone else, through refundable tax credits and matching deposits to encourage college education, home ownership, business ownership, and retirement saving.

But the next step has to be bolder: a Homestead Act for the twenty-first century. Here's how it might work. Every one of the four million babies born in America each year would receive an endowment of $6,000 in an American Stakeholder Account. If invested in a relatively safe portfolio that yielded a seven percent annual return, this sum would grow to more than $20,000 by the time the child graduated from high school, and to $45,000 by the time he or she reached thirty (assuming that the account had not yet been used). Funds in the American Stakeholder Account would be restricted to such asset-building uses as paying for the cost of higher education or vocational training, buying a first home, starting a small business, making investments, and, eventually, creating a nest egg for retirement. Withdrawals would of course decrease the account; work and saving would build it back up. Family members and others could also add money to the account.

Although the program would be universal, giving every American child a tool to help meet his or her lifelong asset needs, it would especially benefit the 26 percent of white children, the 52 percent of black children, and the 54 percent of Hispanic children who start life in households without any resources whatsoever for investment. For these children and others, an asset stake would provide choice, a ticket to the middle class, and, most important, hope.

Prime Minister Tony Blair has proposed a variation on this idea in England, and it could be done in the United States for only about $24 billion a year—a very small amount by the standards of federal programs, and only about a sixth of what the government gives in tax breaks to corporations every year. The American Stakeholder Act, like the Homestead Act and the GI Bill before it, would be a smart investment in our nation's future. Nearly a quarter of all American adults today have a legacy of asset ownership that can be directly linked to the Homestead Act. The GI Bill has generated returns to our country of up to $12.50 for every dollar invested. If asset building were started at birth, even greater returns could be expected from the American Stakeholder Act. Moreover, research indicates that asset ownership increases educational attainment, civic involvement, health quality, and life satisfaction, while decreasing marital breakup. And assets, unlike public assistance, can be passed from one generation to the next.

Americans readily tolerate inequality of *outcomes*, accepting that it's a necessary by-product of how we reward the hard work, initiative, and creativity that underpin our much envied economy. But we should not accept inequality of *opportunity*. Expanding the ownership of assets through a program of American Stakeholder Accounts would help to ensure that wealth inequality in one generation does not become magnified into gross inequality of opportunity in the next.

14

The Black Gender Gap

Katherine Boo

It may be the greatest policy achievement in recent history: over the past decade significant numbers of formerly welfare-dependent black women have successfully entered the work force. But what about black men?

TEN YEARS AGO shoe-leather urbanologists found their primary source material in the late-night crack market. Today they're better off rising early and divesting themselves of $1.10 in pocket change to ride the U8 bus, a leading economic indicator of the American inner city. The U8, which serves the easternmost corner of Washington, D.C., is what's known in public-transport parlance as a circuit bus. Its African-American riders are among the most isolated of the urban poor: those who not only can't afford private transportation but can't afford to live near efficient versions of the public kind. These men and women rely instead on buses that wend from one remote housing project to another, collecting riders who are eventually deposited at some central location from which they can take subways or straight-line buses to where the jobs are.

Every weekday at dawn the U8 offers its passengers the predictable dystopian ghetto vista: a drug-treatment clinic, its parking lot aglint with spent needles; a mini-mart with a sign on its door begging, "PLEASE!!! No ski masks allowed!!!!" Only the view inside the U8 is novel and promising. Wearing secondhand suits, often accessorized by fold-up strollers, the U8's riders are the sleepy embodiment of what may be the greatest social-policy achievement in recent U.S. history: the upward mobility of what many not long ago deemed a permanent underclass.

From a peak of 5.1 million families in 1994, welfare rolls have dropped to 2 million, while the poverty rate for African-American children has hit an all-time low. African-American teenage childbearing has declined, and the median annual income for African-American households has surpassed $27,000, reaching the highest level ever recorded. The U8's hundreds of daily riders suggest how firmly the idea of work has taken root even in public-housing communities where a decade ago 90 percent of residents lived primarily on government support.

Only when we break down the numbers by sex do these soothing data bare the domestic-policy challenge that has to be seriously engaged. Something vital is missing on America's U8s: black males.

IN THE MOST GENEROUS GLOSS, the 1996 federal welfare-reform act aimed to do more than promote work and reduce the tax burden of welfare payments. Explicitly and ambitiously, it endeavored to strengthen historically fragile low-income families. Last year, declaring the task of getting people to work well under way, the President and congressional Republicans put the promotion of marriage atop their social-policy agenda. But even as they spoke, welfare reform's inroads on poverty were opening a chasm between the status and prospects of black women and those of the men they might marry.

A grim home economics: In the 1990s the employment of young black females dramatically increased, despite the fact that many of those working women were single mothers. Meanwhile, the employment of their less-encumbered male counterparts stagnated, even in a period of unprecedented economic expansion. Today black women are more likely to work than white or Hispanic women, whereas black men are less likely than their counterparts. Among non-college-educated young blacks the gender gap is starker. Findings by the social scientists Paul Offner and Harry Holzer, published recently by the Brookings Institution, indicate that whereas young non-college-educated Hispanic males now work at about the same rate as their white counterparts, the rate for African-Americans is a staggering 30 percentage points lower. In fact, fully half of these young black men are unemployed or not in the labor force—and these figures don't even include men in jail. A

ten-day census of early-morning ridership on the U8 last autumn tal-
lied 2.7 women for every man.

Set aside the profound emotional implications of this gender gap—
the loneliness of newly working women struggling to raise children by
themselves; the resentment of men watching female contemporaries
succeed, with considerable government assistance, in jobs at which they
themselves have failed or from which they've been displaced by women.
The greater poignancy comes as social science increasingly ratifies a
conservative cliché: for children a two-parent household is the most
effective anti-poverty program we know. Three out of four white children are born to such households. Only one in three black children is.

The children of single parents are more likely to be abused, become
sick, use drugs, commit crimes, be imprisoned, and have out-of-wed-
lock children—the litany, from decades of longitudinal study, is familiar. Clearly, two-parent households have the potential to create the
continuity-rich context in which children's intellectual and emotional
qualities may take wing. Yet the grave predicament of the contemporary black male, and its fundamental connection to the fate of black children, has managed to slip quietly through two distinct cracks: the one
between competing special-interest blocs of the poverty industry, and
the one between the hardened ideological categories of right and left.

Paul Offner has felt a chill from both directions. A Princeton-
trained social scientist, Offner is best known in public-welfare circles
for a radical career choice. In 1995 he decided to road-test some of the
policy prescriptions he had devised while working as a senior aide to
Senator Daniel Patrick Moynihan and as the chief health-and-welfare
counselor to the Senate Finance Committee. Offner accepted a job
administering what was then one of America's most dysfunctional
urban bureaucracies: Mayor Marion Barry's District of Columbia
Medicaid office, whose cost overruns had left Washington near bankruptcy. While stabilizing costs and constructing one of the country's
most inclusive health-coverage programs for the poor and the working
class, Offner was struck by how the funding patterns of what he calls
the welfare-industrial complex contribute to the neglect of black men.
"The emotional testimony at congressional hearings on welfare reform
is inevitably going to be about day care, or welfare time limits, or def-

initions of activities that qualify as work," he says, "because women and children are the social-services constituency—the individuals with whom the government and the nonprofits interact. Men are barely on the screen, except as deadbeat dads. But if you go into families' homes"—Offner is a veteran volunteer tutor of Southeast D.C. schoolchildren—"you can't help thinking about how much difference a decent father could make in how a child behaves and develops."

The best contemporary social science on nonworking black males tends to wrestle with causality: Why did so many black men abandon the labor force in the first place? Does the legacy of slavery, which gravely distorted kin and work relationships, weigh more heavily on males than on females? Which came first, and matters more, the decline in the manufacturing sector or the rise in black men's incarceration rates?

If there is less rigorous discussion about how, now, to create opportunity for black males, it may be because the political utility of such a debate is uncertain. Drawing acute distinctions between the deserving and the undeserving poor, the political right resists heavy investment in a child-abandoning, work-resistant, lawbreaking population. But-tressing the right's position is the fact that previous federally funded efforts to put young black males to work have produced few appreciable results. The left, meanwhile, is reluctant to advocate for men in the face of the considerable needs of women—such as the need for better child-care options than the typically stultifying urban centers to which welfare reform's next generation has been entrusted.

Yet there is artifice in the notion that black men and women are pitted against each other in a fight for a limited pool of public aid. After all, the plight of the poor black male translates into the plight of the ludicrously overfreighted poor black female. (Black women now earn 96 percent of what white women earn, but that's still on average only $15,000 a year. Surely they could also use the 70 percent of white male income that black men earn: $20,000.) On the U8 one morning the most animated discussion among young mothers concerned the much anticipated release of a painkiller called Bayer Back and Body. A working, child-nurturing partner would certainly be a stronger anodyne, but the R&D isn't there. Offner notes that whereas he can secure plenty of public and private funding for research on health care, the extensive studies of the poor black male population that he's doing with Harry Holzer have been self-financed.

For those willing to write off a generation or two of children and fathers, a case can be made for policy passivity. The current rift between black men and women may be simply a transitional trauma in the process of birthing a better culture. It's also possible that black women will solve some of their problems by marrying in larger numbers outside their race. But at this moment in history new developments inside and outside the inner city may provide new opportunities for social policy to reach the young black male.

The level of promise can easily be overstated. First, it's harder to help poor black men get jobs than poor black women, in part because many employers perceive women to be more trainable, a better employment risk. Second, as the Harvard sociologist Orlando Patterson persuasively contends, employment does not necessarily make black men more likely to marry. (Whether this is because of slavery's legacy or because the decently employed black male has so many romantic options that he may not be inclined to choose just one is a live sociological question.) Still, inside ghettos the market for crack has significantly weakened in recent years, and no equally profitable illicit product has yet replaced it. Thus the appeal of "the honest eight"—the legitimate job—may be quietly increasing among men, along with the appeal of a breadwinning woman. And outside ghettos, more demonstrably, there's a rich new body of knowledge, gleaned from welfare reform, about how to bring the seemingly unemployable into the economic mainstream.

IT'S WORTH RECALLING that for decades the government failed miserably in a series of schemes to encourage welfare mothers to work. But in the 1990s rigorous evaluations of local welfare-to-work programs provided a detailed blueprint from which the current law was constructed. That new law contained a vital acknowledgment: rectifying disincentives and adjusting outlooks among the poor costs more in the short run than issuing welfare checks. Since 1996 we've been willing to pay that short-term cost in behalf of low-income women. Unfortunately, most poor black men lack the singular qualification that made their female counterparts the object of sustained intellection and public money: consumption of taxpayers' dollars in the form of monthly welfare checks.

What if unemployed fathers who owed child support were mandated to participate in work-related activities or community service? What if they then received stipends while learning skills or searching for jobs with the assistance of community-based programs that have established a track record in helping women? Program evaluations tentatively find that intense, employment-oriented programs for disadvantaged fathers increase the likelihood of their working, paying child support, and—for the most estranged fathers—becoming more involved with their kids. Although the 1996 law allows states to spend welfare-reform money on such programs, a 2000 survey found that most states chose not to mandate them. And in the states that were willing to invest in men, stiff remedies for their disadvantages consistently lost out to soft, milky ones. Thus today poor noncustodial fathers can easily avail themselves of any number of group-therapy-like programs to inculcate responsible fatherhood. But if those fathers take the government hint, find a job, and actually marry the similarly encouraged mothers of their children, the newlyweds will face a significant increase in their tax burden because of the way the Earned Income Tax Credit is structured. As both the old and new welfare systems have demonstrated, financial incentives can change family patterns. But for fathers many of those incentives still run in the wrong direction.

The left used to argue that a narrow population neglected would erupt into a wide public threat. This is perhaps the moment to invoke the specter of long, hot summers and armed, envenomed men. But in truth inner-city women, not outsiders, are the ones who will bear—are bearing—the brunt of the black gender gap.

Nonetheless, and beyond all expectation, many of those women have managed to hold up their end of the new social contract. As they raise the next generation, a generation that of course includes males, it is perhaps not just intimate family ties but larger civic ones that merit re-examination. Low-income men who have dropped out of the labor force obviously lack the innocence and promise of, say, the dozens of tiny riders on the U8, clinging like limpets to mothers who will shortly deliver them to Kiddies Kollege, All My Children, and the other bleak federally funded nurseries clustering around the U8's points of debarkation. But for better or worse, the long-term well-being of those children—and of their country—depends less on their day care than on their fathers.

REINVENTING EDUCATION

15

A Grand Compromise

James P. Pinkerton

Saving American education requires ending the reliance of public schools on local property-tax bases.

IN 1983 A FEDERAL EDUCATION commission warned that "a rising tide of mediocrity" threatened the well-being of the republic. That tide has not ebbed. Nearly two decades later, in 2000, the Program for International Student Assessment found that American fifteen-year-olds ranked fourteenth in science literacy and eighteenth in mathematics literacy among the thirty-two countries administering the test, scoring below the average for developed countries in both categories. And although President George W. Bush and Congress recently united behind the grandiosely titled No Child Left Behind Act of 2001, few observers outside Washington, D.C., believe that the legislation will have anything more than a marginal effect on student performance.

All Presidents claim to be "education Presidents," but the schools drift along, up a bit, down a bit, always costing more money, but never making the sort of dramatic gains witnessed elsewhere in American life. Why should this be?

U.S. schools today are the product of three different educational eras: the agricultural (which produced the nine-month school year), the industrial (which emphasized rote learning and regimentation to fit the rhythms of mass production), and what might be called the experimental (which promoted a range of nostrums, from sex education to Whole Language, often at the expense of basic skills). Each of these has left its own layer of sediment to muck things up in the present. The worst legacy of the past, however, is localized school funding, which not only produces great regional inequalities in spending per pupil but also nurtures the persistent incompetence of many schools.

Today about 45 percent of school funding comes from local sources, such as property taxes. In Virginia, for example, average per-pupil spending in rural Hanover County is only half that in suburban Arlington County. In New Jersey, which has been struggling to equalize school funding for three decades, the schools in Elizabeth spend 70 percent more per pupil than do the schools in Toms River.

Beyond state lines the disparities grow even worse: among school districts with enrollments of 15,000 or more, spending ranges from $3,932 per pupil in De Soto County, Mississippi, to $14,244 in Elizabeth, New Jersey. Rectifying such imbalances requires a national solution. "Most of the resource inequality cannot be resolved at the state level," David Grissmer and Ann Flanagan, analysts for the Rand Corporation, have written. "States spending the least are southern and western states that also have a disproportionate share of the nation's minority and disadvantaged students." Yet the federal government does little to address this systemic inequality, and continues to contribute only about seven percent of the total spent on elementary and secondary schools.

So what's an "education President" to do? Happily, the means of reforming elementary and secondary education does not lie in some obscure theory, or in some other country. It has been right in front of our eyes for decades: the model of the Pell Grant program.

Colleges and universities compete, in effect, in a single national market. The federal government pumps $10 billion a year into college education through Pell Grants. The GI Bill and other aid programs add billions more. Pell Grants have an inherently equalizing effect on per-student funding: every qualifying student in the country has access to the same amount—a maximum of $4,050 a year—and can spend it at the accredited college of his or her choice. Thus much of higher education is more equitably funded than K–12 education. Moreover, because Pell recipients decide where their grants are applied, the program is driven by students, not administrators.

Why not build on the Pell model, and apply it to elementary and secondary education? Total K–12 public school spending, for some 47 million students, is currently about $350 billion a year, slightly more than $7,000 per pupil per year. Expanding on the Pell model would mean giving every American elementary and secondary school student $7,000 to spend at the school of his or her choice. Unlike Pell Grants, this money would be given to all students, regardless of the level of need. This would create, in effect, a grand compromise between left and right, guaranteeing more-equal funding (which the left wants) and more choice for students (which the right wants).

Making this happen, of course, would require a radical reshuffling of financial responsibilities among the various levels of government. But such a reshuffling is not unprecedented; after all, though states and localities once bore the cost of raising militias, national defense is now a federal responsibility. Since 9/11, of course, federal responsibility for homeland defense has increased, to the point where a new Cabinet department has been legislated.

Education is no less a national priority than defense. Education reformers should not shrink from the full implications of their goals; it's time for the federal government to do more for education—and for state and local governments to do less. It is true that the $350 billion a year in spending that the federal government would have to take on from state and local governments is no small amount. But at three percent of GDP, it is less than the annual U.S. military budget, and less than what the federal government spends on health care each year. And because state and local governments would be able either to spend the money currently allotted to education on other priorities or to rebate money to taxpayers, any federal tax increases or spending cuts made to accommodate this new system would be at least partially offset.

Of course, many conservatives and some liberals might object to the loss of local control over schools. But local control is in some ways detrimental to education and to equity. In the Jim Crow South, after all, local control was synonymous with "separate but equal"; today an insistence on local funding ought not to be a cover for maintaining separate and obviously unequal schools.

Moreover, conservatives ought to be pleased with the second element of the grand compromise: expanded choice. The current method of funding K–12 education balkanizes school districts into pockets of excellence or indifference; a federal grant program would make all schools part of a national system, in which no child would be forced by accident of region or neighborhood to attend a bad school.

Because students in such a system could attend the schools of their choice, they would create a self-correcting market. If a given school was inadequate, students could go elsewhere, taking their funding with them. The fragmentary evidence of the past few years suggests that schools faced with competition will struggle to retain "market share."

Of course, if schools in Mississippi are substandard at $4,000 per pupil, there is no guarantee that they would be better at $7,000 per pupil. One of the bitter lessons of the twentieth-century welfare state is that a bureaucracy has an apparently infinite capacity to absorb extra money without producing additional output. But under this proposal schools would have a compelling interest in responding to an exodus of students; a school that failed to respond positively would lose its financial base.

Critics of this plan will say that it is a form of vouchers—and they will be correct. But this plan can't be derided as an attempt to under-

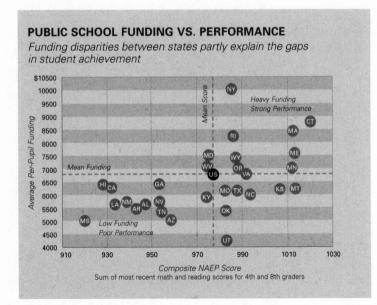

PUBLIC SCHOOL FUNDING VS. PERFORMANCE
Funding disparities between states partly explain the gaps in student achievement

mine the public schools by bleeding away their students. Rather, it's an attempt to lift all schools into the mainstream by equalizing funding across the country, improving the odds that every child receives an education appropriate for this century.

What schools would be eligible to receive this grant money? Public schools only? Religious schools? Home schools? Ideally, every kind of school, though as a practical matter certain schools would not be made eligible right away. The politics of reform must sometimes yield to the slower-moving politics of the possible. But once the principle of federally funded choice was established, its application would expand as the education market reacted to the new incentives.

This is just the outline of a grand compromise on education. If the right celebrates "liberty" untrammeled by bureaucracy and the left celebrates "rights" guaranteed, if necessary, by the government, the two can come together in behalf of a system of federally funded equal opportunity. Although neither side will like everything about this proposal, both might yet decide they like the status quo even less. And federally funded choice is a bold assault on the orthodoxies of the status quo.

16

A New Deal for Teachers

Matthew Miller

Here's how to fix our desperate urban schools: attract better teachers by paying them more—much more—but tie compensation to performance and allow districts to fire bad teachers quickly.

No ONE SHOULD NEED CONVINCING that schools in the nation's poor districts are in crisis. A recent Department of Education study found that fourth-grade students in low-income areas tested three grade levels behind students in higher-income areas. "Most 4th graders who live in U.S. cities can't read and understand a simple children's book," a special report in *Education Week* concluded a few years ago, "and most 8th graders can't use arithmetic to solve a practical problem."

There are probably a hundred things these schools need, and ten things that could make a very big difference, but if we had to focus on only one thing, the most important would be improving teacher quality. Owing to rising enrollments and a coming wave of retirements, more than two million teachers must be recruited over the next decade—700,000 of them in poor districts. That means fully two-thirds of the teacher corps will be new to the job. Finding top talent and not simply warm bodies is a tall order, especially in urban districts, where half of new teachers quit within three years (and studies suggest that it's the smarter half). Research shows that much of the achievement gap facing poor and minority students comes not from poverty or family conditions but from systemic differences in teacher quality; thus recruiting better teachers for poor schools is not only the biggest issue in education but the next great frontier for social justice.

The obstacles to improving teacher quality are great. Good teachers in urban schools have told me with dismay of the incompetence of many of their colleagues. The state competency requirements that aspiring teachers must meet are appallingly low. The late Albert Shanker, the legendary president of the American Federation of Teachers, once said that most of the state tests are so easy to pass that they keep only "illiterates" out of teaching. Yet even these minimal standards are routinely waived so that districts can issue "emergency credentials"; in our biggest cities as many as half of new hires, and up to a quarter of city teachers overall, aren't properly trained or credentialed.

The situation may soon get even worse, because many of the teachers now reaching retirement age are among the best in the system. Until the 1960s and 1970s schools attracted talented women and minority members to whom most higher-paying careers weren't open. Now people who might once have taught science or social studies become doctors, lawyers, and engineers. Salaries that start, on average, at $29,000 simply can't compete with the pay in other professions. In 1970 in New York City a lawyer starting out at a prestigious firm and a teacher going into public education had a difference in their salaries of about $2,000. Today that lawyer makes $145,000 (including bonus), whereas the teacher earns roughly $40,000. Sandra Feldman, the president of the American Federation of Teachers, is quite open about the problem. "You have in the schools right now, among the teachers who are going to be retiring, *very* smart people," she told me. "We're not getting in the same kinds of people. In some places it's disastrous."

How should we address this crisis? Most discussion so far has revolved around improving the skills of the teachers we already have. But upgrading the skills of current teachers can get us only so far when so many new teachers will be needed. Although changing the kind of person who goes into teaching may be hopelessly beyond the power of local school budgets and policies, we need to seize this moment of generational turnover in the teaching ranks to lure top college graduates to our toughest classrooms.

How to do this? Let's stipulate first that pay isn't everything. Teachers are the only category of people I've ever met who routinely say, without irony, that their jobs are so fulfilling they hardly care how little they make. For many of them, too, job security, good health benefits and pensions, and free summers offset the low income. But fulfillment and fringe benefits will never suffice to attract and retain hundreds of thousands of talented new teachers for poor districts.

There's no way to get large numbers of top people without paying up. Conservatives rightly worry that pouring more money into the system will subsidize mediocrity rather than lure new talent—especially when union rules make it next to impossible to fire bad teachers. "Dismissing a tenured teacher is not a process," one California official has said. "It's a career." The effort can take years and involve hundreds of thousands of dollars. Rather than being fired, bad teachers are shuffled from school to school. In a recent five-year period only sixty-two of the 220,000 tenured teachers in California were dismissed.

A grand bargain could be struck between unions and conservatives: make more money available for teachers' salaries in exchange for flexibility in how it is spent. For instance, the standard "lockstep" union pay scale, whereby a teacher with a degree in biochemistry has to be paid the same as one with a degree in physical education if both have the same number of years in the classroom (even though the biochemist has lucrative options outside teaching), should be scrapped. Better performing teachers should make more than worse ones. And dismissing poor performers—who, even union leaders agree, make up perhaps 10 percent of urban teachers—should be made much easier.

If the quality of urban schools is to be improved, teaching poor children must become the career of choice for talented young Americans who want to make a difference with their lives and earn a good living too. To achieve that the federal government should raise the salary of every teacher in a poor school by at least *50 percent*. But this increase would be contingent on two fundamental reforms: teachers' unions would have to abandon the lockstep pay schedules, so that the top-performing half of the teacher corps could be paid significantly more; and the dismissal process for poor-performing teachers would have to be condensed to four to six months.

In Los Angeles teachers currently earn about $40,000 to start and top out, after thirty years and a Ph.D., at about $70,000. Under this new deal those teachers would start at $60,000, and the top-performing half of teachers would make $85,000 to $90,000 a year, on average. A number of the best teachers could earn close to $150,000 a year. The plan is designed to pay America's best teachers of poor students salaries high enough to allow them to put aside a million dollars in savings by the end of their careers.

How much would this plan cost? Roughly $30 billion a year, which would lift the federal share of K-12 spending from seven percent to 14 percent of the total nationwide—only right, given that on their own poor districts can't afford the skilled teachers they need. This federal investment looks modest beside the $80 billion a year that some representatives of corporate America say they spend training ill-prepared high school graduates to work in modern industry. The plan could be administered through a program similar to Title I, which provides supplementary federal funds to poor schools. We might call it Title I for Teachers.

To FIND OUT whether this basic plan is politically feasible, I presented it to big-city superintendents, high-ranking union leaders, and assorted education experts and teachers.

"I'd endorse something like that in a hot minute," said Day Higuchi, the president of the Los Angeles teachers' union from 1996 to 2002. "Right now L.A. Unified is the employer of last resort. People who can't get jobs elsewhere come here. If we did this, we'd become the employer of first resort. High-powered college students will be taking the job." Arne Duncan, the CEO of the Chicago Public Schools, told me that now there's "very little incentive outside of pure altruism" to get someone into teaching. This proposal "would dramatically change the face of the teacher profession," he said.

To gauge the conservative reaction, I spoke with Chester E. Finn Jr., a longtime school reformer on the right. Finn is the president of the Thomas B. Fordham Foundation, and served as an assistant secretary of education in the Reagan Administration. He expressed several concerns. "The troubling part of this proposal," he said, "is a 50 percent boost for just showing up for work, without any reference to whether anybody you teach learns a damned thing."

I replied that the offer was designed to make it worthwhile for the unions to accept real reform in pay and dismissal practices. And the pay increase would subsidize mediocrity only briefly, because under the new dismissal rules bad teachers could much more easily be fired.

Finn had his own variation to offer. "If you wanted to make this plan really interesting," he told me, "job security and tenure would be traded for this raise. The swap here ought to be that you take a risk with your employment and you don't have to be retained if you're not good at what you do. If you are good and you get retained, you get paid a whole lot more money. If current teachers can't swallow that tradeoff, make this a parallel personnel system for new ones coming in and for the existing ones who want to do it."

How might that work? I asked.

"Any current teacher is free to join this new system on its terms," Finn said, "or to stick with the old arrangement, in which they have high security and low pay. That's just a political accommodation to an existing work force for whom this might be too abrupt a shift. Over time you'll get a very different kind of person into teaching."

"It sounds tempting from a union point of view," Sandra Feldman told me of Finn's parallel approach. "The more voluntary you can make a system like this, the easier it is to sell. But I worry that something like that could create resentment between the people in the different tracks." Other union and district leaders, however, told me they thought that virtually every new hire would opt for the new system, as would perhaps a quarter of the senior teachers—meaning that most of the urban teacher corps would be on the plan within five years.

THAT UNION LEADERS THINK it makes sense to move toward serious pay differentials for teachers is important. But educators are concerned about two related questions. In determining pay rates, who will decide which teachers are better performers? And what standards will be used to assess teachers?

I asked Sandra Feldman if there was a consensus in the faculty lounges at most schools about who the best teachers were. "Absolutely," she said. The question is how to evaluate performance in a way that is objective and untainted by cronyism.

The superintendents and conservative reformers I spoke to agreed that serious weight should be given to students' test scores. In theory, so-called "value-added analysis"—the effort to track the impact of teachers on student achievement each year—is the holy grail of accountability, and thus the ideal basis for performance pay. But in reality, many people think it has serious limits. "There's just no reliable way of doing that right now," Feldman told me. This isn't only a union view. Joseph Olchefske, the superintendent of schools in Seattle, has studied the issue; he believes it would be hard to measure the value added by individual teachers. Others, however, think individual value-added analysis may soon be practical. Day Higuchi, the former L.A. union leader, argues that in elementary school, where each child has essentially one teacher, the right testing could constructively measure that teacher's impact.

Finn and others suggested a blended approach to teacher assessment. "You could have value-added analysis at the school level, which is clearly going to be done," Finn said, "combined with some other kind of performance reviews." Adam Urbanski, the president of the Rochester Teachers Association, who has spearheaded union-reform efforts for two decades, said, "It would be a fatal mistake not to include student learning outcomes as the ultimate test of this. It would be equally fatal to use only test scores, because you would have a huge invitation to cheating and manipulation." He and others proposed that various indicators regarded as germane to teacher assessment by educators and the public—such as dropout rates, graduation rates, peer review, specialized training, teaching technique, and student work—be considered along with test scores.

The superintendents all told me that principals should be the final arbiters of teacher performance. This is a sticking point with the unions. The problem with giving principals control is that many teachers think principals don't know the first thing about good teaching. Jene Galvin, a teacher who has worked in the Cincinnati school system for twenty-seven years, told me, "We don't really believe that the principals are the experts on pedagogy or classroom teaching or classroom management. The reason is they just didn't do it very long." The solution might be to have peer evaluators—mentor and master teachers—do the evaluations along with principals.

Experts I spoke with, including Finn, thought that all these challenges ultimately seemed surmountable. Finn said that a key to his supporting such a plan would be "that it included the ability for managers of schools to have a whole lot of control over who is working in their school."

IF THIS AGENDA were presented as a federal challenge, in which the President or congressional leaders said, "We're putting this pot of money on the table for those communities that can come together around a plan that meets its conditions and make it work," school districts would almost surely step forward. If unions declined to come to the table, local media and business leaders could ask why they were balking at billions of dollars. Rank-and-file teachers, who might earn an extra $20,000 to $50,000 a year, would obviously have a huge stake in the plan's adoption. They might tell union leaders they supported finding ways of speedily dismissing poor performers.

Some Republicans may resist. After all, teachers' unions are big Democratic donors and the chief foes of Republican efforts to introduce school vouchers. The last thing we need, these Republicans might say, is a bunch of teachers with more money to spend on making sure that Republicans never get elected.

But some savvy Republicans think the time for a plan like this is ripe. Rick Davis, a political adviser to Senator John McCain, believes that such a plan may be inevitable. "Anybody who has looked at teacher pay as an element of the overall problem in education realizes that money matters," Davis told me. "Other than the voucher debate, we've exhausted the Republican position on education. So sooner or later we're going to get to teacher pay, because we can't be against teachers' making money. The American public is going to figure out that their teachers make less than their garbage collectors, and they're not going to be for that."

17

The Tuition Crunch

Jennifer Washburn

For low-income students college is increasingly out of reach.

A FOUR-YEAR COLLEGE DEGREE has become all but a necessity for getting ahead in the information age. Since the 1980s the average real income of workers with only a high school diploma has fallen, while salaries among those with at least a college degree have risen: they now earn 75 percent more than high school graduates. At the national level, having a highly educated work force is critical in order to sustain our technological edge in the global economy.

America's higher-education system ranks among its greatest achievements. But in the past two decades our commitment to equal opportunity in postsecondary education has deteriorated markedly. In 1979 students from the richest 25 percent of American homes were four times as likely to attend college as those from the poorest 25 percent; by 1994 they were ten times as likely.

Part of the problem is the skyrocketing cost of college. Since 1980 tuition and related charges have increased at more than twice the rate of inflation, rising by nearly 40 percent in real terms in the past decade alone. Public attention has focused largely on the $35,000-plus annual cost of elite schools like Harvard and Brown. The bigger problem rests with the public colleges and universities that serve 80 percent of the nation's students. In 2003 the University of Arizona's average annual tuition rose by 39 percent, to $3,604, and Iowa State's rose by 22 percent, to $5,028. For many low-income families increases like these are difficult to absorb. Indeed, the cost for such families of sending a child to a four-year public institution shot from 13 percent of family income in 1980 to 25 percent in 2000 (for middle- and high-income families the percentage barely increased).

Congressional Republicans, led by Representative Howard McKeon, of California, contend that universities are largely to blame for these tuition hikes. However, most experts agree that fluctuations in state spending are the principal cause of tuition increases at public institutions, which depend heavily on appropriations to subsidize their operations. As Arthur Hauptman, an expert on college financing, explains, in each of the past three economic recessions—in the mid-1970s, the early 1980s, and the early 1990s—state higher-education spending per student declined, forcing students and their families to shoulder more of the cost in the form of double-digit percentage hikes in tuition. Increases during the recent recession reflect the same pattern.

The tuition spiral is not the only impediment to equality of opportunity. More significant perhaps is the nation's backsliding on need-based financial aid. In 1975–1976 the maximum federal Pell Grant award (for low-income students) covered 84 percent of the cost of attendance at a public four-year college; by 1999–2000 it covered only 39 percent. This is part of a broader shift to a system dominated by loans, which has left a generation of students struggling to finance heavy debt.

Hardest hit are low-income students, whose numbers are expected to increase dramatically over the next decade. From 1989 to 1999 the average cumulative debt of the poorest 25 percent of public college seniors grew from $7,629 to $12,888 (in constant 1999 dollars). Studies find that when financial-aid packages inadequately cover expenses, students work long hours, attend school part time, and opt for two-year as opposed to four-year programs—all of which reduce their chances of acquiring a bachelor's degree.

Federal efforts during the past decade or so to address rising tuition have done little to help low-income families. Both the Clinton and the George W. Bush Administrations promoted tax breaks and saving incentives encouraging families to set aside money for college. These programs largely benefited middle- and upper-income families, who have both taxable income and resources to save. With the Higher Education Act up for renewal this year, Congress should focus on aiding those students unlikely to complete—or attend—college without greater financial support, and should encourage universities to do the same. To begin with, it should restore the purchasing power of Pell Grants by raising the maximum award from the current $4,050 to $8,000. Many will argue that the cost—roughly $15 billion in additional annual spending—is unrealistic. Historically, however, our nation's investments in expanding access to higher education have paid off many times over. And the money required, according to a new Century Foundation publication, is roughly equivalent to the annual revenue lost to the Treasury from tax and savings benefits that currently help those higher on the income ladder. To relieve the extraordinary debt burden that many students face, Congress should also put the college-loan system under federal administration, and let every student consolidate loans and pay them off on an income-contingent basis, as one federal loan program already allows.

Broadening access to higher education has never been the answer to inequality, but it *is* the way to ensure that every young person has a chance to move upward in society. Either we can continue to ignore the persistent disparities in post-secondary training and rely increasingly on foreign students to fill our graduate-level science and engineering programs, or we can renew our commitment to educating the young people who are already here.

A NEW HEALTH CARE
PARADIGM

18

The Overtreated American

Shannon Brownlee

One of our biggest health-care problems is that there's just too much health care. Cutting down on the excess could arrest the spiraling cost of health care while improving the quality of medical treatment.

AMERICANS ENJOY THE MOST sophisticated medical care that money can buy—and one of the most vexing and expensive health-care-delivery systems in the world. We spend more than one trillion dollars each year on health care, two to four times per capita what other developed nations spend, yet we can't find a way to provide health insurance for more than 40 million citizens. After a brief respite in the 1990s when HMOs held down expenses by squeezing profits from doctors and hospitals, medical costs are once again rising by around 8 percent a year. Yet reforms proposed by Congress and the White House are only nibbling around the edges of the problem.

Such political timidity is understandable, given the experience of would-be reformers of the past. Any attempt to expand coverage for the uninsured while holding down costs inevitably raises fear in the minds of voters that the only way to accomplish these seemingly opposing goals is by restricting access to expensive, life-saving medical treatments. Sure, we feel bad about the 18,000 or so of our fellow citizens who die prematurely each year because they lack health insurance, and about the seniors who are forced to choose between buying food and buying medicine. But Americans want nothing to do with a system like England's, which, for example, is reluctant to provide dialysis to the elderly, and most of us who are now covered by either Medicare or private insurance have little stomach for health-care reform that contains even a whiff of rationing. Behind this fear lies an implicit assumption that more health care means better health. But what if that assumption is wrong? In fact, what if more medicine can sometimes be bad not just for our pocket-books but also for our health?

An increasing body of evidence points to precisely that conclusion. "There is a certain level of care that helps you live as long and as well as possible," says John Wennberg, the director of the Center for Evaluative Clinical Sciences at Dartmouth Medical School. "Then there's excess care, which not only doesn't help you live longer but may shorten your life or make it worse. Many Americans are getting excess care." According to the center, 20 to 30 percent of health-care spending goes for procedures, office visits, drugs, hospitalization, and treatments that do absolutely nothing to improve the quality or increase the length of our lives—but which nonetheless drive up costs. At the same time, the type of treatment that offers clear benefits is not reaching many Americans, even those who are insured.

That's a sobering thought, but it opens the possibility of a new way to look at the conundrum of health-care reform. Lawmakers, insurers, and the health-care industry might be able to save money if they were to concentrate on improving the quality of medicine rather than on controlling costs. Better health care will of course mean more medicine for some Americans, particularly the uninsured; but for many of us it will mean less medicine. The trick, of course, lies in figuring out what constitutes quality.

Support for the idea that many Americans are getting too much medical care can be found in *The Dartmouth Atlas of Health Care*, a compendium of statistics and patterns of medical spending in 306 regions of the country. The atlas is generated by a group of nearly two dozen doctors, epidemiologists, and health-care economists, using data from Medicare, large private insurers, and a variety of other sources. Wennberg is the group's leader and the patron saint of the idea that more medicine does not necessarily mean better health—a view that has not exactly endeared him to the medical establishment over the years. These days, however, his ideas are bolstered by the Institute of Medicine and other independent researchers, and by new results coming from his Dartmouth research team, which is showing precisely how the nation misspends its health-care dollars.

Take the regions surrounding Miami and Minneapolis, which represent the high and low ends, respectively, of Medicare spending. A sixty-five-year-old in Miami will typically account for $50,000 more in Medicare expenses over the rest of his life than a sixty-five-year-old in Minneapolis. During the last six months of life, a period that usually accounts for more than 20 percent of a patient's total Medicare expenditures, a Miamian spends, on average, twice as many days in the hospital as his counterpart in Minneapolis, and is twice as likely to see the inside of an intensive-care unit.

This type of regional variation would make perfect sense if regions where citizens were sickest were the ones that used the most medical services. After all, it's only fair that we should spend more and do more in places where people need more medical attention. But, as Wennberg and his colleagues Elliott Fisher and Jonathan Skinner point out in a recent paper, "Geography and the Debate Over Medicare Reform," which appeared online in the journal *Health Affairs*, rates of underlying illness do not account for the differences in spending among regions. If they did, the region around Provo, Utah, one of the healthiest in the country, would get 14 percent fewer Medicare dollars than the national average because its citizens are less likely to smoke, drink, or suffer from strokes, heart attacks, and other ailments. Instead it receives seven percent more than the national average. In contrast, elderly people in the region around Richmond, Virginia, tend to be sicker than the average American, and should be receiving 11 percent more—rather than 21 percent less—than the national average. Nor are regional differences explained by variations in the cost of care. Provo doctors are not, for example, charging significantly more for office visits or lumpectomies than doctors in Richmond, and their patients aren't getting costlier artificial hips.

Rather, much of the variation among regions—about 41 percent of it, by the most recent estimate—is driven by hospital resources and numbers of doctors. In other words, it is the supply of medical services rather than the demand for them that determines the amount of care delivered. Where neonatal intensive-care units are more abundant, more babies spend more days in the NICU. Where there are more MRI machines, people get more diagnostic tests; where there are more specialty practices, people see more specialists.

When the Dartmouth researchers looked in detail at these patterns, they found that more care does not mean longer life. More neonatal intensive care units, for instance, and more neonatologists (doctors who specialize in the care of low-birth-weight babies) do not improve infant mortality rates, according to research by Dartmouth pediatrician and associate professor David Goodman and colleagues. Goodman and his collaborators found that too few neonatologists—below about 2.7 per 10,000 births—increased the chances that a low-birth-weight baby would die by about 8 percent, but having more than about 4.3 neonatologists per 10,000 births did not improve a low-birth-weight baby's odds. (And some parts of the country have as many as 11.6 specialists per 10,000 births.) Similarly, too few beds in the NICU put low-birth-weight infants at heightened risk of dying, but extra beds simply meant that more relatively healthy babies are put into the NICU, with no improvement in the overall mortality rate.

At the other end of life, an overabundance of medical resources and doctors is not helping Medicare recipients live longer or healthier lives. During the last six months of life, a period when it's safe to assume that most people are gravely ill, Medicare beneficiaries see, on average, twenty-five specialists in Miami versus two in Mason City, Iowa, largely because Miami is home to a lot more specialists. Even though Medicare patients visit doctors more frequently in high-cost regions, they are no more likely than citizens in low-cost regions to receive preventive care such as flu shots or careful monitoring of their diabetes.

In fact, living in a high-cost region may lead to a slightly shorter life, according to a paper published last year in the *Annals of Internal Medicine*. The study, which was conducted by Fisher and several colleagues at Dartmouth and the Veterans Administration Hospital in White River Junction, Vermont, found that mortality in high-cost regions appears to be about 2 to 6 percent higher than in the lowest-cost regions of the country. In other words, too much medicine appears to be killing people. The most likely explanation for the increased mortality seen in high-cost regions is that elderly people who live there spend more time in hospitals than do citizens in low-cost regions. And hospitals, says Wennberg, "are risky places." Patients who are hospitalized run the risk of suffering from medical errors or drug interactions, receiving the wrong drug, getting an infection, or being subjected to diagnostic testing that leads to unnecessary treatment. As Henry Aaron, a health care economist at the Brookings Institute puts it, "We've got the most sophisticated and advanced medicine in the world, but at the high end we've just got more of it, not better medicine."

An obvious way we might cut excess medical care and improve the quality of our health care is to change the way we pay hospitals and doctors. "Medicine is the only industry where high quality is reimbursed no better than low quality," says David Cutler, a health economist at Harvard. "The reason we do all the wasteful stuff is that we pay for what's done, not what's accomplished." Although that's clearly the case, figuring out the right incentives for health-care providers is by no means easy. But there is an even more fundamental problem, a problem so basic that is has largely been ignored in all health care reform efforts to-date: namely, we lack the information we need even to know what constitutes high quality health care.

What's missing is not just any kind of information, but data on outcomes—how well different doctors and hospitals accomplish the task of keeping patients healthy, and the effectiveness of the various treatments they administer. It has been more than a decade since the manifesto of "evidence-based medicine" was published, yet much medical care is still based more on intuition than science. Doctors still don't know, for example, whether regular mammograms for women in their forties save lives, or whether or not the statins, or cholesterol lowering drugs, protect patients against heart attacks and strokes any better than changing their diet and exercising. Many doctors are unaware that calcium channel blockers, a class of drug that's widely prescribed for high blood pressure, are no better than diuretics, which cost considerably less. When common medical practices are put to the test—as only a small fraction have been—many turn out to be either ineffective or excessively risky, at least for some patients. For instance, a clinical trial that ended in 2002 showed that hormone replacement therapy, a drug that generated $1.2 billion in sales in 2000 and that post-menopausal women have been taking for more than 30 years, not only does not lower the risk of heart attack, as previously believed, it appears to *raise* it.

At the same time, health care consumers—patients, employers, and insurers—lack the information they need to choose the best care at the most reasonable price. Insurers have no rational basis for adjusting reimbursement for high- and low-quality care, because they track neither patient outcomes nor the performance of individual hospitals and doctors. Their costs keep rising because they have few data for judging the effectiveness of all the hospitalizations, tests, office visits, and procedures they are paying for, and thus only limited leverage in denying coverage. Patients have no meaningful way of choosing a doctor or a hospital—despite the proliferation of such guides as *U.S. News & World Report's* "America's Best Hospitals"—so that purchasing health care is a little like trying to buy a cell phone and wireless service without the benefit of consumer reports.

More information would increase both the quality of health care and the system's efficiency—if only someone would gather the data. But most insurers, with the exception of Medicare and a handful of the largest private companies, don't compile the records that might help them improve health care quality, largely because they lack the expertise and manpower, but also because they can make a profit without bothering to perform time-consuming and expensive reviews of medical practices. A few groups are already trying to assess the effectiveness of common medical practices—the Cochrane Collaboration, for instance, an international consortium of researchers, compiles evidence from randomized controlled clinical trials to determine the efficacy of various practices—but such efforts are too few and too underfunded to provide all the information that's needed. The National Institutes of Health, which have traditionally focused on finding cures rather than improving existing medical practices, set aside only one-thirtieth of their combined budgets—about $800 million annually—for clinical research. The Agency for Healthcare Policy and Research, the one government agency that was devoted to gathering outcomes data, saw its budget slashed in 1995 in the face of lobbying by a determined and influential group of neurosurgeons, who didn't like the results of one of the agency's assessments of medical evidence.

The first step toward improving the quality of health care in America—and reining in overtreatment—would be to create a National Clinical Sciences Institute, which would serve as a clearinghouse for outcomes data. Such a national institute could be funded by either the federal government alone or in concert with private insurers, but it would need the political insulation of the Federal Reserve Board if Medicare is to use its data in setting guidelines for covering drugs and medical procedures. With data from the institute, doctors, patients, and insurers would finally have the information they need to know what works in medicine, what doesn't, and what treatments provide only uncertain benefit.

The institute's first task would be gathering information on patient outcomes from hospitals and doctors to determine who is delivering the most effective—and safest—care. It would also pull together all available evidence for current medical practices. If existing data can't determine the effectiveness of a treatment or a test, the institute would then fund a clinical trial to get the answer. It should initiate clinical trials like the one that found hormone replacement therapy increases the risk of heart attack, and head-to-head comparisons of drugs and their cheaper equivalents, Celebrex and Vioxx versus ibuprofen, for example. With real evidence in hand, doctors could base standards of care more on science than intuition. Insurers would have a rational basis for deciding which drugs and procedures to cover—and they could adjust reimbursement to hospitals and doctors according to who does the best job. And patients would know which doctors and hospitals to choose.

The danger, of course, is that weighing cost against the effectiveness of treatments and drugs will raise the specter of medical rationing.

But patients might feel differently about all the medical care they think they want—and deserve—if they had access to clear and accurate information showing that the most expensive drugs aren't necessarily the best, and that many treatments and tests pose unseen risks without much proof of potential benefit.

There's growing evidence that this is the case. Some doctors are now testing a new method of care called "shared decision making," which is showing that the choices patients make are connected to what they know. Rather than the doctor trying to determine what the best course of action is—whether to perform an angioplasty, say, or a P.S.A. test—a doctor gives the patient a videotape to watch at home that lays out in clear and simple terms what is known about the test or procedure being considered, and what the potential dangers are. Patients, it turns out, are often more wary of the risks of medical intervention than their doctors are. In a recent study conducted at the Dartmouth-Hitchcock Medical Center in Hanover, N.H., researchers compared two groups of people with severe back pain caused by a ruptured disc. One group simply talked to their surgeons about having a back operation. The other group took home a video that described the possible risks and benefits. The group that saw the video was 30 percent less likely to choose surgery compared with the other patients.

A National Clinical Sciences Institute would also help reduce what the Dartmouth group calls "supply-sensitive" care—the excess procedures, hospital admissions, and doctor visits that are driven by the supply of doctors and hospital resources rather than by medical need. Its data would allow such organizations as the American Medical Association and Kaiser Permanente to set benchmarks for quality, giving them the leverage for getting doctors to provide not only fewer procedures that don't work but also more treatments whose benefits are proven. Three recent studies, conducted by the Institute of Medicine, the Rand Corporation, and the President's Advisory Commission on Consumer Protection and Quality in the Health Care Industry, report widespread underuse of evidence-based treatment, such as balloon angioplasty to open blocked arteries in heart-attack victims, even among citizens with gold-plated health insurance.

Put into the practice, information provided by a Clinical Sciences Institute would improve the quality of care, and might even trim billions of dollars that are now wasted on unnecessary medicine. Here's just one example: A recent study found that carotid endarterectomy, a $15,000 surgery performed on about 150,000 patients a year to prevent stroke, turns out to pose a greater risk of triggering a stroke than preventing one in two-thirds of patients. If Medicare stopped paying surgeons to perform this procedure on the wrong patients, it could save the system $1.5 billion.

Even so, the hardest part of reforming health care will be persuading policymakers and politicians that improving the quality of care can also save money. The Medical Quality Improvement Act, introduced last July by Vermont Senator James Jeffords, is a step in the right direction. It would call on several medical centers around the country to model high-quality medicine that also reins in costs.

But evidence already exists that improving quality can hold down costs. Franklin Health, a company based in Upper Saddle River, New Jersey, manages so-called "complex cases" for private insurers. Complex cases are the sickest of the sick, patients with multiple or terminal illnesses, who are also the most costly to treat. They typically make up only one or two percent of the average patient population while accounting for 30 percent of costs. Franklin employs a battalion of nurses, who make home visits and spend hours on the phone, sometimes every day, to help patients control pain and other symptoms and stay out of the hospital. For this low-tech but intensive service the company charges insurers an average of $6,000 to $8,000 per patient—but it saves them $14,000 to $18,000 per patient in medical bills.

How much money is at stake for the nation? If spending in high-cost regions could somehow be brought in line with spending in low-cost regions, Medicare alone could save on the order of 29 percent, or $59 billion a year—enough to keep the Medicare system afloat for an additional ten years, or to fund a generous prescription-drug benefit for seniors. And there's no reason to believe that doctors and hospitals behave any differently toward their non-Medicare patients. That means the system as a whole is wasting about $400 billion a year—

more than enough to cover the needs of the 40 million or so uninsured citizens.

The last attempt at reforming the U.S. health-care system failed in large measure because of fears of rationing. Reform was viewed as an effort to cut costs, not to improve health, and voters believed, rightly or wrongly, that they would end up being denied the benefits of modern medicine. Future efforts at reform are going to have to persuade Americans and their doctors that sometimes less care is better.

19

Insurance Required

Laurie Rubiner

How to achieve universal health insurance without relying on a single payer system.

THE NUMBER OF AMERICANS without health insurance continues its stubborn climb. Despite the fact that the United States spends more on health care than any other nation, more than 43 million Americans, one in seven U.S. citizens, including 12 million children, lack even basic coverage. People without health insurance receive fewer preventive services and less regular care for chronic conditions such as diabetes and asthma. They also delay needed care and, as a result, have poorer health outcomes and die prematurely. When a severe illness or injury necessitates resort to the health system, the uninsured are often socked with hospital bills up to twice as high as those insured patients would incur for the same services. Some patients are lucky enough to receive charity care, often subsidized by taxpayers; others end up in financial ruin.

The lack of universal coverage, however, is not just an issue for the uninsured, but for the insured as well. Those with insurance are paying more every year for less coverage and are increasingly vulnerable to losing health insurance altogether. In 2002, premium costs, which are being passed on to employees, rose at double-digit rates for the third year in a row. Not surprisingly, polls show Americans who have insurance are nervous about their continued ability to afford their employer-sponsored coverage. Others worry about losing their coverage entirely, because in our voluntary, employer-sponsored system, losing a job often means losing your health insurance as well.

While the majority of Americans support the idea of universal coverage, there is little agreement on how best to achieve this goal. A decade ago, President Bill Clinton made health care reform a centerpiece of his administration, but was unable to agree with Congress on a plan. Since that time, some incremental steps have been taken to expand coverage, such as enactment of the Children's Health Insurance Program in 1997 to cover low-income, uninsured children who don't qualify for Medicaid. While these piecemeal programs have made strides toward covering some of the uninsured, the number of uninsured is actually higher today than it was ten years ago.

Guaranteeing universal coverage is not an unrealistic goal and need not break the bank. There is in fact a pragmatic and politically appealing route to universal coverage: mandatory individual insurance made affordable by a new social bargain among employers, insurance companies, and the government. Such an approach would have four basic elements: All Americans would be required to have insurance. Employers would be required to offer all employees health insurance or contribute a fixed amount to an employee's individual plan. The government would subsidize the cost of coverage for those who cannot afford it. And insurance companies wishing to take advantage of publicly subsidized applicants would be required to accept all comers, regardless of their health status or pre-existing conditions. The underlying logic of this new social bargain is: universal coverage for universal responsibility.

The centerpiece of such a universal coverage system would be a self-insurance mandate—a requirement that every adult, individually and on behalf of his or her dependents, must have adequate health insurance coverage. Just as drivers are required to have auto insurance, an individual has a responsibility not to impose the burden of uncompensated health care costs on society. While many of the uninsured truly cannot afford health insurance, more than 30 percent of those who are now uninsured have annual family incomes of more than $50,000 year. This suggests that approximately a third of the uninsured could afford health insurance on their own but choose to play Russian Roulette with their health, a gamble that too often forces them into bankruptcy or leaves the taxpayer footing their bill in the event of injury or illness. As a duty of citizenship, these higher-income individuals should be required to maintain an adequate level of health care coverage and should be expected to contribute a modest amount of their income toward the cost of this insurance.

A major benefit of compelling the 43 million uninsured Americans to get insured is that it would lower premiums for all. Why? Because the vast majority of the uninsured are relatively young and healthy: 12 million are under the age of 18, and another 17 million are between the ages of 18–34. By creating a larger and more diverse national risk pool, risk would be distributed more evenly among the entire population, which would reduce the cost of premiums for those with insurance and make insurance more affordable for those without.

Naturally, making basic coverage mandatory for all individuals requires making such coverage available and affordable to all. In this regard, employers, the government, and private insurance companies all have an important role to play. While a self-insurance mandate would open the way for a new approach to health insurance that is no longer strictly employer-based, employers would remain an integral part of any social contract for universal coverage. Employers currently contribute approximately $350 billion annually toward their employees' coverage, a third of overall healthcare spending. Withdrawing this contribution would be disastrous for the market and unfair to employees who have come to depend on it. Employers who are already offering benefits and wish to continue providing them could do so, but others who want to get out from under the cumbersome administration of health care benefits or who have chosen not to offer their employees coverage would instead be required to contribute a fixed amount to a pool or to the plan of their employee's choice. This requirement would also help level the playing field by eliminating one form of cost-shifting whereby companies offering good family coverage are effectively subsidizing those who don't. For those employers who are already offering coverage, stabilizing their contribution would be an attractive alternative to the double-digit premium increases that have become the norm in recent years.

The government also has an important role to play in making insurance both accessible and affordable. For those who cannot afford to shoulder the full burden of basic coverage, the federal government would offer tax credits and vouchers to help pay the cost of insurance. In addition, it would help establish large-scale purchasing pools to lower the costs of insurance and to make the market work more efficiently. As it is now, individuals and smaller employers typically face substantially higher premium charges than those participating in the risk pools of larger firms. The government can remedy this problem by helping to create health insurance purchasing cooperatives that would pool smaller groups into larger ones. Insurance companies that wanted to service these cooperatives and take advantage of government subsidized insurance purchases would need to agree not to discriminate against applicants based on health or pre-existing conditions.

Contributions to the cost of this new health insurance system would be divided, as it is today, among three sources: the federal government (in the form of federal tax subsidies), employers (in the form of an employer contribution), and individual payments that would never exceed a modest share of a family's adjusted gross income. A citizen-based, universal system is estimated to cost roughly $80 billion in additional spending each year. While some may argue that taxpayers can't afford this price tag, the uninsured are already costing the public approximately $35 billion a year in uncompensated care, costs that are reflected in the increasing premiums paid by employers and their employees. Add to this the benefits to society as a whole of having a healthier and more productive population, allowing us to recoup in tax revenues some of the $65–130 billion every year the Institute of Medicine estimates we are losing as a result of lack of health insurance, and we are close to having the money we need to provide everyone with health insurance.

Over the long run, the benefits of this new social contract for universal coverage would far outweigh the costs. In addition to ensuring coverage for all Americans and lowering the cost of premiums for most of them, it would give citizens more control over their own health security. Today's voluntary, employer-based system would give way to a citizen-based system, in which the insurance and the subsidy for that insurance follow the individual rather than the job. This would enable all Americans to select and keep the health insurance provider of their choice and to take advantage of group rates, which are now available only to those with employer-sponsored coverage. This would help American workers at all levels: from the highly compensated executive changing jobs to the single mother working two part-time jobs to the independent contractor who can't afford the prohibitive costs of getting insured in today's individual market. Never again would an American need to fear that losing or changing of a job would mean losing his or her health insurance.

By delinking health insurance from employment, a citizen-based system would also solve one of the most vexing by-products of employer-based health insurance—the inability to take your doctors and your health plan with you when you change jobs. According to a recent study in the Annals of Family Medicine, 20 percent of people with insurance change health plans each year, resulting in higher costs and lower quality care. By enabling individuals to stay with a single insurer, a system of portable and continuous coverage would increase insurers' incentives to invest in disease prevention and long-term preventive care, investments that decrease the cost of care over time. And moving away from the employer-based system means employees would not be confined to the plan their employer chooses, empowering individuals to select their own plan and level of coverage.

Mandatory health insurance is far from a radical concept, and it is an idea that has already been embraced at least in part by both Democrats and Republicans. Senator John Edwards and General Wesley Clark, Democratic candidates for President in 2004 would require all children to be insured. And before that, Bob Dole, the Republican nominee for President, once co-sponsored legislation with the late Republican Senator John Chafee to require all Americans to secure health insurance by the year 2005. At the time, Dole and Chafee were joined by 18 of their Republican colleagues, half of whom remain in the Senate today. This suggests that a mandatory insurance is not only the most promising way to solve the problem of the uninsured but also is the approach most likely to garner bipartisan support.

We are already required to purchase automobile insurance if we wish to own a car and homeowner's insurance if we need a mortgage. Applying the same principle to a far more valuable asset—our health—

should become second nature. Undoubtedly, there will be critics who decry such a system as yet another government intrusion into the lives of Americans. But properly understood, a system of mandatory insurance would provide citizens more choice and more freedom and would allow the United States to catch up to the rest of the developed world in providing universal health insurance to its citizens.

20

Aging Productively

Phillip J. Longman

As the American population grows older, it's time to refocus health care expenditures on rewarding fitness.

NEARLY EVERY WEEK BRINGS new warnings about the future of old age in America. Government economists have recently calculated, for example, that the U.S. Treasury would have to put aside $44.2 trillion dollars today in order to cover the cost of unfunded pension, health care, and other benefits promised to Americans over the next 75 years. This is more than four times the entire annual output of the U.S. economy. Medicare is the biggest culprit, accounting for more than 80 percent of the shortfall—not even counting the cost of its new prescription drug benefit. To close this long-term deficit, these same economists conclude that "an additional 16.6 percent of annual payrolls would have to be taxed away forever, beginning today."

Or perhaps there is a better way. The long-term outlook for an aging society is not ultimately a question of finance. It's a question of biology: how many children are born, and for how long after they grow up do they remain healthy, productive adults?

We know with great certainty how many Americans will be over age 65 in 2050, because those people have already been born. By mid-century, one out of every five Americans will most likely be over the age of 65, making the U.S. population as a whole much older than Florida's is today. Yet what we don't know, but can influence, is how many of those 65 year-olds will be, in today's sense, "elderly." How many will suffer from disabilities? How many will be able to, or want to, continue working?

Even modest changes in the rate at which we age could make enormous differences. During our last six months of life, for example, we may consume $50,000 worth of high tech health care at taxpayers' expense, but if those last six months come when we are 85 instead of 75, and we have meanwhile been able to continue to contribute to society, then what's the harm in our increased longevity? In an aging society, there will be fewer children to support. And there could be fewer adults to support as well if the threshold of true old age recedes and the average life span includes more productive years.

Is there any reason to believe this will actually happen? Let's start with the good news. Health and wealth for a vast cross section of those over age 65 are improving, creating what some gerontologists call a "Second Middle Age," or what others call a "Third Age." People who are experiencing this new life stage are not hard to spot. These are folks who contemptuously reject the "golf and drinks" model of retirement. They may have lost some of their youthful drive and vigor, but they don't feel old or out-of-date, and want to remain productive. Many enroll in flourishing "Elder Hostel" programs. Many others serve as consultants, volunteers, small business owners, or launch long delayed careers in the arts or helping professions.

How extensive is this phenomenon of productive aging? There are several indicators. The average age of retirement, after trending downward for 50 years, is now moving back up, at least in the United States. Whereas less than a quarter of all American men age 65 to 69 were still in the labor force in 1985, nearly a third are today. Some of this change may be due to less generous pensions and health care plans, but clearly most older Americans are not putting off retirement because they have to. In 1984, the median net worth of households headed by a person 65 to 74 was slightly less than that of households headed by a person 45 to 54. Now it's the older households that are the wealthiest by far, enjoying exactly double the net worth of the younger group.

There are also many signs that older Americans are less frail than in the past. According to several well-publicized recent studies, disability rates among older Americans declined by more than one percent annually during the 1990s. Older Americans are also becoming more involved in the lives of their grandchildren. Between 1970 and 1997, the number of children living in households headed by their grandparents increased by 76 percent. Today's older Americans are also far better educated than the elderly of previous generations, which is very positive, since health strongly corresponds to education.

In the face of all these trends, one might reasonably conclude that we have little to fear from population aging. With fewer younger workers available, employers in the future will pay an ever-higher economic penalty for age discrimination, and will have new incentives to create flexible, part-time jobs suitable to older workers. To keep their classrooms full, universities will be forced to reach out to older students and promote lifetime learning. If all these current trends continue, the percentage of the population over 65 may still increase, but the percentage of the population that is "elderly"—that is, frail, and economically dependent—may not.

Yet overshadowing all this good news is another trend that must be reversed if the promise of productive aging is to amount to more than just happy talk. Productive aging is not just for old people; everyone is aging all of the time, and if we look at how today's working-aged people, and even children, are going about it, the picture is alarming.

In the last 20 years, the U.S. population has grown much more sedentary, and much heavier. The percentage of overweight and obese adults has doubled to 61 percent, while the percentage of adolescents who are overweight or obese has tripled. Americans are smoking fewer cigarettes, but they are eating many more Big Macs and spending much more of their lives in their cars. Between 1972 and 1997, the number of fast food restaurants per American doubled. Largely because of the growth of sprawl, the number of trips people take on foot has dropped by 42 percent between 1977 and 1997.

In today's sprawling suburbs, almost no one walks or takes a bike, and for good reason. Only 6 percent of all trips are made on foot or by bicycle, yet pedestrians or cyclists account for 13 percent of all traffic fatalities. Not surprisingly, metro areas marked by sprawling development are the most dangerous regions to walk or bike today.

But, of course, rarely walking, or taking a bike, is even more deadly. Among women, walking ten blocks per day or more reduces the chance of heart disease by a third. While taking at least 10,000 steps a day (the equivalent of a five-mile walk) is widely considered by public health officials to be a baseline for maintaining health, a typical, sedentary American takes only about 3,500–5,500 steps per day. The risk of a sedentary lifestyle is comparable to and, in some studies, greater than, the risk of hypertension, high cholesterol, diabetes, and even smoking.

The next generation of elders in America will presumably have access to more sophisticated medical interventions, but there is little medicine can do to combat the chronic diseases of aging if people do not change their habits. Scientists estimate that up to 75 percent of all cancer deaths are caused by human behaviors such as smoking, diet, and lack of exercise. This helps to explain why life expectancy among American women over age 65 actually decreased slightly in the 1990s (there were more women with a history of smoking, and more women leading sedentary lives). It also helps to explain why, a generation after President Nixon first declared "War on Cancer," the percentage of the U.S. population dying of cancer is still higher than it was in 1970. Moreover, it is why the age-adjusted incidence of many specific forms of cancers, including female breast and lung cancer, are getting worse year after year. Although modern medicine can help some people to put off the day they will die from the consequences of their behavior and environment, rarely can it make those consequences go away.

What is to be done? As Prohibition and the War on Drugs prove, simply criminalizing unhealthy behavior doesn't work. Similarly, imposing sin taxes on undesirable behavior, while effective, can only go so far without creating black markets. Yet there are many policy levers government can use to promote more productive aging, some of which might at first seem to have little to do with health.

Consider, for example, how containing sprawling, auto-dependent development would promote public health. For the elderly, living in an environment in which it is possible to get around without a car is particularly important. One reason is that loss of night vision afflicts many who would otherwise be able to hold down a job or remain active in community affairs. Another reason is that routine exercise is especially important to maintaining health at older ages. As a report sponsored by the AARP and other leading health and aging groups concludes: "Scientific evidence increasingly indicates that physical activity can extend years of active independent life, reduce disability, and improve the quality of life for older persons."

One must add that sprawl is also associated with high levels of social isolation, which also has a strong correlation with poor health. Indeed, as Robert Putnam, a professor of public policy at Harvard University, has shown in his well-known book, *Bowling Alone*, for every 10 minutes spent driving to work, involvement in community affairs drops by 10 percent. What's the public health implication? A large literature shows that the health risks of being socially isolated are comparable to the risks associated with cigarette smoking, high blood pressure, and obesity. In fact, Putnam finds that an isolated individual's chances of dying over the next 12 months is cut in half by joining one group and cut by two-thirds by joining two groups.

Thus, among the biggest policy levers available for improving public health and promoting productive aging involve reducing subsidies to sprawl. These include gas taxes that are nowhere near high enough to compensate for even the environmental cost of driving, let alone the direct and indirect toll in injury, chronic disease, and premature death. And they include ending over-investment in new roads and highways, and directing more investment to mass transit, bike trails, and sidewalks. Instead of transit users having to feed a fare box, they should receive a dollar's credit, for up to three rides per day, financed by drivers, who will enjoy less traffic, cleaner air, and a reduced burden on the health care system. The government could also offer greater home mortgage deductions to homeowners who move to cities and compact developments served by mass transit.

There are many other ways to encourage Americans to take better care of themselves. Take, for example, the question of exercise. Already some private health insurers are offering everything from discounted health-club memberships to European vacations for those who exercise, lose weight, or quit smoking. Why not mandate that all insurers, including Medicare, adjust their premiums on an actuarially fair basis to reward those who can establish regular gym attendance? Simultaneously, we could require that all companies employing 25 workers or more provide either on-site exercise rooms or tax-free employee benefits covering gym membership.

Moreover, with today's technology, it would not be difficult to pay people for using their bike or taking the stairs. Just create individual exercise accounts and install reverse, electronic tolls on bike trails and stairwells: the farther you peddle or the more stairs you climb, the bigger the credit automatically credited to your account. To expand opportunities and incentives to exercise, we could use abandoned railroad right-of-ways to create an Interstate Bicycle Highway System with reverse tolls. We could also pass legislation mandating that all new planned urban developments contain a set length of sidewalks and trails per resident.

We could be equally creative when it comes to encouraging Americans to improve their diet. For example, why not ask the Food and Drug Administration to develop an operational definition of "junk food," based on fat, salt, and sugar content. We could then require health warnings on junk food, and make it subject to sales taxes commensurate with those imposed on cigarettes and alcohol. We could also ban sales of junk food in school cafeterias as well as junk food advertising on children's television. Moreover, just as most jurisdictions hold down concentrations of liquor stores through licensure and zoning, we could do the same for fried meat shacks. Restaurants serving items meeting the FDA's definition of "junk" would require a special license to operate, with the supply of new Burger Kings and McDonalds strictly limited by regional quotas.

These are just a few of the ways we could encourage more productive aging of the U.S. population. But we also need to think how to make it easier for older people to continue to work and be active in their communities. As studies show, any measures that will lead more people to work at older ages are likely to bring large dividends in public health. If you doubt that work benefits the elderly, consider the experience of so-called "Notch babies." These are people who were born just after January 1, 1917 who, due to a change in Social Security benefit formulas, wound up receiving substantially smaller Social Security benefits than those born during the years just prior to that date. One might imagine that notch babies as a group would suffer poorer health as result of their loss of benefits, but the opposite is true. If one compares the mortality rates of cohorts born in the six months prior to January 1, 1917, with the mortality rates of those born in subsequent six months, a startling disparity emerges. Up until age 65, these two cohorts showed no difference in their mortality, but after age 65, men in the group with the lower Social Security benefits enjoyed significantly better health. The reason, researchers speculate, is that many notch babies responded to their benefit cut by delaying retirement or taking on part-time jobs, which helped them to avoid the unhealthy consequences of inactivity and social isolation.

An argument for cutting Social Security? Perhaps, especially since the program on its current course offers progressively more generous benefits to each new generation of retirees. But it is also an argument for better job retention, better mass transit, more rigorous enforcement against age discrimination, as well as reforms to health insurance markets that will make it easier for employees to offer flexible, part-time employment to older workers.

Such approaches would bring far higher returns to public health, and do far more to promote productive aging than, say, expanding Medicare to pay for mood-altering or sex-enhancing drugs. Population aging need not break the Treasury or cause vast poverty among the elderly, but only if we take more responsibility for the rate at which we age.

AMERICA'S CHANGING
DEMOGRAPHIC LANDSCAPE

21

The New Continental Divide

Michael Lind

Overcrowded cities on the coasts. Dying rural communities in the interior. The way to save both may be to create a post-agrarian heartland.

TWO OF OUR COUNTRY'S most cherished dreams are at risk. One is the American dream of upward mobility. The other is the romantic dream of settling the American heartland. These two dreams cannot be separated in the information age any more than they could be in the frontier past. Indeed, for many Americans in this century moving up may mean moving inland.

Today much of the Great Plains is undergoing a catastrophic demographic collapse. Stretching 1,600 miles from central Texas to the Canadian border and 750 miles across at its widest point, and containing all or most of ten states, this region accounts for a fifth of the land area of the United States, but only four percent of the population—about 12 million people. To put this in perspective, the population of the Los Angeles region is now greater than that of the Great Plains, an area five times the size of California.

Sixty percent of the counties in the Great Plains declined in population in the past decade. In 2001, ninety-nine U.S. counties had populations in which four percent or more of residents were eighty-five or older; most of these counties were in rural areas in the Great Plains. Many heartland communities face the prospect of becoming ghost towns, as older inhabitants die and younger residents move away. Already more and more of what early Americans called "the Great

American Desert" fits the nineteenth-century definition of frontier territory: an area with no more than six inhabitants per square mile.

Meanwhile, the coasts are rapidly filling up. Although coastal counties occupy only about 17 percent of the territory of the contiguous
United States, they contain about 53 percent of the nation's population. By 2015 the coastal population will have increased by the equivalent of two Californias—71 million newcomers—since 1960. In the
same period the Pacific Coast alone, adding more than 28 million people, will have undergone a 158 percent increase in population.

The percentage of the U.S. population living in coastal counties has
remained relatively constant since the 1960s. But the increase in
absolute numbers means that the coasts are getting crowded. The official population density of the United States is only seventy-six people
per square mile—compared with 134 in Europe and 203 in Asia. Density on the coasts, however, is much greater (and in the interior is much
less) than the average suggests. By 2010, when California has 50 million people, it will have a coastal population density of 1,050 per square
mile—considerably greater than the average in Europe or Asia. The
Northeast currently has twice the population density of any other U.S.
region; with 654 people per square mile, it is as crowded as Germany.

The crowding is intensified by immigrants, who are concentrated
in a small number of "gateway" cities and states that are generally on
the coasts. Owing to a high rate of immigration, which accounts for 70
percent of U.S. population growth today, the United States is experiencing a population increase just as other democratic nations are
watching their populations decline.

The future demographic pattern of the United States may be a
largely empty interior surrounded by a handful of densely populated
metropolitan areas: "Bosnywash," the Boston—New York—Washington corridor; "San-San" (San Diego to San Francisco); a "Texas Tri-
angle" defined by Dallas, Houston, and Austin—San Antonio. The
suburbs of expanding cities may fuse together, whereupon a process of
inexorable "densification" may begin.

As a result of coastal growth and heartland decline, a new geographic divide is appearing in American society at the beginning of the
twenty-first century: not the familiar rivalry between the rugged West

and the effete East, or the Yankee North and the Confederate South, but a growing divergence between the coasts and the interior. Beyond the slow death of many of America's small towns, this divide raises a number of serious issues.

The most obvious relates to national politics, as the stark contrast in the 2000 election between densely populated "Gore country" and thinly populated "Bush country" suggests. Al Gore could fly from California to Washington, D.C., without passing over a single state in between that gave him its electoral votes. That power in Washington is only partly related to population density does not clearly benefit any region, but it does undermine the very essence of the democratic process. On the one hand, the Electoral College and the U.S. Senate exaggerate the political power of the prairie, the Great Plains, and the Mountain States. Wyoming's senators represent about half a million people; California's represent 34 million. Yet every state has exactly the same number of Senate votes. On the other hand, many heartland politicians raise much of their money from the wealthy in coastal enclaves, prompting questions about whether they represent their local constituents or their distant donors.

The geographic divide is also an economic divide. During the past decade seventeen of the twenty fastest-growing counties in the United States were on the coasts, as were eighteen of the twenty counties that lead the nation in per capita income. Many CEOs and Hollywood stars seek a change of scenery at private ranches and resorts in the interior, where the descendants of once proud farming and ranching families wait on their tables or scrub their floors. As ambitious young people move out, entire regions enter an economic death spiral, characterized by an aging population, a shrinking tax base, and contracting public and private investment.

Meanwhile, inequality is growing on the coasts themselves. The 2000 census revealed a startling drop in median income in New York City, the result of depressed wages in neighborhoods in Brooklyn, the Bronx, and Queens where the immigrant population has grown the most. The census revealed a similar phenomenon in other northeastern cities and in southern California—also areas of high immigration. Even if wages in densely populated cities and states were not being driven down by mass immigration, crowding would inevitably raise both real-estate prices and the cost of living—to the detriment of working-class Americans and the poor.

The nightmarish result might be an America in which the same wealthy elite lords it over both a largely nonwhite proletariat of maids, nannies, gardeners, and janitors in the coastal cities and over a mostly white working class of janitors, dude-ranch employees, and tourist-trap workers in the interior. This, in turn, might produce a hardening economic and racial hierarchy or even a class war. Whatever the outcome, the American dream of a middle-class society might be threatened.

THE HEARTLAND NEEDS PEOPLE—and many Americans on the coasts need affordable housing. Why not bring them together?

Imagine a federal program that would help poor and working-class Americans to move not from crowded cities to suburbs in the same general area but from crowded states to low-density states where homes are cheaper and the general cost of living is lower. Compare the proportion of homes that a median-income family can afford in Kansas City (82.1 percent) with the number in Boston (51.3 percent), New York City (42.1 percent), Los Angeles (40.2 percent), and San Francisco (10.3 percent). The people who moved would not be the only ones to benefit financially. If the coastal areas did not replace those lost workers with migrants from elsewhere in the country or the world, wages there might rise as the labor market grew tight; and financial barriers to home ownership would decline even in big coastal cities.

Today only about six percent of America's land is residential (urban, suburban, and rural). About 20 percent is farmland, another 25 percent is rangeland, and the rest is wilderness and woodland. The United States grows far more food today than it did in 1954—on about three quarters the acreage. Since 1950, even as agricultural production has increased by more than 100 percent, land has been taken out of agriculture eight times as fast as it has been consumed by suburban development. Much of that abandoned farmland has gone back to forest, particularly in the Northeast. In the twenty-first century most of the land that is liberated from unnecessary agriculture can continue to be restored to wilderness—prairie, forest, or desert—even if a significant portion is reserved for new, low-density housing for migrants from the crowded coastal states.

The federal government subsidizes many farms and ranches that should have been shut down long ago. At best, farm subsidies provide life support for comatose communities. The government is planning to spend at least $171 billion on direct farm subsidies alone over the coming decade. In much of the continental interior this money would be better used to promote a combination of service and manufacturing industries, as part of an ambitious economic development program for the region.

Washington should also phase out the roughly $2 billion in annual irrigation subsidies to western agribusinesses—of which almost half is used for surplus crops. Subsidized irrigation is rapidly depleting the High Plains aquifer under Texas, Oklahoma, New Mexico, Kansas, Colorado, South Dakota, Wyoming, and Nebraska, which now provides about 30 percent of the groundwater used in the United States. The experiment with agriculture in the semi-arid Great Plains from the late nineteenth century onward was a mistake; it produced the Dust Bowl during the Depression and today's regional demographic decline. Cutting off such subsidies would not only end the western water wars but also drive agriculture eastward to states like Illinois and Iowa, where water is abundant and renewable. Within those states market pricing for water would encourage crop diversification and technological innovation in agriculture. Residential and industrial use, not agricultural use, should be the priority of water policy in the Great Plains and the desert and Mountain West, including major portions of California and Texas. And diverting water from agriculture to industry has the potential to generate far more jobs: according to the U.S. Geological Survey, for example, the same amount of water that supports a sixty-acre alfalfa farm with only two workers could support a semiconductor factory with 2,000 workers.

The money saved by reducing direct and indirect agricultural subsidies could help to pay for a new high-tech infrastructure in the American heartland. All too many rural areas lack, for example, high-speed broadband access. The federal government, which subsidized the railroad in the nineteenth century and the electric-power grid and interstate highways in the twentieth, needs to build a transcontinental infrastructure once again. A hydrogen-based transportation system might be constructed from nothing in many rural areas, which would be spared the transition costs necessary in developed regions. And the government could encourage an air-taxi system, such as James Fallows has proposed in *The Atlantic Monthly* (see "Freedom of the Skies," June 2001), in which thousands of small regional airports would supplement our major hubs, potentially turning dying small towns into new centers of commerce and culture. An "interstate-skyway system" might be to America in the twenty-first century what the interstate-highway system was in the twentieth.

RURAL KANSAS WILL NEVER be as scenic as San Francisco, or as crowded with libraries as Boston. But a post-agrarian heartland would be a nice place to live for the children and grandchildren of many of today's struggling coastal families. Fortunately, most jobs in the service economy can be performed anywhere. By 1997, 39 percent of Great Plains farm owners were already designating their main job as "other," rather than "farmer," on their tax returns. By the middle of the twenty-first century the archetypal Plains dweller might be a telecommuting professional.

Thomas Jefferson's idea that population dispersal would promote economic and social equality was shared by Abraham Lincoln, who signed the Homestead Act to provide western land to settlers from the East, and by Franklin Delano Roosevelt, who in 1925 expressed admiration for Canada's policy of seeking "distribution of [its] immigrants throughout every portion of Canada." By means of rural electrification, interstate-highway construction, tax benefits for homeowners, and the nationwide distribution of military plants and government contracts, FDR and his successors made it possible for immigrant slum dwellers and poor tenant farmers to become today's home-owning suburban majority.

In a second inland movement, wired professionals and well-paid service workers might make new lives in wide open spaces that are slowly reverting from monotonous expanses of wheat and corn to wilderness. The first wave of heartland settlement was in the long-term perspective a failure, with consequences that are evident today. The high-tech pioneers of the twenty-first century, unlike their agrarian predecessors, may be able to reconcile the myth of the heartland with the American dream.

22

Mongrel America

Gregory Rodriguez

The most important long-term social fact in America may be the rising
rates of intermarriage among members of ethnic and racial groups. A
glimpse into our mestizo future.

ARE RACIAL CATEGORIES still an important—or even a valid—tool of
government policy? In recent years the debate in America has been
between those who think that race is paramount and those who think
it is increasingly irrelevant, and in the next election cycle this debate
will surely intensify around a California ballot initiative that would all
but prohibit the state from asking its citizens what their racial back-
grounds are. But the ensuing polemics will only obscure the more fundamental question: What, when each generation is more racially and
ethnically mixed than its predecessor, does race even mean anymore?
If your mother is Asian and your father is African-American, what,
racially speaking, are you? (And if your spouse is half Mexican and half
Russian Jewish, what are your children?)

Five decades after the end of legal segregation, and only thirty-
seven years after the Supreme Court struck down anti-miscegenation
laws, young African-Americans are considerably more likely than their
elders to claim mixed heritage. A study by the Population Research
Center, in Portland, Oregon, projects that the black intermarriage rate
will climb dramatically in this century, to a point at which 37 percent
of African-Americans will claim mixed ancestry by 2100. By then more
than 40 percent of Asian-Americans will be mixed. Most remarkable,
however, by century's end the number of Latinos claiming mixed

ancestry will be more than two times the number claiming a single background.

Not surprisingly, intermarriage rates for all groups are highest in the states that serve as immigration gateways. By 1990 Los Angeles County had an intermarriage rate five times the national average. Latinos and Asians, the groups that have made up three quarters of immigrants over the past forty years, have helped to create a climate in which ethnic or racial intermarriage is more accepted today than ever before. Nationally, whereas only eight percent of foreign-born Latinos marry non-Latinos, 32 percent of second-generation and 57 percent of third-generation Latinos marry outside their ethnic group. Similarly, whereas only 13 percent of foreign-born Asians marry non-Asians, 34 percent of second-generation and 54 percent of third-generation Asian-Americans do.

MEANWHILE, AS EVERYONE KNOWS, Latinos are now the largest minority group in the nation. Two thirds of Latinos, in turn, are of Mexican heritage. This is significant in itself, because their sheer numbers have helped Mexican-Americans do more than any other group to alter the country's old racial thinking. For instance, Texas and California, where Mexican-Americans are the largest minority, were the first two states to abolish affirmative action: when the collective "minority" populations in those states began to outnumber whites, the racial balance that had made affirmative action politically viable was subverted.

Many Mexican-Americans now live in cities or regions where they are a majority, changing the very idea of what it means to be a member of a "minority" group. Because of such demographic changes, a number of the policies designed to integrate nonwhites into the mainstream—affirmative action in college admissions, racial set-asides in government contracting—have been rendered more complicated or even counterproductive in recent years. In California cities where whites have become a minority, it is no longer clear what "diversity" means or what the goals of integration policies should be. The selective magnet-school program of the Los Angeles Unified School District, for example, was originally developed as an alternative to forced busing—a way to integrate ethnicminority students by encouraging them to look beyond their neighborhoods. Today, however, the school district is 71 percent Latino, and Latinos' majority status actually puts them at a disadvantage when applying to magnet schools.

But it is not merely their growing numbers (they will soon be the majority in both California and Texas, and they are already the single largest contemporary immigrant group nationwide) that make Mexican-Americans a leading indicator of the country's racial future; rather, it's what they represent. They have always been a complicating element in the American racial system, which depends on an oversimplified classification scheme. Under the pre–civil-rights formulation, for example, if you had "one drop" of African blood, you were fully black. The scheme couldn't accommodate people who were part one thing and part another. Mexicans, who are a product of intermingling—both cultural and genetic—between the Spanish and the many indigenous peoples of North and Central America, have a history of tolerating and even reveling in such ambiguity. Since the conquest of Mexico, in the sixteenth century, they have practiced *mestizaje*—racial and cultural synthesis—both in their own country and as they came north. Unlike the English-speaking settlers of the western frontier, the Spaniards were willing everywhere they went to allow racial and cultural mixing to blur the lines between themselves and the natives. The fact that Latin America is far more heavily populated by people of mixed ancestry than Anglo America is the clearest sign of the difference between the two outlooks on race.

Nativists once deplored the Mexican tendency toward hybridity. In the mid nineteenth century, at the time of the conquest of the Southwest, Secretary of State James Buchanan feared granting citizenship to a "mongrel race." And in the late 1920s Representative John C. Box, of Texas, warned his colleagues on the House Immigration and Naturalization Committee that the continued influx of Mexican immigrants could lead to the "distressing process of mongrelization" in America. He argued that because Mexicans were the products of mixing, they harbored a relaxed attitude toward interracial unions and were likely to mingle freely with other races in the United States.

Box was right. The typical cultural isolation of immigrants notwithstanding, those immigrants' children and grandchildren are strongly oriented toward the American melting pot. Today two thirds of multiracial and multiethnic births in California involve a Latino parent. *Mexicanidad*, or "Mexicanness," is becoming the catalyst for a new American cultural synthesis.

In the same way that the rise in the number of multiracial Americans muddles U.S. racial statistics, the growth of the Mexican-American mestizo population has begun to challenge the Anglo-American binary view of race. In the 1920 census Mexicans were counted as whites. Ten years later they were reassigned to a separate Mexican "racial" category. In 1940 they were officially reclassified as white. Today almost half the Latinos in California, which is home to a third of the nation's Latinos (most of them of Mexican descent), check "other" as their race. In the first half of the twentieth century Mexican-American advocates fought hard for the privileges that came with being white in America. But since the 1960s activists have sought to reap the benefits of being nonwhite minorities. Having spent so long trying to fit into one side or the other of the binary system, Mexican-Americans have become numerous and confident enough to simply claim their brownness—their mixture. This is a harbinger of America's future.

THE ORIGINAL MELTING-POT CONCEPT was incomplete: it applied only to white ethnics (Irish, Italians, Poles, and so forth), not to blacks and other nonwhites. Israel Zangwill, the playwright whose 1908 drama *The Melting Pot* popularized the concept, even wrote that whites were justified in avoiding intermarriage with blacks. In fact, multiculturalism—the ideology that promotes the permanent coexistence of separate but equal cultures in one place—can be seen as a by-product of America's exclusion of African-Americans from the melting pot; those whom assimilation rejected came to reject assimilation. Although the multicultural movement has always encompassed other groups, blacks gave it its moral impetus.

But the immigrants of recent decades are helping to forge a new American identity, something more complex than either a melting pot or a confederation of separate but equal groups. And this identity is emerging not as a result of politics or any specific public policies but because of powerful underlying cultural forces. To be sure, the civil rights movement was instrumental in the initial assault on racial barriers. And immigration policies since 1965 have tended to favor those immigrant groups—Asians and Latinos—who are most open to intermarriage. But in recent years the government's major contribution to the country's growing multiracialism has been—as it should continue to be—a retreat from dictating limits on interracial intimacy and from exalting (through such policies as racial set-asides and affirmative action) race as the most important American category of being. As a result, Americans cross racial lines more often than ever before in choosing whom to sleep with, marry, or raise children with.

Unlike the advances of the civil-rights movement, the future of racial identity in America is unlikely to be determined by politics or the courts or public policy. Indeed, at this point perhaps the best thing the government can do is to acknowledge changes in the meaning of race in America and then get out of the way. The Census Bureau's decision to allow Americans to check more than one box in the "race" section of the 2000 Census was an important step in this direction. No longer forced to choose a single racial identity, Americans are now free to identify themselves as mestizos—and with this newfound freedom we may begin to endow racial issues with the complexity and nuance they deserve.

23

Alienated Muslims

Geneive Abdo

A new generation of Muslim immigrants is challenging the ideal of America as a melting pot.

AMERICA'S RELATIONSHIP WITH ISLAM, once confined to grainy images of bearded men on the evening news pouring out of mosques in far-off lands, is now up-close and personal. It is common to see veiled women at supermarkets and universities, or to read in the local newspaper of zoning battles pitting plans for a new mosque against the unease of long-time residents. Islam is the fastest growing religion in the United States and is likely to outpace Judaism in the coming decades as the second faith to Christianity. But, for now, it is not the sheer number of Muslims in America, estimated by scholars at up to six million, which explains why they have suddenly become so visible.

Rather, a new and distinct Muslim identity has been taking shape steadily across America, almost by stealth until it exploded onto the national consciousness on the morning of 9/11. For years, the nation's Muslim population had been undergoing a subtle yet decisive shift, as a new generation of immigrants brought the experience of religious revival underway at home to their adopted land. For the most part, the immigrants of the 1960s and 1970s were drawn from elite, educated professionals from South Asia and the Arab world, eager to climb the career ladder and to assimilate into the American mainstream. By contrast, the next two decades saw the arrival of a new type of immigrant, largely drawn from the deeply devout middle classes caught up in the worldwide Islamic resurgence and better immunized against the lure of melting-pot America. The experience of Western Europe, where this process has a head start of 10 to 15 years, paints a bleak picture of what America might expect: mounting social and sectarian tensions; increased alienation of Muslims; and the creation of a volatile underclass tucked away in isolated ghettos and fueled by an alien ideology.

While the shift toward a more authentic Islamic lifestyle was already well underway, the political climate created by the attacks in New York and Washington have sharply accelerated the process. If they once were determined to assimilate, as other ethnic and religious groups have done for two hundred years, America's Muslims now seek to recreate the Islamic revivals underway in the countries they left behind in the Middle East and on the subcontinent. Attendance at mosques is exploding, so much so that Islamic institutions are furiously building more to keep pace with demand. Even secular Muslims who prayed in mosques only on rare occasions now look to the weekly *khutba*, the Friday sermon, as a way to reconnect with their co-religionists. More Islamic schools, designed to serve as an alternative to a public educational system that fails to meet the community's needs, are being established. Islamic organizations, some focused on politics and others on religion, are mushrooming. There are some 2,000 Islamic Student Associations active on university and college campuses.

The make-up of the American Muslim community is today hotly debated, but a 1992 study, considered to be the most authoritative, put African Americans at 42 percent; South Asians at 24.4 percent; Arabs at 12.4 percent; and Iranians at 3.6 percent. Although African Americans constitute the largest number, their Islamic traditions generally differ from immigrant Muslims, and they have devoted much of their effort to issues of race and class struggle. As a result, they have remained on the fringes of the profound cultural shifts shaping their fellow Muslims.

For decades, the Islamic community was content to exist in the shadows, if not on the margins of American life, and the U.S. government and American society were perfectly content to let them. Today, this comfort zone no longer exists for either side. Muslims in the United States and those in Islamic countries are now more intertwined than ever, posing new challenges for the government's "war on terrorism." The greatest task facing the FBI in its quest to track down any al-Qaeda sleeper cells is how to distinguish the pious Muslim from the potentially militant one.

Of the thousands of Muslims who have been detained by law enforcement agencies since 9/11, only a handful have been charged with terrorist-related crimes, and fewer have been convicted, according to a study released by the Migration Policy Council. Countless FBI raids on Muslim homes and offices—most of which turned out to be false alarms, often sparked by tips from suspicious neighbors—have only encouraged Muslims to believe they are targets of racism and illegal profiling. Legislation, such as the USA Patriot Act, which created broader police powers that have now been turned on Muslims in general, has also given credence to the community's sense of being under siege in their adopted land.

Ordinary Americans also have contributed to the widespread discrimination. Stories abound of public insults and racist remarks: the Muslim woman who has been mocked so many times for wearing a headscarf that she sends her husband to the supermarket; or the university professor who was asked in his posh Washington, DC, apartment building if he were a terrorist. The Committee on American-Islamic Relations, the Washington-based lobby, keeps a daily log on its Web site of hate crimes and other forms of discrimination by law enforcement and private citizens.

The Muslim community has responded in different ways to violations of their civil liberties. Many prominent Muslim leaders have expressed public gratitude for the freedom they enjoy in the United States, liberties that do not exist in their homelands. As part of an attempt to separate Muslims in America from those in the broader Islamic world, they go to great lengths to assert that Islamic militancy has nothing to do with Islam. Rather, they say, extremism is aberrant behavior practiced by a few on the fringes of Islamic societies.

This commonly expressed position, however, glosses over the profound theological debate raging today within Islam, represented in part by the ideas of Osama bin Laden and other extremists. It may play well among ordinary Americans, but is not believed by most educated Muslims, here or abroad. For centuries, Islam has produced radical thinkers and activists who advocate violence in either battling non-believers or

Muslim leaders they deem to be illegitimate in religious terms. While this is not generally part of mainstream Islamic thinking, the presence beneath the surface of this profound struggle—one of Islam versus Islam—cannot be ignored.

Rather than seeking acceptance among Americans, the majority of Muslims have turned to the mosques and Islamic centers for solace, in an attempt to recreate the spiritual lives—real or imagined—they left behind. Even after they have received an American education or become part of the workforce, they remain spiritually and emotionally tied to their native countries. Seeking what they regard as a more authentic reading of the faith, they generally spurn American-born religious teachers in deference to imams and theologians back home, the vast majority of whom have no understanding of contemporary American society.

Through the Internet, satellite television, and international radio programs, the religious decrees, or *fatwas*, from sheikhs across the Islamic world are easily accessible here in America. Believers also turn to the al Jazeera television network and other Arabic satellite channels for daily news from the Islamic world and the Middle East. These programs offer harsh criticism of U.S. policies toward the Palestinian-Israeli conflict and the occupation of Iraq, and report the unprecedented anti-Americanism sweeping the region. These news programs stand in stark contrast to what is reported in the mainstream American media.

Yet, despite the great divide between American Muslims and American society, many argue that the Islamic community will eventually assimilate just as Eastern Europeans, Chinese, Irish and Italian Catholics, and other ethnic and religious groups have done throughout American history. To make this claim, however, is to underestimate the many dimensions of Islam, for it is not merely a religion to be practiced once a week during an hour-long service at the mosque. It is a total belief system that encompasses spirituality, culture, and politics and remains intact even when faced with the material lures of the Western world. When President Bush declares that Muslim extremists have targeted U.S. interests at home or abroad because they are envious of America's freedoms, he misreads modern history. In fact, they are taking aim at what many see as U.S.-imposed obstacles—commercial and cultural dominance and political support for illegitimate leaders—to the Muslim pursuit of religious salvation.

Muslim sentiment in the United States bears some resemblance to that of the late Sayyid Qutb, the Egyptian ideologue and the godfather of the modern jihadist movement. Qutb's brief experience in the 1940s in the United States led to his radicalization when he returned to Egypt to lead a revolt against the secularist government. Qutb had only con- tempt for American culture, reflected in his memoirs of life in the United States. "How much do I need someone to talk to about topics other than money, movie stars, and car models," he wrote to a friend in Cairo. Later, he wrote: "Nobody goes to church as often as Americans do . . . Yet no one is as distant as they are from the spiritual aspect of religion."

The most solid indication that the Islamic identity will withstand the forces of Americanization lies in the young generation of American Muslims. Young Muslims born in the United States or raised most of their lives here are often more observant of conservative Islamic prac- tices than their parents. Young women are wearing headscarves in increasing numbers, even if their mothers did not wear them. Arranged marriages are becoming more common, so much so that Islamic match- making agencies advertise their services in many Muslim newspapers and magazines. And Muslim Student Associations, linked nationwide through a network of Web sites, offer support groups to encourage lifestyles free of alcohol, drugs, and pre-marital sex. Activities these groups sponsor on campuses include lessons in the Koran and the hadiths, the teachings of the Prophet Mohammed, and *iftar* dinners to break the fast during Ramadan, as well as protests against U.S. policy in the Middle East and the Islamic world.

This younger generation, along with older Muslims who have now joined an Islamic awakening in the United States, are pursuing two strategies at once to achieve their goals. As they become increasingly observant of Islamic practice and tradition, they are also working to achieve political power in the United States. On the surface these two pursuits might seem contradictory: While they are seeking to carve out a distinct identity apart from the American mainstream, they are try- ing to gain a stake in the political system, which requires some degree of assimilation.

But for Muslims the two go hand in hand. Increasingly, believers are demanding electoral power to protect and expand their rights and to influence U.S. foreign policy in the Middle East and the broader Islamic world. Caught up in the anti-terrorist dragnet of the "war on terrorism" and enraged by the occupation of Iraq and the Bush administration's unconditional support for Israel at the cost of Palestinian aspirations, Muslims are seeking political influence to match their growing numbers. Already, Muslim voters are poised to play a key electoral role in certain swing states, like Michigan and Illinois, where they represent sizeable voting blocs. Statistics released in October by the Bliss Institute in Akron, Ohio, show that 83 percent of Muslim voters backed Democratic candidates in the 2002 congressional races. Pollsters expect this trend to continue in 2004.

The danger lies in the American public's response to an increasingly visible Muslim political and social agenda, with the very real risk that resistance or outright hostility would alienate Muslims further from their fellow Americans, and create the conditions for withdrawal and religious extremism. As Muslims gain more political power, they will certainly demand a change in American policy toward Israel and the Palestinians. While many Muslim countries have never actively supported the Palestinian demand for independence, the conflict over the last decade has come to play a key role in relations between the West and the Islamic world. America's Muslims are also likely to fight more aggressively for an end to US government support of repressive Arab regimes, such as Egypt, Saudi Arabia, and Jordan. Without US support, Muslims in America and abroad believe these governments would collapse, paving the way for free elections that would bring Islamists to power.

By organizing politically to seek changes in American policy, Muslims in the United States have set daunting tasks for themselves that are certain to present unprecedented challenges to America's notions as a melting pot and a land of freedom for all.

TESTING OUR
CIVIC HEALTH

24

The Angry American

Paul Starobin

Social rage as a measure of the country's moral and political well-being.

Is AN ANGRY SOCIETY an unhealthy one? So we're often told. Feeling angry? Well, then, say those earnest experts who seek to soothe our roiled spirits, calm down. Take a pill. Try yoga. In *The New York Times* the op-ed columnist Nicholas D. Kristof begs us to "hold the vitriol," which, he worries, "discourages public service." And yet where would America be without its anger? Perhaps still under Colonial rule, if those rowdy upstarts had never tossed British tea into Boston Harbor. Perhaps still mired in a slave-based economy, if not for the prodding of yes, vitriolic abolitionists. Okay—I'm exaggerating to underscore a point. But the point is worth considering: the presence of anger can indicate a society's moral and political well-being, and its absence can be a worrisome sign of complacency. Indeed, the democratic idea rests on the proposition that the well-placed anger of the citizenry can be an appropriate and useful instrument of change. Aristotle certainly thought so. "The man who is angry at the right things and with the right people . . . ," he wrote in Book IV of the *Nicomachean Ethics*, "is praised."

Praise be, America's social-anger thermometer is on the rise. No, the mercury has not reached the level of the 1960s, America's previous Decade of Anger. But there is an appreciable warming of the economic, political, and cultural climate zones. Let's start with a brief definition of terms. By "social anger"—or, let's say, "public anger"—I don't mean incidents of road rage or obscene chants directed by Boston Red Sox bleacher bums at New York Yankees outfielders. My concern is with the anger that is directed at the institutions of political, legal, economic, and cultural power; at the practices and policies that such institutions pursue; and at the people in charge of them. This is, broadly speaking, anti-establishmentarian anger. Ripe targets include the Pentagon, the Republican Party, George Bush, multinational corporations, the California car-tax collector, and the Massachusetts Supreme Judicial Court judges who in November 2003 revoked a state ban on same-sex marriages.

The prospect of gay marriage infuriates religiously motivated conservative traditionalists. Manufacturing workers are angry about jobs lost to a resurgent China. ("A SEETHING POLITICAL ANGER RISES IN AMERICA'S INDUSTRIAL HEARTLAND," the trade publication *Manufacturing & Technology News* recently declared.) Perhaps the most sensitive issue of all is the mounting casualty list in U.S.-occupied Iraq, which is generating antiwar wrath at the powers that be in Washington. Some of this anger is deeply personal, born of grief; it is acquiring a public, political cast as relatives of U.S. soldiers killed in Iraq speak out in the newspapers and on radio and television. "The President don't care," Vecie Williams, the cousin of Sergeant Aubrey Bell, of Tuskegee, Alabama, who was shot and killed in front of an Iraqi police station, told *The New York Times*. "You see him on TV. He says this, he says that. But show me one tear, one tear."

Ahead of us promises to be an invigorating election season in which the prizes go to those candidates able to tap the anger while managing to avoid becoming its target. Howard Dean, the front-runner for the Democratic nomination, who at any moment looks ready to sink his teeth into the nearest available thigh, is banking his campaign on the "I'm mad as hell" (about Iraq, the economy, Bush, you name it) vote. Other Democrats are certainly doing their best to imitate his snarl. "The angry voter is back," the veteran pollster John Zogby reports. "He and she have been on sabbatical." Zogby says the sabbatical began with the economic boom that started in the mid-1990s, but the boom petered out nearly three years ago, and the discord has been growing ever since. And the terrorism threat seems to have only exacerbated partisan rivalry. The Washington-based Pew Research Center found in a recent survey that "national unity was the initial response to the calamitous events of Sept. 11, 2001, but that spirit has dissolved amid rising political polarization and anger."

Although public anger tends toward cyclical peaks and troughs, its varieties fall into well-established taxonomical grooves. There really aren't any altogether new kinds of anti-establishmentarian anger in America—a country that since its birth has been a congenial breeding ground for this sort of animosity. But even if such anger is a fixed part of America's genetic code, mutations occur as the various strains adapt to a changing political, social, and cultural environment. A catalogue of the forms of social anger in America circa 2003 reflects the nation's evolution as the ultimate middle-class society. It turns out that public anger doesn't dissipate as the average house size (and waistband) expands; it simply fastens onto new targets. Perhaps, as some analysts argue, the anger of an affluent post-industrial society is inevitably rooted more in cultural identity than in economic discontent—but then again, never underestimate the rage of an American who senses a threat to material livelihood. At least three forms of anger in the catalogue, updated for the times, are classic breeds.

TRADITIONAL AMERICAN POPULISM was born on the prairie, as struggling nineteenth-century farmers focused their ire on the large, alien, impersonal forces of a rapidly industrializing economy—namely, the extortionist freight-hauling railroads and Wall Street banks to which the farmers were hostage. Today's prototypical angry worker is the laid-off factory worker; since March of 1998 the U.S. manufacturing sector has shed 3.1 million jobs. The blue-collar manufacturing sector endured a similar downsizing in the early 1980s, but now there is a growing white-collar component to the trend, with Boeing, Microsoft, and IBM all "outsourcing" software-programming and engineering jobs to lower-wage havens like India and Russia. In an Internet society it is possible to contract abroad for almost any work that deals principally in digitized data, such as insurance claims. The future of populist anger may thus lie in Redmond, Washington, and Hartford, Connecticut. Born of economic fear and insecurity, this anger has an eternal future in a dynamic capitalist society in which "structural change" is inescapable.

In the here and now, though, the anger is concentrated in places like Rockford, Illinois, a once thriving center of machine-tool industry about an hour's drive from Chicago. The Rockford area has lost 10,000 jobs in the past three years—at Motorola, Textron, and other companies—and many of those laid-off workers who have found new employment are generally working for lower wages, without health and other benefits. "We're on our way to becoming a Third World nation," says Donald Manzullo, a Republican member of Congress who was born in Rockford in 1944 and has represented the district since 1993. Manzullo is a lawyer; his father was a machinist. Although he counts himself a free-trader, he blames China, as do many others in his district, for keeping its currency artificially undervalued, thus boosting exports. What's the state of mind of his constituents? "They are angry because they lost their jobs," he says, "angry because the jobs are going overseas, and angry because the Chinese work for such a low wage." The anger is starting to turn inward, into depression: "A lot of people have given up hope."

Although the pain from which populist anger springs is certainly real, the anger itself tends to be misplaced. Rapacious railroads damaged but did not destroy the yeoman farmer; he fell prey to mechanization, which raised the productivity of American agriculture so much that many fewer workers were needed to produce the same quantity of, say, corn. Similarly, the main reason today's manufacturing workers occupy a shrinking share of the work force is that automation has vastly improved productivity in factories—a trend also inexorably in motion in Japan and Europe.

Still, populist anger tends to serve a useful social purpose. Agrarian populism generated political momentum for the trust-busting and other good government reforms of the Progressive era. Angry U.S. manufacturing workers are helping to stimulate an overdue debate on the sweatshop conditions in which many products are made in China and elsewhere—a debate that has already prompted Nike and other multinationals to upgrade their overseas labor standards, and that may yield a more balanced trade policy (if not one that restores the industrial vitality of Rockford). And if health-care benefits ever become "portable" (that is, migrate with workers wherever they go), the populist anger of permanently anxious workers forced to change jobs half a dozen times during their careers probably will have been responsible.

IN THE BEGINNING, the Angry American Liberal was a Christian human-rights zealot embarked on a crusade ordained by a wrathful

God against the original sin of the new republic: slavery. Harriet Beecher Stowe, the daughter of an evangelical Protestant preacher, helped to support her family by writing for religious periodicals. She shook the country with her first novel, the antislavery tract *Uncle Tom's Cabin* (1852), but her writing, suffused with a Christian sentimentality, has scant appeal for the modern liberal. Outside the African-American community, whose religious leaders continue to embrace a liberal politics of righteous indignation rooted in the Bible, the voices of modern liberalism are almost entirely secular. The creeping secularization of liberal anger, which brings the values of the white American liberal into rough alignment with those of Northern Europe's mainstream political culture, stands as political anger's most impressive adaptation in the past century. Indeed, religious fervor is a central animus for this liberal, who associates it with intolerance and inexplicable (to the modern liberal mind) conservative obsessions such as abortion and school prayer.

Perhaps not since the 1960s has liberal anger been so intense. Its grievances have blended into a potent brew: first the 2000 election, which liberals believe George Bush stole; then the inattention to environmental concerns, as symbolized by the Bush Administration's abandonment of the Kyoto Protocol; and now the Iraq War, which liberals widely view as manufactured by the Bush team to benefit nefarious crony interests, including the oil-services company Halliburton, Vice President Dick Cheney's former employer. The Republican Party itself is seen as a font of evil.

To take a sounding of this anger I spoke with one of modern American liberalism's most articulate—and imposing—representatives: the novelist Jane Smiley, who stands over six feet tall and regularly dispatches angry letters on politics to *The New York Times* and other news organizations. Smiley's novels have not so far tackled explicitly political themes, but the writer offered a modern commentary on patriarchal rage in *A Thousand Acres,* which loosely uses the plot of *King Lear* for a story about a midwestern father's tempestuous dealings with his three daughters. "I woke up early this morning, and I lay awake anxious and angry about political matters," Smiley told me in a telephone chat from her home in Carmel Valley, California, on a Thursday in early November, the day after she learned that the Republicans had won gubernatorial elections in Kentucky and Mississippi. "I see people who are Republicans as people who have aligned themselves with the worst features of the American character. I call them the gruesome threesome: toxic patriotism, toxic religion, and toxic racism." Smiley conceded that her anger is in some sense problematic; it's disturbing her sleep, for one thing, and it disagrees, she said, with the liberal's temperamental preference for placid tolerance. But on the whole, she said, "I don't actually mind being angry. I don't think liberals mind. I think it's a good thing."

This current wave of anger has been a long time coming, with liberals finally responding in kind to the generation of smash-mouth conservatives who have been assaulting them since the Reagan era. Before there was Howard Dean there was Al Franken, the former *Saturday Night Live* writer and performer who in 1996 published his mold-making *Rush Limbaugh Is a Big Fat Idiot and Other Observations.* That book, Franken told me recently, grew out of his anger at the Gingrich revolution of 1994, for which he saw Limbaugh as "the mouthpiece." Franken's current anti-Bush, anti-Republican best seller, *Lies and the Lying Liars Who Tell Them*, prepared with research assistance from students at Harvard (where Franken was a fellow at the Kennedy School of Government's Shorenstein Center on the Press, Politics and Public Policy), is relatively low on humor and in the vein of a political-activist tract. It is a favorite among Dean's well-read supporters, who are disproportionately drawn from the wealthiest, best-educated wing of the Democratic Party.

The bane of modern liberal anger is its tendency to closet itself in elite, marginal causes, such as those espoused by the various societies opposed to anyone's wearing fur. But liberal anger at its best is drawn from the deepest and purest source of all: love. No one has ever expressed this anger better than Charles Dickens. With his scathing indictments of the numerous institutional injustices of Victorian Britain—from debtors' prisons to dreadful factories dependent on child labor—he moved a society toward its better self, and toward reform. In America a kind of Dickensian anger appeared in the civil-rights movement of the 1960s, which laid bare the injustices of institutionalized racism. The last sermon that Martin Luther King Jr. wrote (he was murdered before he could deliver it) was titled "Why America May Go to Hell." But King's central vision was of a new Promised Land, which could be reached only through a redemptive journey paid for in the coin of love. Today's wrathful liberals are unlikely to broaden their appeal unless they can transcend their penchant for satire and sarcasm—which are indirect ways, after all, of taking a poke at a target. Michael Moore's best seller *Dude, Where's My Country?* doesn't quite cut it.

JUST HOW LONG can social conservatives stay angry? Conservative anger at such venerable targets as Harvard, Hollywood, and the TV networks began well before the ascent of Rush Limbaugh, in the mid-1980s—its roots are in the Goldwater and Nixon campaigns of the 1960s and even before that, in young-Republican activism on college campuses. In an earlier era, when Darwinism was a fresher concept, conservative Bible Belt anger welled up at the teaching of evolution in the public schools.

Conservative anger persists because core elements of the conservative world view—which is grounded in an abiding religious belief—are in fact under steady assault (and have been ridiculed since at least H. L. Mencken, with his barbs at Bible Belters). The conservative bid (led by southern Democrats) to thwart racial integration was lost decades ago, so thoroughly lost that Mississippi Senator Trent Lott and other old-style conservatives are nowadays embarrassed to be reminded that so many in their ranks supported the struggle to maintain segregation. The effort to limit abortion achieves an occasional success (such as the recently enacted restriction on so-called partial-birth abortion), but the overall trend is altogether in favor of the liberal feminist vision enunciated by Betty Friedan & Co. in the 1960s. Conservative attempts to keep smut from invading the household faltered with the coming of the Internet, a pure-gold pipeline for the pornography industry.

And in a society as culturally fluid as America's there will always be new causes for anger on the right. These days gay rights seem to be taking the place once occupied by racial integration as a focus for conservative rage, with the anger meter rising especially rapidly on the volatile issue of gay marriage. One stalwart opponent of gay marriage, Sandy Rios, the president of Concerned Women for America, a Washington-based group whose motto calls for "prayer and action,"

says she possesses "a righteous anger" that "comes from serious fol-
lowers of Jesus." A divorced fifty-four-year-old mother of two who
grew up in southern Illinois, Rios says that she herself has seen how the
permissive values of the 1960s have broken up families and damaged
children. Why such strong sentiments on gay marriage in particular?
Because traditional marriage, between a man and a woman, is like "the
support beam in a big house," she says. "If you take the support beam
out, the structure will fail."

At its worst conservative anger detracts from well-being not only
by embracing stereotyped and in some cases hateful images of certain
groups of people but also by drawing from the tainted well of nostalgia. The well is tainted because the nostalgia is usually for a society
remembered or imagined as much better than it ever actually was. Nostalgia can make for poignant art, but it tends to produce a perverse and
impractical politics. In 1930 a group of southern writers at Vanderbilt
University, including John Crowe Ransom and other "fugitive poets,"
railed against a faster-paced modern life in their deservedly discarded
political manifesto *I'll Take My Stand*, which offered the South "in its
very backwardness" as a pathway to "the reconstruction of America."

But at its best conservative anger has forced a rigorous, Old Testa-
ment-like moral accounting on issues incautiously advanced by modern liberal secularists. America, which does sometimes seem close to
motoring full throttle over a secular cliff, is richer for the debate that
angry and uncompromising social conservatives have forced on abortion and euthanasia. As inflamed as the question of gay marriage is
likely to become, committed conservatives will force lawmakers,
courts, and the large number of citizens who are unsure of their stance
to do some hard thinking about the legal and moral meanings of marriage and its larger significance for the social health of America. We're
probably going to get where the liberal secularists want to take us, but
at a more measured, more deliberate pace.

Is SOCIAL ANGER REALLY, on balance, a public good? Certain variants
seem entirely devoid of merit. Cynicism—at least one part the anger of
the disillusioned spirit—is generally corrosive, although a populace
that errs on the side of suspiciousness toward its leaders is not alto-

gether a bad thing. (Better a cynical than a credulous nation.) Then there's a loathing of our nation's leaders, which is often linked to a sense of betrayal. A violent, visceral hatred has at times exacted the steepest of prices: the assassination of Abraham Lincoln came during a campaign of unremitting vilification, in which haters portrayed the President as a traitor to his race and drew caricatures of him as a Negro and an ape. In the 1990s a wave of presidential loathing resulted in the character assassination of Bill Clinton, who was hated with a particular intensity by fellow southerners who viewed his liberalism and his embrace of selected aspects of 1960s counterculture (even if he never inhaled) as a threat to their region's native conservatism. Clinton of course provoked them with his behavioral lapses and subsequent lies— but the loathing was out of proportion to the offenses. And now George Bush, who strikes a fair number of people as a genial guy, is the target of loathing on the left, with the haters gleefully confessing to an obsessive animosity. ("I hate George W. Bush," Jonathan Chait wrote at the outset of his September 29 *New Republic* cover story, "Mad About You.") Loathing tends to focus on the minutely personal as emblematic of the political; in Bush's case, his strut seems to be a particularly infuriating trait, a signifier of the cockiness and arrogance the loathers see in his stance on Iraq and other matters. "He's a smug bastard—you can tell by the way he walks," said Peter Nelson, a thirty-five-year-old massage therapist who showed up at Faneuil Hall, in Boston, to cheer on Howard Dean at a debate there on November 4. (To demonstrate, Nelson puffed out his chest and swung his arms wide, mimicking a cowboy saunter.) It may be that loathing of the President is an unavoidable byproduct of the pursuit of bold change. Few Presidents have faced more vitriol than Franklin Delano Roosevelt, whom fellow patricians considered a betrayer of his class for his embrace of the New Deal. It's hard to remember much loathing of the mild Calvin Coolidge.

True, social anger in America today too often betrays the impatience and ingratitude of a spoiled-brat society. In almost every corner of the planet live people who would sacrifice a good deal to trade their list of daily public angers for that of the average American. Has the good life ever been lived better than in California, which despite its laid-back image has for many years been a pacesetter for the anger agenda? California's per capita income—$32,702—puts it well ahead of the United Kingdom, Germany, and France. Yet Californians were so angered by a proposed tripling of the state's car tax that they recalled Governor Gray Davis and replaced him with Arnold Schwarzenegger, the former bodybuilder best known for his movie role as the Terminator. As for the despised levy, it meant that the owner of a 2003 4x4 Chevrolet Suburban, retailing at $40,665, would have to pay a tax of $813.30 rather than $264.32. Small change, one might think, for the sort of consumer quite willing to add on such features as heated leather seats, an XM satellite radio system, and a DVD player for the kids. But flashpan anger in response to even slight threats to material well-being ultimately reflects the country's distinctive determination—sanctioned in its founding charter—to pursue happiness. (The Terminator's first official act as governor, needless to say, was to roll back the car tax.)

Of course, more might be accomplished if Americans could somehow manage to become as united in their anger as Californians seem to have been on the car tax. The clash between angry secular liberals and angry religiously motivated conservatives sometimes seems to generate little more than media din. But the rising partisanship of the American voter is probably a positive development. A country as big and diverse as the United States cannot avoid contentious fights over public-policy issues. A broad sorting of voters into a Red team and a Blue team—a trend harking back to the intense partisanship of the nineteenth century—is better than a European-style fragmentation of the electorate into numerous small parties, able to govern only after patching together fragile coalitions. The same Pew Research Center survey that found—tut-tut—a surge in the intensity of partisan feelings also turned up a decline in cynicism about government.

That makes sense. The Pragmatic American wouldn't be investing energies—and angers—in partisan causes if he or she didn't believe in the decent possibility of a payoff. America works as well as it does because of the practical use it makes of its anger. Now the country is getting angry again. Perhaps it is not angry enough.

25

Suspicious Minds

Jedediah Purdy

Too much trust can actually be a bad thing—a polity of suckers is no better than a nation of cynics. But Americans' steadily declining faith in one another is a warning.

WITHOUT TRUST, SOCIAL LIFE is all but impossible. We walk down the street unarmed, invest our money with strangers, and pay taxes— all because we trust that nobody will mug us, take the cash to Cancun, or use government revenue to enrich a family company. The only other way to coordinate complex activity is coercion—which, as the Soviets learned, is neither efficient nor pleasant. Today, when your credit-card number makes regular trips to Bangalore and Ghana, startups get their money from millions of pensioners and private investors, and you put your life in the hands of several federal bureaucracies whenever you fly or take a train, trust is holding up the world. We had all better hope this Atlas does not shrug.

Yet in recent decades Americans have expressed declining confidence in government, business, civic institutions, religious establishments, and one another. Trust in the government has fallen by about half since its peak, in 1966. Sixteen percent of Americans—compared with 55 percent in 1966—say they have "a great deal of confidence" in major companies; and the share that trusts organized religion is down by almost half, to 23 percent. These declines embrace a fair amount of jumping about, but they are declines nonetheless. Meanwhile, the proportion of Americans who believe that most other people are trustworthy has fallen steadily since 1960, from about 55 percent to just above 30 percent.

Trust in government peaked before the controversy over Vietnam got ugly and has since dragged through two troughs: 1974 to 1980 (the seven years after Watergate) and 1990 to 1994. It has recently been rising. Trust in business was very low in the late 1980s and bottomed out in 1991, following the Black Monday stock crash of 1987 and the savings-and-loan scandals. It rose smartly through the 1990s, until the NASDAQ collapse and the latest round of corporate-accounting scandals. Trust in organized religion was higher in the late 1990s than at any time since the mid- 1970s, reflecting a general conservatism in cultural attitudes, although the scandals within the Catholic Church have since brought mistrust on all religious authority. Only trust in other people has steadily fallen.

"Trust," of course, has many meanings. Take trust in government. When people say they "mistrust" the government, they may mean that they are mildly skeptical, profoundly disaffected, or on the verge of revolt. Before 9/11 the public's trust in government was low, but in the first months afterward it soared to its highest levels since the mid-1960s. That suggests that the earlier mistrust was not a deep conviction but a casual attitude born of secure times. It is easy to mistrust what we think we don't need.

Mistrust is not bad in itself. A polity of suckers is no better than a nation of cynics. But both mistrust and trust should be thoughtful, not automatic. During the post–9/11 jump in trust one poll found that 80 percent of Democrats thought that Al Gore should not criticize President Bush; 39 percent of all voters and 37 percent of Democrats said in December of 2001 that it would be inappropriate for *anyone* to disagree publicly with the President's military decisions. Avoiding debate is never a sign of robust civic culture. The argument over foreign policy and domestic security that has returned in recent months is much better than a rote profession of faith in whoever holds power.

Collective mood swings about government are probably the norm for a modern democracy, which is designed to get along well enough while most citizens focus on their private lives. We look up occasionally from our own business, and what we see then—a revolution of civil rights, a distasteful scandal, a terrible attack—can shape our attitudes for years. If there has been a systemic change, it is that scandal-hungry reporting and a tell-all culture have drawn attention to the personal limitations of public figures, encouraging us to be smug in the conviction that the appetitive Bill Clinton or the inarticulate George Bush cannot deserve our confidence, even if their shortcomings have little to do with making sound political decisions. The American oscillation between glib cynicism and naive trust, though, is an old and basic habit.

Mistrust of business has always been driven by events, most recently the rash of corporate-accounting scandals. The unrecorded peaks and valleys from 1927 to 1931 must have outdone those of the past decade, but today the stakes may be higher. For more than a decade American business has been the world's gold standard, providing a model of successful low-regulation capitalism. For that reason we Americans have been able to rely on enormous foreign investment while saving almost none of our own money and maintaining a vast trade deficit. If the United States were perceived to have come down with a case of raging crony capitalism, investors everywhere would think about withdrawing their funds. Without foreign subsidy for American consumption, we could go into a long recession, which would also sink export manufacturers around the world.

The recent scandals raise that danger, and their genesis shows how important the difference is between intelligent trust and thoughtless trust. In 1994 the percentage of people who said they trusted the federal government most or all of the time reached by far its lowest point since 1958, when the National Election Studies—which asks questions about trust in government—began. At the same time, confidence in major companies was picking up, about to begin its strongest run in almost three decades. The following six years, full of reflexive skepticism about government and uncritical euphoria about private enterprise, produced a burst of deregulation and a wave of stock-market investment. The fashionable belief was that markets always got it right and government almost always got it wrong.

We now know what that produced: Enron, WorldCom, and the NASDAQ bubble, to name a few. The companies that were supposed to herald a changed world turned out to be old-fashioned pyramid schemes. The lesson is that if business is to deserve public trust, it must be regulated by a trustworthy government. Without that foundation, trust in business is superstition. It is bad to mistrust those who deserve trust, but worse to trust those who don't.

The important question, then, is what fosters a trustworthy government. At least part of the answer appears to be interpersonal trust— the supposition that most other people are trustworthy. Suspicious people are less likely to join associations, follow public events, get to know their neighbors, or make contact with their congresspersons. In fact, they are less likely than others to do just about anything except watch TV and flip off other drivers on the highway. That means they are not the kinds of citizens who are likely to hold government accountable, intelligently and regularly, and thus keep it trustworthy.

This is worrisome, since interpersonal trust is the one attitude that has steadily fallen since social scientists began measuring it. Moreover, it appears to be driven not so much by episodic events as by formative personal experiences. Interpersonal trust does not change much through life: the trusting young adults of the 1950s are the trusting retirees of today, and their children and grandchildren have expressed less trust in others—with a slight uptick among people just now coming of age. This suggests that the decline is related to basic changes in American life.

For instance, most older people developed their habits of trust in small towns or tightly knit urban communities. Whether or not the neighborhood shopkeeper is a good person, he can usually be trusted, because he will have to deal with you again and again. The same does not go for a telemarketer calling from India or from prison, or the summer employee at The Gap in a mall twenty miles from your home. In a wired economy many of us give credit-card numbers every day to people we will never encounter again, about whom we know nothing. How are you to tell whether the unshaven pedestrian on your suburban street is a child molester or an investment banker from the next subdivision, enjoying an afternoon walk in a bear market? When people say they don't trust others, some are describing this new situation: they may still trust most of the people they know, but they know fewer of the people they deal with.

Mobility and anonymity are related to today's great achievements: meritocracy and racial equality. We probably can't have the good without the bad. There is plenty of trust among homogeneous elites, whether small-town businessmen or Boston Brahmins, who do their business together and exclude outsiders. There was also in-group trust in the racial solidarity of an America that within living memory publicly embraced white supremacy. Freedom and opportunity have eroded those unjust forms of community, and have at the same time made us more of a nation of strangers.

Another source of mistrust has no redeeming side: economic segregation. Expensive new suburbs and urban gentrification are only the extremes of a trend that is now several decades old: rich neighborhoods, like rich families, are getting richer, and poor neighborhoods poorer. Because the poor tend to be mistrustful, economic segregation produces untrusting communities cut off from wealthier (and generally more trusting) populations. That is not a formula for a good civic life.

WHEN GOVERNMENT BUILDS or undercuts interpersonal trust, it is shaping its own future. Half of what government can do in this area is to avoid dangerous mistakes. Asking people to spy on one another spreads mistrust—as it did under the surveillance-heavy and paranoid communist regimes of East Germany and Romania. So does reinforcing pernicious inequalities, whose victims, understandably, mistrust everyone, often including one another. The other half of what government can do is more affirmative. Funding AmeriCorps and other volunteer programs will help. So will creating opportunities in schools and other institutions for civic involvement, because people involved in common projects learn to trust one another. The greatest challenge, though, is to find a way of overcoming economic segregation.

America's democratic capitalism asks civic diligence and mutual concern of people who are, reasonably enough, mostly interested in looking out for themselves in a moneymaking society. Naturally, it disappoints almost everyone sometimes. However, the future of interpersonal trust and its twin, civic involvement, is everyone's concern. A vivid way to imagine the alternatives is to look beyond America's borders to Norway, where 65 percent of people say they trust their fellow citizens, and to Brazil, where three percent do. Climate aside, most people would prefer the orderly, egalitarian society to the crime-racked and corrupt nation of well-protected rich and restless poor.

We know that in the 1990s, without faith in government, trust in business turned out to be groundless. The question now is, If we don't trust one another enough to keep civic culture strong, will our growing faith in government prove equally misguided? Then we could fall back only on the weak reed of our solitary selves.

26

Overflowing Jails

Margaret Talbot

The inevitable consequence of America's high incarceration rate is a
high prison-release rate—and the prisoners getting out are often more
violent or antisocial than they were before. It's time to rethink—and
rebuild—rehabilitation and parole.

EVERY DAY IN AMERICA some 1,600 people will leave state and federal
prisons. Most will start their journey with "gate money" (from $20 to
$200), a one-way bus ticket, and little else. Many will be drug abusers
who received no treatment for their addiction while on the inside, sex
offenders who got no counseling, and illiterate high school dropouts who
took no classes and acquired no job skills. A lot of them will be sick: rates
of HIV, tuberculosis, and hepatitis C are all considerably higher among
prisoners than in the general population. Many of them will be obdurate
"churners," who have already been reincarcerated for a new crime or a
parole violation and are now being let out again. Only about 13 percent
will have participated in any kind of pre-release program to prepare them
for life outside. Nearly a quarter of them will be sent home unconditionally and with no supervision. And two thirds (up from one half in
1984), according to the Urban Institute, will return to just a few metropolitan areas in their states, where they will be further concentrated in
struggling neighborhoods that can ill afford to accommodate them.

It's not quite fair to say that no one thought about these sorts of
things when the rage for incarceration began to dominate American
crime policy, in the early 1980s, but it's not far from the truth either.
Almost all prisoners get out eventually. What happens when they do,

however, is not a topic that held the interest of the legislators who passed mandatory-sentencing laws, abolished parole boards, and eliminated funding for prisoner education. As a result, prison sentences have grown longer while prisons have become places where nothing is done to reprogram criminals for the life outside to which 95 percent of them will return. "Our contemporary prisons basically replicate the social order that produced the offenders to begin with," says Mark A. R. Kleiman, a professor of public policy at the University of California at Los Angeles. "Their signal qualities are violence, idleness, and noise."

Until the early 1980s prison education and rehabilitation programs were deeply embedded in American corrections. But over the past twenty years—a period in which the U.S. prison population has increased fourfold—vocational and educational programs for prisoners have dwindled steadily. Funding once earmarked for such programs has gone instead toward constructing new facilities and providing health care for an older and sicker inmate population.

Prison programs lost their funding partly in response to research in the 1970s that implied they had scant success in cutting recidivism. But new studies suggest that certain kinds of programs do work to increase employment and reduce criminality. Adult literacy and GED classes, vocational training with a realistic eye to the job market, cognitive therapy for sex offenders, and drug-abuse counseling that continues after release have all shown modest but cost-effective success. A recent study sponsored by the Virginia Department of Correctional Education, in which ex-inmates were tracked for fifteen years, found that recidivism among those who had pursued an education while in prison was 59 percent lower. More-comprehensive studies on prison educational programs have shown that reincarceration is 20 percent less frequent for participants. Even allowing for the inevitable selection bias (those who enroll in optional prison programs are more motivated to succeed in the first place), these are pretty encouraging results. "It's an ironic story," says Todd Clear, a professor at the John Jay College of Criminal Justice, in New York, "in that just as the evidence for programs that reduce recidivism was growing, the willingness and capacity to fund them shrank."

MEANWHILE, THE CULTURE OF PAROLE has changed too. Resources for supervising parolees have not kept pace with the growing numbers

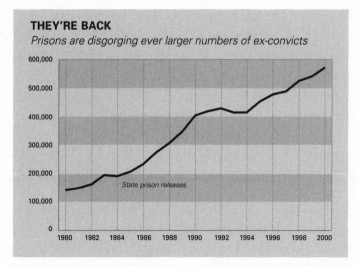

THEY'RE BACK
Prisons are disgorging ever larger numbers of ex-convicts

State prison releases

of them, so caseloads are bigger. In the 1970s the average parole officer oversaw forty-five ex-offenders, according to the Urban Institute,
whereas today the number is about seventy. One consequence has been
an emphasis on surveillance rather than more time-consuming personal relationships between officers and parolees, which has meant that
many more parolees are charged with technical violations. Indeed,
parole violators make up a rapidly growing class of prisoners: in 1980
they accounted for 18 percent of admissions; today they account for a
third, and most of them have been sent back on technical grounds. But
many technical violations—leaving a designated area, not showing up
for a meeting with the parole officer—aren't crimes, and it's not at all
clear that improving the capacity to detect technical violations or locking up more parole violators enhances public safety. What we can say
is that this approach is expensive: California, which sends more parole
violators back to prison than any other state, spends some $900 million
a year to house them, for average stays of about five months.

The larger problem, though, is that in many places we have
replaced discretionary parole, in which parole boards decide when a
prisoner is ready for conditional release, with a regime that eliminates
much of the discretion not only from parole but also from sentencing.
In so doing we have removed some powerful incentives for prisoners to
become the sort of people we would want to send home again. Parole
boards came under attack in the 1970s: the right criticized them for

being too lenient, the left for being too hard on minorities, and good-government types for being too beholden to the narrow political interests of the governors who appointed them. In 1977 parole-board decisions still accounted for 88 percent of all prisoner releases; by 2000 they accounted for only 24 percent.

In some ways this was an improvement: it removed an element of arbitrariness from the parole process. But the social cost was high. As Joan Petersilia, a criminologist at the University of California at Irvine, explains in a forthcoming book, *When Prisoners Come Home:*

> A majority of inmates being released today have not been required to "earn release" but rather have been "automatically released." Parole boards used to examine a prisoner's "preparation" for release, including whether she or he had a place to live, a potential job, and family support. With determinate sentences [fixed prison terms in which parole boards have no say], these factors are not relevant to release. When offenders have "done their time," they are released no matter what level of support is available to them or how prepared they are for release.

One ramification of this is that in a growing number of cases prisoners have "maxed out" on their sentences and are being released unconditionally. Because of new so-called truth-in-sentencing laws (mandating that a prisoner serve most of his or her sentence behind bars and not on parole), by the time some prisoners get sprung, the penal system no longer has any hold over them. In 1977 only four percent of prisoners maxed out; by 1999, 18 percent did. "We have about 150,000 people getting out scot-free each year now—no supervision, nothing," Petersilia told me recently. And although some of these are minor offenders who served short sentences, many are what the former assistant attorney general Laurie Robinson calls the "baddest of the bad"—prisoners who failed to qualify for any early-release credits, or who had committed such violent crimes that they were ineligible for early release. "In Massachusetts," Mark Kleiman says, "you can graduate from a super-max facility at Walpole—where the lights are on all the time, you never see another human face because all the guards are wearing hockey masks, and you leave your cell one hour a day for exercise—straight to the street. And that is not atypical. But nobody ought to be able to walk straight from a prison to the street. Inmates need to decompress. That's what halfway houses were supposed to be for."

OVER THE PAST YEAR OR SO some of the dismal facts about "prisoner re-entry" have come under new scrutiny and have begun to generate some creative thinking. For one thing, parole clearly needs to be reformed. It is not working: more than 40 percent of released inmates are back in prison within three years. Part of the problem is the all-or-nothing response to technical violations. "We need a system that does not have as its only sanction ending the experiment of parole for someone entirely," says Kleiman, who advocates a range of prescribed and immediate but less drastic sanctions, such as short confinements in "halfway-back houses," for people who have been caught in technical violations of parole.

A handful of jurisdictions around the country—including Richland County, Ohio, and Fort Wayne, Indiana—are now experimenting with a promising institution called re-entry court, which is charged with overseeing a prisoner's reintegration into society. Here "conditions of parole are openly agreed to and openly enforced," as Jeremy Travis and Sarah Lawrence, of the Urban Institute, write. "If a new crime is committed, all bets are off and the parolee is prosecuted for the new crime." The violations of parole that now fill prisons, though, are handled differently—with "support services, close judicial monitoring, graduated sanctions for failure to meet conditions, and local detention where needed to enforce the orders of the court." Travis has argued for a twist on this approach: making sentencing judges responsible for coming up with a re-entry plan for prisoners. Judges would tell men and women they had just sentenced that they must begin preparing in prison for the return home, and would order drug rehabilitation, job training, or whatever other programs were called for.

At the same time, prison programs have been experiencing a renewal. A few prisons are involving families and community groups in an inmate's release plan before he is let out. The Vera Institute of Justice's Project Greenlight, for example, brings representatives of community organizations into the Queensboro Correctional Facility, in New York, to talk to prisoners about jobs they might seek once they're free. It also provides counseling for prisoners and their families before the prisoners' release. When prisoners serve longer sentences, as they have done in recent years, family ties are likely to be more attenuated, meaning that inmates are likely to require more help to reconstruct them. Of course, not everybody wants to participate in easing a relative's transition from prison; often family members have been the inmate's victims. But when prisoners can go home to families, they seem to fare better, both in the crucial first few months after release and later.

A few prison systems, notably Oregon's, have been trying out more-practical kinds of vocational training, geared to job openings in fields such as telemarketing and computer-aided mapping of water and tax districts. This has cut recidivism. Meanwhile, Missouri's prison system, under the leadership of Dora Schriro, has come up with a more comprehensive approach whose premise is that prison life should actually resemble real life as much as is practicable. Every offender engages "during work and non-work hours in productive activities that parallel those of free society," as Schriro describes the rules in a paper written for the National Institute of Justice. "In work hours offenders go to school and work and, as applicable, to treatment for sex offenses, chronic mental-health problems, and drug and alcohol dependencies. In non-work hours they participate in community service, reparative activities, and recreation."

Schriro says that from 1994 (when the program went into effect) to 1999 the proportion of inmates returned to prison in Missouri for felony offenses fell from 33 percent to 20 percent. That's impressive in itself. Still more promising, however, is the larger idea this approach evokes. It may be that as a society we want to keep our incarceration rates higher than those of other industrialized democracies (though not, surely, as high as they have been, given how many prisoners are parole violators and drug offenders). After all, there is fairly good evidence that the prison boom was responsible for about a quarter of the decline in crime in the 1990s. But if we do want to keep our prisons full, we must endow them with a purpose broader than incapacitation. We will have to take up again, in new form, the goal of remaking prisoners for life beyond bars. We will have to accept that the question before us is not only how stringently we want to punish people in prison but also what kind of people we want to see emerge from it.

AMERICA AND
THE WORLD

27

Beyond Dominance

Sherle R. Schwenninger

To fashion a world order favorable to American interests, the United States must ask other countries to do more and rediscover its talent for establishing alliances and institutions committed to common international goals.

THE CENTRAL IDEA UNDERLYING American grand strategy since the end of the Cold War has been dominance—the notion that the United States is so powerful and virtuous that it can pretty much remake the world on its own terms. For most of its two terms in office, the Clinton administration pursued a form of soft dominance, in that it sought to legitimize its policies through America's traditional alliances and through the use of international bodies like the International Monetary Fund. The Bush administration has opted for a more explicit form of dominance, arguing that the United States must remain the world's dominant military and economic power, not only to discourage the emergence of other rival powers but also to maintain world order. In pursuing dominance, it has sought to free itself from the constraints of alliances and multilateral institutions, preferring to emphasize the benefits of coalitions of the willing and the ability of the United States to act with maximum freedom, whether it be against rogue states or international terrorist groups.

Dominance may be a seductive idea that has won the support of Democrats and Republicans alike. But as a guiding concept for American grand strategy, it has resulted in bad, and sometimes even reckless, policies that have in the end weakened America's position in the world.

There are two fatal flaws with the notion of dominance. The first is that it does not reflect the realities of today's world. The second is that it does not work.

For most observers of American foreign policy, dominance is an inescapable fact given America's overwhelming military, economic, and cultural power. The only question is how the United States uses that power. But this triumphalist view of American dominance rests not only on a misunderstanding of power and influence in today's world, but also on a misconception of America's relative power position vis-à-vis other states. The United States may be the world's most powerful country, but that does not mean that American supremacy or unipolarity is the defining feature of international relations today.

To begin with, military power has limited utility with respect to most international problems and thus yields less influence than it once did. Unlike during the Cold War, America's wealthy allies in Europe and East Asia do not face a specific military threat. Nor do they see one on the horizon, residual worries about China in East Asia notwithstanding. Instead, their security problems arise from the disorder and violence that accompanies failed states and failed development, and from unsettled nationalist and separatist struggles. U.S. military power is largely irrelevant to most of these problems. To be sure, U.S. military force was arguably helpful in restoring order in the Balkans in the late 1990s, but European countries have now assumed the overwhelming burden of peacekeeping and nation-building in Bosnia, Serbia, Macedonia and, increasingly, in Afghanistan as well.

The situation in East Asia is more complex in that the American military presence there arguably adds a dimension of security reassurance for China, Japan, Taiwan, and South Korea that still gives the United States leverage in the region. But even in East Asia, there is a growing sense that the United States may no longer be the stabilizing force it once was. China has abandoned its previously confrontational posture toward many of its neighbors, particularly over its territorial claims in the South China Sea (although its stance toward Taiwan still remains worrisome), and has generally assumed a more responsible role in the region, particularly with regard to North Korea. Meanwhile, Washington's new emphasis on preventive war, with its on again/off again tough talk toward North Korea has made many East Asians uneasy.

While America's allies see U.S. military power as less central to their own security, they have actually become more important to our own. Indeed, there has been something of a reversal of security roles over the past decade. The United States now needs the help and security cooperation of Europe, Russia, China, South Korea, and Japan more than they need our military protection. The noted foreign policy analyst Robert Kagan, in his book *Of Paradise and Power,* attributes the European preference for softer forms of power to Europe's military weakness. That may be so, but it is also a product of two much larger trends. The first is the growing realization on the part of most Europeans that they are no longer vulnerable to any foreseeable conventional military threat, and that they have a more than adequate military capability for achieving their principal regional security goals. To be sure, they could reorganize their militaries to project power better, but they have been reasonably successful in fulfilling their peacekeeping and nation-building missions in the Balkans and Afghanistan. Secondly, they believe, with some justification, that potential threats to European security are best handled by a combination of political, economic, and diplomatic measures tailored to each case: constructive engagement, as with Iran and Libya; conflict resolution and economic support with regard to the Palestinians and Israelis; nation-building and peacekeeping, as in the former Yugoslavia; and economic development and political reform in Eastern Europe and North Africa.

If many supporters of dominance overstate the role of military power in securing world order, they also tend to discount American weaknesses. In addition to bearing burdens for world security, dominant great powers generally export capital, investing in the infrastructure and industries of less developed countries. At the height of its imperial power, in 1913, Britain exported capital on a scale equal to nine percent of its GDP, financing much of the infrastructure of the United States, Canada, Australia, and Argentina. By contrast, the United States imports capital, not just from Europe and Japan but also from capital-poor emerging economies, to the tune of nearly six percent of GDP. Its international debt is approaching 30 percent of GDP, a level normally associated with developing economies, and which will make it vulnerable to the political decisions as well as to the financial problems of other countries in the decades to come.

By investing so heavily in military power, the United States has undercut its international influence in other critical ways. Foreign assistance has been out of favor for years in nearly all political circles in the United States, but it still matters when it comes to building influence in many parts of the world. Washington's spending on foreign assistance is just one-nineteenth of its military budget and ranks last among OECD countries as a percentage of GDP. And U.S. assistance is heavily concentrated in just a few countries: Israel, Egypt, Colombia, and Jordan. The United States does serve as a large market for many economies, which gives it leverage and influence, but it is constrained from using that leverage because it is dependent on the world market for so many essential goods as well as for financing its external deficit. More than 50 percent of the manufactured goods that Americans now buy are made outside the United States, up from 31 percent in 1987, and the United States needs to import nearly $600 billion in capital annually to cover its external deficit.

By virtue of its lopsided investment in military power, the United States does not have very much, in terms of financial assistance, to offer many countries in the world today, or, for that matter, very much to threaten them with either. This is one of the reasons why so many countries on the U.N. Security Council felt safe in defying the United States on the war against Iraq. Nothing exposed the myth of American dominance more than Washington's inability to get the votes of countries like Chile and Mexico, not to mention Guinea and Cameroon.

A GRAND STRATEGY OF DOMINANCE ultimately rests on the simple idea of a unipolar world, the idea that the United States is the only power that counts in the world today. That is why some advocates of dominance are so critical of France's avowed goal of creating a multipolar world, attributing it to France's superpower envy. Yet for all practical purposes, a multipolar world already exists. On a global plane, the United States may appear to be the world's only superpower, spending more than the next 15 countries combined on military power. But viewed at the level of its key strategic relationships with Europe, Russia, China, and Japan, the United States in each case needs them to achieve its foreign policy goals as much or more than they need the United States. In other words, at the bilateral level, the other established and emerging powers of the world enjoy either strategic parity with the United States or a favorable balance of power and interest. The balance is likely to tilt even further in favor of Europe, Russia, Japan, and China in the future—in part because the American market will become less important to them—and in part because America's growing dependence on foreign capital will increase its international debt burden, making it more vulnerable to the policies and attitudes of its principal creditors.

Take the case of America's relationship with the European Union. Unipolarists like to focus attention on Europe's military weaknesses and the lack of a unified European foreign policy. But, contrary to conventional wisdom, Europe enjoys an attractive position vis-à-vis the United States in that Washington needs the help and support of Europe more than Europe needs the United States. If looked at objectively, Europe is no longer dependent on the United States for any real security or defense needs. In fact, the European nations of NATO and the European Union now have primacy over their own security and over the security of the immediate European Rim region stretching from Ukraine in the north to the Balkans in the south. As much as certain Europeans might like the United States to do more to help create stability in Ukraine or maintain peace in Kosovo and Macedonia, Washington has essentially removed itself from these security-related concerns. Europe's main security worry vis-à-vis the United States today is of an entirely different nature—not that Washington will abandon Europe, but that it will use its power in the Middle East in a way that will destabilize the region and create greater Western-Islamic tensions.

But even in this case, Europe may have more influence and leverage over the United States than has been commonly recognized. Even though Washington is trying to build a flexible military structure that is less dependent on its allies, the United States still relies on European bases and infrastructure for non-NATO missions, and it still needs a measure of European support and participation to gain domestic support for those missions. Beyond this, Washington depends upon European Union members for peacekeeping and nation-building tasks, not just in the Balkans but in Afghanistan and most likely eventually in Iraq, and it benefits from European assistance for other U.S. security-related concerns, such as support for the Palestinian Authority. This is not to mention the importance of Europe's active cooperation in stopping international terrorism and nuclear weapons proliferation.

In many ways, Europe is better positioned to pursue a project to build democracy in the Middle East than is the United States. While the United States has had very little success in helping create stable democracies in any part of the world over the last two decades, the European Union has a solid track record when it comes to democracy building, particularly as it relates to the candidate countries of Central and Eastern Europe, its earlier missteps in the Balkans notwithstanding. For much of the last decade, the world has heard repeatedly about the superiority of the American model. But it has been the European Union that has had the most success in exporting democracy and fostering economic reform.

Moreover, as a continent made up of several of the larger creditor economies, Europe has the financial wherewithal to do more in North Africa, the Middle East, and Eastern Europe. While the United States is dependent upon European as well as East Asian capital to fuel U.S. growth and to pay for its international policies, the nations of the European Union continue to export capital to the developing world as well as to the United States. In addition, the European Union now has as much or more influence with other key members of the international community—such as Brazil, Russia, and Turkey—than the United States does and often pursues policies that better reflect their interests than American policies do. It thus would be able to enlist them in European projects in a way that the United States has not been able to do.

What is true in the case of America's relationship with Europe is true to a lesser degree with respect to its relationships with Russia, China, and Japan. The United States needs a reasonably strong Russia not just to maintain the safety of its nuclear weapons but to help balance an increasingly powerful China, check Taliban-like extremists and terrorists in Central Asia and the Caspian Sea, help stop nuclear proliferation in Iran, and help stabilize the world oil market. In return, Washington has very little to offer Moscow now that Russia has recovered its economic independence from the International Monetary Fund and has begun to repatriate its own capital, except possibly for its blessing of Moscow's sometimes misguided effort to crush the Chechen separatists and support for Russia's bid for membership in the World Trade Organization.

In recent years, the balance of interest and power with China has shifted to one of mutual dependence. China has neutralized American power in a number of ways: by modernizing its nuclear forces; by adopting a good neighbor policy in East Asia; by stepping up its diplomacy toward the resolution of the North Korea crisis; and by becoming both one of the largest suppliers of consumer goods to the United States as well as one of its biggest creditors. Over the past year, the central bank of China has become the largest purchaser of U.S. Treasury bills and, together with the Japanese central bank, funded 45 percent of the U.S. current account deficit in the second quarter of 2003. China has also become an increasingly important destination for Japanese goods and capital, including for Japanese companies relocating production abroad, and China has also taken the lead in establishing a free trade zone with the countries of Southeast Asia. This has reduced Japan's dependence on the United States and strengthened the foundations of an emerging East Asian economic community that one day may represent another challenge to America's international economic position.

Many advocates of dominance would prefer to ignore these developments because they contradict the appealing notion of a unipolar world. But viewed from the perspective of American strategic relations with Europe and Asia, the central feature of international relations today is not American unipolarity but the once popular notion of interdependence. Elsewhere, the troubled underdeveloped regions of the world, struggling with disorder, bad governance, and arrested development, if not outright poverty, do not seem to be the beneficiaries of American dominance. In these regions, the central challenge is not so much a great power competition for influence than it is the collective weakness of the developed world to do anything about their problems.

THE ULTIMATE LEGITIMATING APPEAL of American dominance—of American empire, if you will—is that it is good for the world. Tellingly, however, two of the regions where the United States has enjoyed dominance over the last three decades—the Middle East and our own neighborhood—are two of the most troubled areas of the world. The problems of the Middle East are well known: an increasingly bloody conflict between the Palestinians and Israelis; authoritarian Arab governments that are fearful of greater democracy; its ranking near the bottom in regional lists of human development; feudal allies that fund Islamic fundamentalists and that breed bitter and disillusioned young men who dream of destroying the United States and establishing a single Islamic state.

The record of dominance in our neighborhood is no less discouraging. Colombia is the victim of a seemingly endless civil war fueled in part by America's drug habit. Venezuela suffers from deep-seated civil strife and is unraveling economically. Fidel Castro continues to preside over a failed socialist experiment in Cuba, propped up in part by American hostility. Other countries in the Caribbean still struggle with underdevelopment and are too reliant on a shadow economy of drugs, arms, and money laundering. Haiti is one of the poorest and most miserable places on the planet. Mexico might seem to be one of the few bright spots in this picture in light of its progress toward democracy until one considers that the standard of living of 80 percent of its population has fallen over the last 15 years and that it survives only by exporting its people to the United States.

This points to the second problem with dominance as a strategic policy: that wherever it has been tried it has failed. Even the softer form of dominance practiced by the Clinton administration led to bad policies and overreaching. The Clinton administration thought it could remake the international economic order by pushing financial liberalization and other policies known as the Washington Consensus onto the emerging economies of Asia and Latin America. But that effort helped produce the Asian financial crisis, which almost brought down the global economy. As a result of this overzealous and misguided effort, the United States now has less influence in Asia than it did a decade ago and is more dependent on Japan and China for their capital, even though their financial markets remain largely closed to American financial institutions. Meanwhile, the Washington Consensus has been discredited in most parts of the world, especially in those Asian producer-oriented economies that would benefit from some liberal reforms.

The Bush administration has made a similar mistake in waging an unnecessary war in Iraq, tying down a significant portion of its military power, and making American forces an easy target for Islamic extremists as well as for disgruntled Iraqis. The United States may ultimately pay a heavy financial price, as the costs of the occupation will be a drain on American finances for years to come. This will not only constrain needed investments at home but undermine America's ability to finance other important foreign policy goals.

Over the last decade, the United States has benefited from a "foreign policy bubble"—from an exaggerated sense not only of its power and influence but of its contribution to international peace and security. The Clinton and Bush administrations alike fueled that bubble with endless spin about America's foreign policy accomplishments and the superiority of the American way. But with the Clinton administration's ill-fated program of international financial liberalization, followed by the NASDAQ crash and the revelations of corporate governance scandals, the bubble of American economic dominance burst. And now by showing the limitations of American military power, and its dependence upon other countries to secure Iraq and Afghanistan, the Bush administration may have pricked the bubble of American military dominance as well.

THE ARCHITECTS OF DOMINANCE are correct that American foreign policy works best when it combines high moral goals with real world national interests. But, as we have seen, they are wrong to make dominance the central organizing principle of American grand strategy. In doing so, they are ignoring the foundations of world order that enabled the United States to become a secure and prosperous society while establishing the basis for a lasting peace among the great powers of North America, Europe, and East Asia. The generally peaceful orientation of the foreign policies of today's China, India, and Russia as well as of Europe, Japan, and South Korea is the product not of American military dominance (although America's military power played a role) but of the pull of a global economy and a system of commerce that offered their people middle-class prosperity. These countries have for the most part subordinated ideology and great power ambition to economic development and commercial prosperity, and emerging powers—including middle-level powers like Malaysia, Indonesia, Turkey, and even Iran—are beginning to follow suit.

The greatest accomplishment of American foreign policy has been the creation of a system of political and economic cooperation that tied together Europe, East Asia, and the United States into a growing world economy and that has acted as a magnetic pull for other countries. This system, of course, has not been perfect, but it has created the conditions for a great power entente—a global concert of powers committed to creating wealth and managing international conflict. The central overarching challenge of the early twenty-first century is how to update the foundations of this system so that it offers a secure place not just for the already prosperous countries of Europe, North America, and East Asia but for emerging powers and struggling developing countries as well.

But to do that successfully, U.S. policy thinkers must put aside such seductive notions as dominance and avoid solitary American military crusades against rogue states and terrorist networks. Instead, it must rediscover its talent for world order building—for establishing alliances, institutions, and networks of government and non-government actors committed to common international goals. What threatens the American-inspired system in not a rival military power or even a set of potential military powers, but disorder and failed development. And at the heart of the specter of disorder is a growing governance gap that cannot be filled by American power alone.

This governance gap is the result of the growing complexity of world affairs and the global economy, on the one hand, and the weakness of existing international and regional institutions, including such informal organizations as the G8, on the other. Everywhere one looks there are problems that call out not just for international cooperation but for more collective action and resources: failed states in Africa, Asia, and Latin America; separatist conflicts in Central and South Asia, including one that could lead to nuclear war between Pakistan and

India; AIDS and other epidemics; pollution and global warming; energy shortages; underdevelopment and recurrent financial crises in the developing world; and global criminal gangs trafficking in arms, drugs, and women. Indeed, the principal problem of world order is the huge gap between the demand for international public goods (from military protection to international development assistance) to help rectify these problems and their supply.

The agenda of dominance has exacerbated this gap in two ways: by denigrating international law and many international institutions, and by discouraging the emergence of other responsible powers willing to bear a greater share of the burden for order keeping and the management of the world economy. As outlined earlier, the defining feature of the international system is not American dominance but multipolarity and the collective weakness of the great powers to deal with the many transnational problems of failed development and failed states. Washington's insistence upon American dominance has provoked three counterproductive reactions on the part of the potential contributors to world order. It has caused countries to resist American power or to free ride on it—or, even worse, to both resist and free ride. Neoconservatives in the Bush administration do not seem to understand that Europe and, to a lesser degree, Japan, Korea, and Russia are powerful enough to resist many American initiatives that threaten their interests and strong enough to go it alone in their own regions if need be. This is why the United States has lost influence in the two regions that matter most—in Europe and East Asia—even as it flexes its military muscles in Iraq, and why the governance gap will grow wider if the United States continues to insist on dominance.

If anything, the troubled American occupation of Iraq should underscore the fact that the United States lacks the resources and order-keeping capabilities to deal with the problems of disorder and failed governance alone. The first principle of American foreign policy, therefore, ought to be to encourage the development of other responsible centers of power and authority capable of working together to expand zones of peace and prosperity and to manage the instability caused by failed governance in the developing world. This, in turn, means harnessing the efforts of the world's other great regional powers—the

European Union, Russia, China, India, Japan, South Korea, Australia, Canada, and Brazil. Many of these efforts will be regional in scope, but they would be part of a larger system of international governance committed to common world-order goals. Indeed, it is only by sharing power and building international institutions, not by insisting on American dominance, that we can hope to close the international governance gap.

THE FIRST STEP TOWARD putting this first principle into practice is to recognize that the answer to rogue states and terrorist groups, like al-Qaeda, is not the unrestrained exercise of American military power, but the building of elaborate networks of regional cooperation embracing understandings relating to police and intelligence collaboration, as well as to the exercise of economic and military power. Just as containment and political and economic engagement brought about peace between Europe, Russia, China, Japan, and the United States, a new grand strategy must manage potentially revisionist powers by embedding them in regional security orders that constrain them while offering them the stability and encouragement needed for successful economic development. The most pressing challenges in this regard relate to the suspected nuclear ambitions of Iran and North Korea, and the need for new security arrangements in the Persian Gulf and East Asia.

There are no easy answers for dealing with the nuclear aspirations of these vastly different countries. A rogue-state strategy aimed at isolating and pressuring North Korea and Iran is likely to be counterproductive and ultimately destabilizing for the regions concerned. On the other hand, a policy of engagement would require us to overlook some unpleasant features of both regimes, and in the case of North Korea would smack of giving in to blackmail. The way out of this seeming dilemma is to think of engagement as a part of a larger multilateral process of establishing a new security order involving great power cooperation in each region. The eventual reunification of Korea must be at the core of a regional security order that further establishes cooperation between China, South Korea, Japan, Russia, and the United States. And the peaceful evolution of Iran is central to a new security order for developing the oil resources of the Caspian Sea and the Persian Gulf, and for curbing Taliban extremists in the region. Such a security order in turn requires the cooperation and support of the European Union, Turkey, Russia, the United States, India, and China.

Each region, of course, has its own unique challenges. But in each case American policy should be guided by three overriding ideas. The first is to elevate common economic development objectives over geopolitical rivalry. The second is to create common security arrangements that reduce the relevance of military power and nuclear weapons to each country's security. And the third is to create a true concert of regional powers by internationalizing the American leadership role, by sharing responsibility with Europe and Russia in the Persian Gulf, and with Japan, China, South Korea, and Russia in East Asia.

In the case of the Persian Gulf and the Caspian Sea region, the United States needs to see a reforming and modernizing Iran as part of the solution to regional instability, despite differences over Tehran's support for Hezbollah and some other aspects of Iranian policy. The United States needs to understand that Iran's drive for nuclear weapons is not mainly an anti-American act but a much more complex response to regional relations: a mixture of a desire for greater regional influence; worries about a resurgent and U.S.-allied Iraq, which after all invaded Iran in the 1980s; and concerns about the other nuclear powers that surround it. Finally, the United States also must understand that an effort to establish a new set of security understandings between Iraq and Iran and their neighbors cannot be an American project alone, but must be a regional effort that is supported by the European Union and Russia.

In East Asia, the challenge facing the United States and its regional partners is how to simultaneously manage the nuclear weapons ambitions of North Korea and its possible economic and social implosion. The Bush administration has been correct to address the question of North Korea by means of a multilateral process, but for too long it was wrong to refuse to consider the kind of security guarantees that a paranoid North Korean leadership may feel it needs in order to give up its nuclear weapons program. The administration also failed by not supporting a broader program of economic and political engagement that Seoul and Beijing had suggested. The principal elements of a new framework for the Korean peninsula would entail both a Korean peace agreement with security guarantees for both North Korea and South Korea, and an economic program aimed at opening up North Korea to trade and investment. This in turn would create the foundation for a broader regional security order that would eventually include multilateral arms control and other common security understandings that would constrain future geopolitical rivalry in the region.

THE UNITED STATES, similarly, needs to adopt a new collective approach to the growing rejectionism of the Arab and Islamic worlds to an American-inspired international system of entente and middle-class prosperity. The United States has a very large stake in the outcome of the struggle within many Arab and Islamic societies between the modernists, on the one hand, and the reactionaries (those who oppose modernization) and the revolutionaries (the Osama bin Ladens, who want to create a single theocratic state), on the other. But, an American project to democratize and remake the Middle East, as suggested by the Bush administration and as supported by some neoliberal hawks, is likely to be counterproductive and possibly even catastrophic for both the United States and the people of the region—in part, because the United States lacks the legitimacy it needs to promote democracy in this part of the world and in part because it alone does not have the resources or experience to do so.

The challenge is how to support and encourage the modernists without making the United States the issue in such a way that strengthens the reactionaries and the revolutionaries instead. Even under the best circumstances, this will be difficult to achieve. The answer broadly is for the United States to internationalize its Middle East policy—to reduce America's dominant, in-your-face presence in the region by sharing responsibility with the European Union, NATO, Russia, and the United Nations. In fact, American policy in the Middle East has been most successful when Washington has actively involved its European partners and the United Nations. Such was the case with the progress on the Israeli-Palestinian conflict from the Madrid conference in 1991 to the signing of the Oslo Accords in 1993, and with the substantial disarmament of Iraq that occurred in the early years of the UN containment and inspections regime.

The first step in this process of internationalization, of course, must involve an early and successful end to the American occupation of Iraq, combined, ideally, with an effort to give the United Nations and the Arab League a larger role in overseeing the transition process. An equally important element of internationalization would involve turning the current American road map for peace, which began as the European-inspired Quartet Plan, into a real international solution to the Israeli-Palestinian conflict. Under Washington's leadership, the road map has unfortunately come to replicate all the problems of the American-sponsored Oslo process, enabling Israel to concoct endless excuses for delaying the dismantling of settlements and its occupation of the West Bank and Gaza. A better approach would be to turn over the occupied territories, including the Israeli settlements within them, to a UN/NATO trusteeship and to establish an American-led NATO peace force for ensuring security, with the goal of establishing a recognized Palestinian state within six to eighteen months.

Only such a bold internationalist approach is likely to break the grip extremists on both sides have over the current peace process and to ensure Israel's long-term security. There is no way to overstate the importance of a viable Palestinian state to the political future of the Arab world, or to America's hope for normalizing its relationship with the Islamic world. If, in two years, there are still Israeli tanks in Hebron, Ramallah, and other Palestinian towns, any modernization or democratization that occurs in the Arab world will take a decidedly anti-American direction. The United States needs to help Israel understand, by pressure if necessary, that its future lies not with the subjugation of Palestinians in the occupied territories, but as the engine for commerce and economic growth in the Middle East.

This raises the final dimension of internationalizing American policy in the Middle East—namely, joining forces with the European Union and the world's financial institutions in putting together a program for regional economic development that would take priority over an American effort to democratize Arab societies. As suggested earlier, an American effort at democratization may only further radicalize the region, and force painful policy choices on future administrations. The current deplorable state of democracy in the region is less a function of

Arab political culture than of failed development, and thus our first priority must be development and jobs as well as free elections.

The idea of internationalizing American policy in the Middle East will be bitterly resisted by powerful figures in and around the Bush administration. But many of these same figures are responsible for the current failed order in the region. Americans not concerned solely with recycling Saudi petrodollars into arms sales or with perpetuating Israel's occupation of the West Bank should welcome this effort because it would serve American interests better than does the current American monopoly. The United States needs a Europe and Russia that can act as a check on America's worst tendencies in this part of the world. For more than three decades now, American policy has been its own worst enemy—embracing the shah of Iran in a misguided authoritarian effort at modernization, befriending and building up a power-hungry Saddam Hussein, arming the Afghan mujahidin and Arab Afghanis, cozying up to Central Asian dictators in a failed bid for control of Caspian Sea oil, stroking a calcified and repressive Saudi royal family even as they export Islamic extremism to other parts of the region, and tolerating, if not giving aid and comfort to, the Israeli occupation of the West Bank and Gaza. This is not to mention the utter failure of the United States to advance democracy and economic development—despite billions of dollars of aid to Egypt and billions of dollars of arms sales to the Saudi, Jordanian, and Kuwaiti governments. In short, the burden of proof should be on those who resist internationalization and continue to insist on the United States having a free hand in the Middle East.

FINALLY, THE NEXT ADMINISTRATION must fully accept the realities of a multipolar world by recommitting the United States to the vision of the world that Franklin Delano Roosevelt and his advisers had when they proposed the United Nations and the Bretton Woods institutions. Many advocates of dominance bitterly oppose the idea of a multipolar world, citing multipolarity as the cause of war and conflict in earlier periods of international relations. This is not just a selective reading of history but ignores America's own interests. In a multipolar world in which the United States may actually suffer from an unfavorable balance of power in each of its key bilateral relationships, it is in America's interest to try to constrain the freedom of other powers with international law and institutions. Indeed, the United States, being the most global power of all, has the greatest interest in a system of global governance.

An appreciation of the importance of global governance to a world order favorable to American interests requires, above all else, a renewed commitment on the part of the United States to the institutional architecture of world order. The United Nations, the International Monetary Fund (IMF), and the World Bank are all still essential, but they are badly in need of updating to reflect today's power relations and to meet today's international challenges. Given the growth of the world economy, the IMF has barely a fraction of the resources it had at its beginning, which helps explain why it has been so ineffective in dealing with the frequent financial crises of emerging economies. The World Bank has become a hodgepodge of feel-good development programs, rather than the catalyst for public investment it was meant to be. Both institutions need to be reshaped to be able to support the extension of middle-class prosperity in the developing world.

Meanwhile, the United Nations struggles with the growing demand for the international community to take on the task of nation-building in countries as diverse as Afghanistan, Iraq, Liberia, Cambodia, and Congo. These institutions will not be reinvented overnight, but the United States needs to devote more time to the questions of global architecture and less time trying to micromanage the remaking of countries that will only resent America's overbearing presence. That global architecture must include not just large multilateral institutions, like the World Bank and the IMF, but also a range of regional and mini-regional organizations. The world has become too complex to be governed either by a single dominant power or exclusively by universal global institutions that in many instances are too big to act effectively or too insensitive to existing regional differences. Indeed, the creation of a new layer of regional institutions holds the key to overcoming many of the problems with today's international organizations. It also holds the key to addressing many of the problems of failed governance and development that afflict so many countries in the developing world.

Recommitting the United States to a project of world order building—by asking other countries to do more both regionally and globally—is the best hope for preserving the best features of an American-inspired system of middle-class commerce and great power entente. It is therefore the best way to secure a world favorable to American interests and values.

28

Opportunity Missed

Michael Lind

Following the end of the Cold War, the United States had an opportunity to preside over the creation of a new and better global system, while putting its own house in order. Here is what could have been.

FROM THE MOMENT the Berlin Wall came down, a succession of U.S. presidents used American economic, military, and cultural primacy as leverage to build a new global system incorporating both the former communist countries and the developing nations of the global South. Over the course of the next decade, America's leaders phased out the Pax Americana alliance system in Europe and East Asia—a temporary Cold War measure—and replaced it with a global great-power concert.

In Europe, the U.S. administrations that came to power after the end of the Cold War transformed NATO by adding post-Soviet Russia, and worked out a common strategy with Europe and Russia to deal with the troubled Middle East region to the south. The civil war in the Muslim world provoked by radical jihadists threatened Europe, Russia, and the United States alike. So instead of responding unilaterally, Washington formed a united front with Europe and Russia against al-Qaeda and similar jihadist groups. Under the auspices of the United Nations and the new NATO, it also worked with Europe and Russia to defuse much of the anger in the Arab world and the wider Muslim world by replacing the Israeli occupation of Palestine with a temporary multinational protectorate until a Palestinian state could be established. The model pioneered in Palestine, in which American, European, and Russian NATO forces presided over a UN-sponsored transition to statehood, was then applied to end the Russian occupation of Chechnya and the Indian and Pakistani struggle over Kashmir.

Multilateral cooperation was also essential to an American-led campaign against the proliferation of weapons of mass destruction. In Iraq, UN weapons inspectors, reintroduced after a few years absence, discovered that UN policy had succeeded in preventing Saddam from acquiring weapons of mass destruction, making unnecessary an invasion of Iraq. The successful disarmament of Saddam Hussein's Iraq by UN inspectors backed up by U.S., European and Russian threats of force permitted the United States to remove its troops from Saudi Arabia and to relocate them in Europe and Russia, removing a source of propaganda for al-Qaeda. The United States joined Europe and Russia in pressuring Israel to cooperate with the nonproliferation regime of the International Atomic Energy Agency in order to reduce the motive for other states in the region to acquire their own nuclear weapons. The admission of Russia to NATO facilitated efforts to dismantle Russian nuclear warheads and to employ Russian nuclear scientists who might otherwise have sold their talents to hostile regimes.

In East Asia as in Europe, the dissolution of the Soviet Union had rendered America's Cold War alliance system obsolete. Realizing that international institutions would be stillborn in the region, Washington began promoting traditional great-power summits involving the United States, China, Japan, and Russia. Multilateral cooperation among the East Asian powers deterred the North Korean regime, even as the United States withdrew most of its forces from South Korea and Okinawa, leaving a small number of troops as a symbol of America's security commitment. Realizing that the United States would probably be isolated in the region and the world if it pursued a policy of confrontation with China, Washington instead adopted a policy of constructive engagement. It followed a similar policy toward Asia's other rising giant, India.

By sharing the burden of policing the Middle East with Europe and Russia, and by replacing confrontation with cooperation in East Asia, the United States was able to demobilize many of its conventional armed forces, freeing up resources for long-term military modernization. The new U.S. military strategy de-emphasized conventional warfare and instead concentrated on high-tech arms and low-intensity conflict. Two previously conflicting schools of thought—the high-tech "revolution in military affairs" and "fourth generation warfare"—were combined in the post-Cold War American national security strategy. Even while adapting the robotics revolution to American national defense, the Pentagon downsized the regular army and focused on special forces capable of fighting alongside, not in place of, allies and proxies in low-level conflicts and peace-keeping operations. Although fewer Americans were employed in the armed forces, the expanded investment in defense R&D enabled the United States to maintain a comfortable lead in military technology and produced valuable spin-offs for civilian industry.

Following the Cold War, America's leaders undertook equally bold structural reforms of the American and world economies. The 1990s were devoted to infrastructure-led domestic growth. To share prosperity and enhance national security, Washington's economic strategy encouraged the decentralization of population and industry from the crowded coasts to the country's interior. It did so by financing the construction of a new national infrastructure that drew on advances in telecommuting practices and small-scale aviation. Washington also undertook a massive investment in hydrogen fuel cell technology in order to reduce America's economic dependence on the volatile oil-supplying countries of the Middle East.

The United States also used the post-1989 moment of great-power peace to reform distorted trade and financial relationships. During the Cold War, Washington bought Japanese geopolitical support for the United States at the price of tolerating Japanese mercantilism (by contrast, America's trade and investment with Europe was more or less in balance). The result was large trade imbalances in Japan's favor. The problem was further exacerbated when the "little tigers" of East Asia—Hong Kong, Singapore, South Korea, and Taiwan—followed Japan's model by protecting their own markets while targeting American consumers. At the same time, American multinational corporations began to expatriate manufacturing to low-wage economies, especially to low-wage economies in East Asia. In order to finance the consumption represented by its large trade deficits, the United States borrowed from Japan and other Asian producer economies upon whose savings it had become dependent for capital.

In the 1990s, visionary American leaders moved quickly to deal with the threats of mercantilism, dependence on foreign savings, and a global "race to the bottom" in manufacturing. Following the advice of strategic trade theorists like James Fallows, a series of presidents abandoned the attempt to force Japan to become a liberal society. Instead, the United States joined with the European Union to form a giant liberal trading bloc, the Trans-Atlantic Free Trade Area (TAFTA), which negotiated specific market-share agreements with mercantilist countries like Japan, which for domestic reasons preferred to play by different rules.

TAFTA, which included the United States and Canada but not Mexico or any other low-income country, accounted for a majority of the world's wealth. The expatriation of industry to developing countries took place, not as a mad scramble in a "race to the bottom" but on the basis of negotiated market-share agreements between TAFTA and nations and regions in the global South. By preserving some market share for domestic manufacturers, the TAFTA regime encouraged industrial companies in the United States and Europe to compete with one another not by lowering wages and benefits but on the basis of efficiency. The result was the rapid automation of First World industries, which produced manufactured goods for the guaranteed market-share of high-wage First World economies.

There remained the problem of America's dependence on foreign capital. Since the Great Depression, American policymakers had been haunted by the fear of underconsumption. By the 1990s, however, it was clear that the longstanding emphasis on consumption needed to be corrected by a new emphasis on savings. A combination of compulsory and voluntary new savings vehicles spread the ownership of income-producing assets throughout American society. By the early twenty-first century, the United States became a net exporter of capital once again, and ordinary Americans profited from investing in the rapid growth of societies in the global South.

Rejecting the attempt of conservatives and neo-liberals to revive discredited Victorian-era notions of laissez-faire, successive American administrations after the Cold War recognized that a truly free global market, even if it was desirable in theory, was not possible in practice, for the reason that many developing nations wanted a share of high-tech industries, much as did all advanced nations. Abandoning the ideal of nondiscrimination among sectors as impractical for political reasons, the United States and its allies worked out new rules for world trade in which individual nations, by means of market-share agreements, domestic-content rules, and other measures, could preserve valuable industries within their borders without resorting to trade-disrupting tariffs or restrictions on investment. In its approach to global development, the United States revived an old American idea—the infrastructure-led development promoted by Harry Truman's Point Four program and symbolized by the New Deal's Tennessee Valley Authority (TVA). The infrastructure that the major economies helped to finance in developing countries consisted, not of giant hydroelectric projects and centralized urban utilities, as in the 1940s and 1950s, but rather of small, decentralized hydrogen-fuel-cell power plants, dispersed small airport systems, and wireless communication systems like those used in the increasingly decentralized United States. By incorporating the technologies of the third industrial revolution, this new development model permitted agrarian societies to evolve directly into high-tech service economies, avoiding a stage of sweatshop factory labor and Dickensian urban agglomerations. At the same time, the marketization of non-traded services, such as housing construction, permitted investors in the global North to profit from the spread of middle-class amenities like single-family homes in the global South.

The result of the post-Cold War reforms in the United States and the world was not a Golden Age. Military rivalries among the great powers, including China and India, continued to exist, along with extensive cooperation in areas of shared interest. Both global security and world trade were governed more by mutual disarmament treaties than by a single set of agreed-upon rules. The civil war in the Muslim world, spilling over its borders now and then, was a disruptive force for decades. Large-scale immigration from the Middle East, South Asia, and Africa, not only to North America and Europe but also in time to Eurasia and South America, created a backlash in the form of xenophobic ethno-nationalist movements. The ideological struggles between capitalism and communism that turned on control of the means of production were replaced by a new ideological struggle over the regulation of biotechnology that revolved around the question of control of the means of reproduction of humans as well as other organisms. These tensions notwithstanding, the system that enlightened American leaders shaped in the years following the Cold War averted great-power conflict for generations, while triggering a sustained growth in global wealth and middle-class living standards without precedent in history.

UNFORTUNATELY, THIS IS FICTION. The story told above is one of an alternate history. Actual history took a different course following the end of the Cold War—and both America and the world are worse off than they might have been.

Consider the fundamental decision confronting American policy-makers following the fall of the Berlin Wall—whether to construct a new global system, or to try to preserve the old Cold War system with slight modifications. Both George Herbert Walker Bush and Bill Clinton chose the latter option. The first Bush, cautious to a fault, initially opposed the reunification of Germany and the secession of the non-Russian nationalities from the Soviet empire, and then insisted that any united Germany must be in NATO. Clinton, instead of incorporating Russia into the Atlantic alliance the way that West Germany had been incorporated in the 1950s, pushed NATO to Russia's borders and pursued an American grab for influence over Central Asian oil resources at Russia's expense. In East Asia, the Clinton administration arbitrarily froze the number of troops at Cold War levels, even though America's Asian troop deployments were not an appropriate response to any threat, including the threat of North Korea to South Korea and its neighbors.

The strategy of the first Bush administration and the Clinton administration can be described as Cold War Plus—the expansion of America's Cold War alliance system into the power vacuum left by the collapse of the Soviet Union. Both administrations had an internationalist veneer, but it was largely a camouflage for American unilateralism. This was especially true of the Clinton administration, as illustrated by the contrast between the Gulf War and the Kosovo War. When the Clinton administration realized that it would not obtain the support of the

UN Security Council for an American-led war against Serbia, Clinton circumvented the United Nations and worked through NATO instead.

At least the elder Bush and Clinton sought to portray themselves as liberal internationalists in the post-1945 bipartisan tradition. George W. Bush, under the influence of neo-conservative ideology, broke with the post-1945 tradition of American liberal internationalism. The neo-conservatives of the Bush administration, based in the civilian leadership of the Pentagon, envisioned a "unipolar world" in which the United States, with "coalitions of the willing," would reserve the right to wage "preventive war" and to "end regimes" that were potential and not imminent threats. Influenced by this radical vision, George W. Bush embarked on a spree of treaty cancellation, went to war in Iraq without UN authorization over the objections of every other great power except Britain, thus crippling NATO by pitting its new Eastern European members against American allies like Germany and France.

In the aftermath of the al-Qaeda attacks on the United States on 9/11, the Bush administration was right to go to war in Afghanistan to topple the Taliban regime, which had permitted Osama bin Laden to use Afghan territory as headquarters for his terrorist army. Unfortunately, however, the United States sought to minimize the role of NATO members in the Afghan war, while expecting its NATO allies to undertake much of the difficult work of peace-keeping and reconstruction in its aftermath.

Following the Afghan war, the Bush administration used the struggle against Osama bin Laden's terrorists as an excuse for two policies that had nothing to do with al-Qaeda: a massive expansion of America's conventional military and the invasion of Iraq, both of which had been planned by neo-conservative policy experts in opposition during the Clinton years. In addition to encouraging the notion that Saddam Hussein somehow was linked to al-Qaeda's attacks on the World Trade Center and the Pentagon, the Bush administration justified the war in Iraq on the grounds that Saddam Hussein was on the verge of obtaining weapons of mass destruction which were likely to fall into the hands of al-Qaeda or other anti-American terrorist groups. But Saddam's secular Baathist regime was not allied with al-Qaeda's Muslim extremists, and apparently Saddam had no weapons of mass destruction—as the

UN weapons inspectors would have soon discovered had their work not been abruptly aborted by the American invasion.

The result of the second Bush administration's policies was a catastrophic diversion of American resources. The two wars in Afghanistan and Iraq stretched the American military to the limits of its manpower and required the expenditure of hundreds of billions of dollars which might have gone to other purposes—including other military expenditures more closely tied to America's actual national security needs. Two of Bush's core constituencies—Protestant fundamentalist "Christian Zionists" in the Bible Belt South and the minority of Jewish-Americans who supported the right-wing Likud government in Israel—applauded the deepening involvement of the United States in the Holy Land. The truth was, however, that the only genuine strategic interests the United States had in the region were shared with Europe and Russia. An American-European-Russian condominium over the weak and turbulent Middle East made sense in terms of American national interest. An Israeli-American condominium, disguised by the addition of small numbers of British, Spanish, Italian, and Polish troops, did not.

The guerrilla war against the American occupiers of Iraq soured the American public on foreign military intervention and tended to discredit the neo-conservatives. It also raised the question of the utility of a regular army designed to wage World War II-style campaigns, in an era in which asymmetric warfare was becoming the norm. In East Asia, the neo-conservatives at first treated China as the next Soviet Union, a superpower that could provide a rationale for massive increases in U.S. defense spending. However, China refused to play its assigned role of villain and sought economic prosperity by inviting multinationals from the United States and other First World countries to take advantage of its huge pool of inexpensive labor. The world's largest surviving communist country was a greater economic threat to the workers of the world than it was a military threat to the capitalists.

In the area of the world economy, American strategy following the end of the Cold War was equally misguided. The 1990s were the years, not only of the stock-market bubble, but also of a "bubble" in economic theory. Anachronistic nineteenth-century notions of a magically self-regulating global market, that had been buried during the Great

Depression and the post-1945 Golden Age of managed, regulated welfare capitalism, were revived in the 1970s by conservatives and attained
intellectual hegemony in policymaking circles by the 1990s. The
"Washington Consensus" held that global free trade would not only
benefit all industrialized nations but would lead to the development of
poor countries as well. The Clinton administration supported regional
free-trade agreements like NAFTA and presided over the formation of
the World Trade Organization (WTO).

In practice, the neo-liberal Washington Consensus did not promote actual global free trade—that would have required an open-
borders policy toward immigrant labor. Instead, the United States
pushed for the global liberalization of investment rules, while leaving
intact the existence of multiple states with more or less immobile populations with different levels of wages and benefits and rights. The predictable consequence of this combination of mobile capital with
immobile labor was a global "race to the bottom" as multinationals
transferred first production and then services to low-wage economies.
Freedom of investment also meant freedom of dis-investment—as
Asian countries discovered, when panic among Western investors led
to a pull-out of "hot capital" and to the worst economic crisis in the
region since the Great Depression.

The Asian economic crisis was followed by new crises, as low-wage
countries that had earlier profited from the expatriation of manufacturing, like Mexico, lost jobs to other low-wage countries like China.
The expatriation of industry, in some form, was inevitable, and often
desirable. But in the world of the alternate history that began this essay,
the globalization of production took place on a negotiated basis, as a
united Euro-American liberal world worked out agreements with low-
wage nations in the global South. In the real world expatriation took
place in an environment more like that of the California Gold Rush—
to the detriment of the industrial and industrializing nations alike.

The contrast between policies promoted by the Washington Consensus and those the United States could have pursued if it had been true
to its internationalist traditions could not have been more extreme. In
the history of what might have been, American policymakers after 1989
revived the view of mid-century Americans like Franklin Roosevelt and

British thinkers like John Maynard Keynes. Roosevelt, Keynes, and the other architects of the post-1945 Bretton Woods financial order believed that capitalism must be made safe for democracy. Currency fluctuations and depressions, by wrecking stable middle classes, fed the kind of political extremism that led to the rise of ideologies like fascism and communism. The mid-century reformers of the world economy, having regulated national economies by policies such as America's New Deal, believed that the regulation of the global market was necessary both to preserve the middle class in industrial nations and to promote a middle class where it historically had not existed, in agrarian, former colonial countries.

By contrast, the actual policies promoted by the United States during the heyday of the Washington Consensus following the Cold War promoted the interests of small elites in both the North and the South, often at the expense of working-class and middle-class citizens in both. Some countries with strong and enlightened governments, like Singapore, were able to use their status as low-wage producers to move up the economic food chain. More often, the foreign investment that flowed into encapsulated export-processing zones in low-wage countries did not necessarily "trickle down" to the primitive economy around it; all too often, the money, monopolized by local partners of multinationals, went to secret offshore accounts.

Ordinary Americans sometimes did benefit from cheap consumer goods made in low-wage countries like China and Mexico. At the same time, however, the expatriation of manufacturing forced many well-paid, unionized manufacturing workers into the poorly-paid, non-unionized service sector. Only a small minority of Americans accounted for most stock ownership, and they reaped the lion's share of the gains from the global economic strategies of the multinational companies they co-owned. Even the rich suffered from the instability of a global trading and financial system in which a devaluation here or a political change there could lead to a rush of capital from one low-wage economy to another, leaving shuttered factories, empty government treasuries, and impoverished populations behind.

The failure of American foreign policy in the past decade and a half has been, at its core, a failure of ideas. The administrations of George

Herbert Walker Bush and Bill Clinton lacked the imagination to envision a new international order other than an incremental extension of the Pax Americana system of the Cold War and a return to laissez-faire economics. George W. Bush suffered from no lack of vision—but his vision, of unilateral American world domination, based on brute force and contempt for international law and diplomacy, was profoundly misconceived.

The new American internationalism that I have outlined would have been easier to promote in the decade following the end of the Cold War than in the changed circumstances of the second half of the first decade of the twenty-first century. The U.S. government is constrained today by escalating budget and trade deficits. The damage to America's prestige in the world and to American alliances that has been done by the belligerent unilateralism of the second Bush administration will take years to repair.

But it is never too late to start doing the right thing. Whether under a Democratic president or a second Bush administration, the United States should repudiate both incrementalism and unilateralism. Belatedly, the United States should accept the challenge of collaborating with the other nations of the world to create a genuine international order that is not merely American hegemony in disguise. Inevitably, the American share of global power and wealth will decline. When it does, it will be in America's interest to have a peaceful and liberal global order in whose preservation and perpetuation every major power, not merely the United States, has a stake.

In the realm of security, the goal of the United States should be to phase out America's Cold War alliances and to replace them with a system of regional and global concerts, in which former Cold War rivals like Russia and China play the role of partners in the peaceful resolution of international crises. The management of a multilateral world will require a style of American diplomacy different in kind than that exercised by Washington either during or after the Cold War. The institutions of U.S. foreign policy-making may need to be reformed, to provide for long-term continuity and to insulate the executive branch to a greater degree from the disruptive influence of domestic special interests and ethnic lobbies.

In the realm of political economy, the supply-side approach to global development associated with the moribund neoliberal Washington Consensus needs to be replaced by a new development strategy based on demand-led growth in the global South, fuelled by the invested savings of the aging populations of the global North. Sustainable global growth may require a "new Bretton Woods," a new multilateral financial architecture that provides long-term stability in exchange rates.

Americans in the bipartisan internationalist tradition of Roosevelt and Willkie and of Truman and Eisenhower can only remain true to their tradition by having the courage to innovate. Twice in the past, after World War I and after World War II, new great-power conflicts prevented American plans for a liberal world from being implemented, except in a partial form and on a small scale. The end of the Cold War, by contrast, brought a period of great-power peace that would have made such a project more feasible. Tragically, when this unprecedented opportunity arose after 1989 America's leaders, for lack of a strategy, were unable to take advantage of it. It is not too late for the United States to promote a new internationalism. But as time passes, America's leverage will dwindle—and with it may diminish the chance for the United States to help create a global system favorable to American interests and values alike.

29

The Population Implosion

Phillip J. Longman

World population may well start shrinking over the next half-century. Long before, the ranks of the elderly will be exploding, even in the developing world. How will global aging change our future?

A NEW CHALLENGE FACES THE WORLD. It is not a problem that can be photographed, reduced to a sound bite, or rendered into the conventional formulations of Left and Right. It has everything to do with sex, death, money, and power, yet is rarely the subject of a headline. Rather, its reality dwells beneath the surface of everyday events, in the realm of what historian Arnold Toynbee once called the "deeper, slower movements that, in the end, make history." The trend, if properly managed, presents many positive opportunities for mankind, but also poses deep risks to the world's standard of living and geo-political order.

In 2003, the number of human beings on Earth increased by roughly 75 million. Thus it is hardly surprising that the prospect of over-population continues to cause widespread alarm around the globe. Yet a closer look at demographic trends shows world population growth has already slowed dramatically over the last generation and is headed on a course for absolute decline. Indeed, forecasts by the United Nations and others show world population growth could well turn negative during the lifetime of people now in their forties and fifties, and is very likely to do so before today's children reach retirement age. Long before then, many nations will shrink in absolute size, and the average age of the world's citizens will shoot up dramatically, as the elderly in many parts of the world become far more numerous than children.

These predictions come with considerable certainty. The primary reason is the unprecedented fall in fertility rates over the last generation that is now spreading to every corner of the globe. In both hemispheres, in nations rich and poor, in Christian, Taoist, Confucian, Hindu, and especially Islamic countries, one broad social trend holds constant at the beginning of the twenty-first century: As more and more of the world's population moves to crowded urban areas, and as the economy demands more and more education from men and women alike, people are producing fewer and fewer children.

Today, global fertility rates are half what they were in 1972. No industrialized nation still produces enough children to sustain its population over time, or to prevent rapid population aging. Germany could easily lose the equivalent of the current population of East Germany over the next half-century. Russia's population is already contracting by three-quarters of a million a year. Japan's population meanwhile is expected to fall by as much as one-third—a decline equivalent, the demographer Hideo Ibe once noted, to that experienced in medieval Europe during the scourges of the plague.

Yet the steepest drops in fertility, and the most rapid rates of population aging, are now occurring in the developing world, where many nations are now growing old before they reach economic prosperity. Today, when Americans think of Mexico, for example, they think of televised images of desperate, unemployed youths swimming the Rio Grande or slipping through border fences. Yet because Mexican fertility rates have dropped so dramatically, Mexico will not only be a less youthful country than the United States by mid-century, its population will be older than Japan's is today. The same is true for much of the rest of Latin America, according to UN projections.

Similarly, those televised images of desperate, unemployed youth broadcast from the Middle East create a misleading impression. Fertility rates are falling faster in the Middle East than anywhere else on earth, and as a result, the region's population is aging at an unprecedented rate. It took the United States 50 years to go from a median age of 30 to today's 35. By contrast, during the first fifty years of the twenty-first century, Algeria will increase its median age from 21.7 to 40, according to UN projections.

China's low fertility, brought on in part by its one-family/one-child policy, has put the country on a course in which by 2020 its labor supply will be shrinking and its median age will be far older than that of the United States. By mid-century, China could easily be losing 20 to 30 percent of its population per generation.

India's fertility rate has dropped by roughly a fifth since the first half of the 1990s. Already, residents of the major southern provinces Kerala and Tamil Nadu produce too few children to replace themselves, as will be true for Indians as a whole by the end of the next decade if current trends continue. Meanwhile, the country's sudden drop in fertility means that its population will be aging three times faster than will the U.S. population over the next half century. By 2050, the median age in India is expected to be 37.9, making its population older than that of the United States today.

All told, some 59 countries, comprising roughly 44 percent of the world's total population, are currently not producing enough children to avoid population decline, and the phenomenon continues to spread. By 2050, according to the latest United Nations projections, 75 percent of all countries in even under-developed regions will be reproducing at below replacement levels.

How will the global economy and balance of power evolve, given current trends in fertility and population aging? Let us begin with the positive possibilities.

SLOWER WORLD POPULATION GROWTH offers many benefits, some of which have already been realized. Many economists believe, for example, that falling birthrates made possible the great economic boom that occurred first in Japan, and then in many other Asian nations beginning in the 1960s. As the relative number of children declined, so did the burden of their dependency, thereby freeing up more resources for investment and adult consumption. In East Asia, the working-aged population grew nearly four times faster than its dependent population between 1965 and 1990, freeing up a huge reserve of female labor and other social resources that would otherwise have been committed to raising up children. Today, China's rapid industrialization is aided by a dramatic decline in the share of dependent children in the population.

Over the next decade the Middle East could benefit from a similar "demographic dividend." In every single country of the Middle East, birth rates fell during the 1990s, often dramatically. The resulting "middle aging" of the Middle East will ease the overall dependency ratio over the next 10 to 20 years, thereby freeing up more resources for infrastructure and industrial development. As young adults account for a declining share of the population, the appeal of radicalism may also diminish, as Middle Eastern societies become increasingly dominated by middle-aged people concerned with such practical issues as health care and retirement savings. Because of population momentum from the past, there will still be considerable strains on water and other natural resources in the region, but much less than if the rate of population growth was not declining.

Yet even if declining fertility rates can bring a "demographic dividend," that dividend eventually has to be repaid. At first there are fewer children to feed, clothe, and educate, leaving more for adults to enjoy. But soon enough, if fertility continues to remain below replacement levels, there are fewer productive workers as well, while there are also more and more dependent elderly, who each consume far more resources than children do. Even after considering the cost of education, a typical child in the United States consumes 28 percent less than the typical working age adult, while elders consume 27 percent more, mostly in health-related expenses. Persons 65 and over receive 11 times more in federal spending per person than do children under age 18.

Largely because of this imbalance, population aging puts severe strains on government budgets. In Germany, for example, public spending on pensions, even after accounting for a reduction in future benefits written into current law, is expected to swell from an already staggering 10.3 percent of GDP to 15.4 by 2040—even as the number of workers available to support each retiree shrinks from 2.6 to 1.4. Meanwhile, the cost of government health-care benefits for the elderly is expected to rise from today's 3.8 percent of GDP to 8.4 percent by 2040.

Theoretically, raising the retirement age could help to ease the burden of unfunded old age benefits, but declining fitness among the general population places severe obstacles to more productive aging. The dramatic increases in obesity and sedentary lifestyles so evident in the United

States today, for example, are now spreading to many other nations, and are likely to overwhelm any public health benefits achieved through medical technology. According to the International Association for the Study of Obesity, an "alarming rise in obesity presents a pan-European epidemic." A full 35 percent of Italian children are overweight. In the case of European men, the percentage who are overweight or obese ranges from over 40 percent in France to 70 percent in Germany. Meanwhile, as Western lifestyles spread throughout the developing world so do Western ways of dying. According to the World Health Organization, half of all deaths in places such as Mexico, China, and the Middle East are now caused by non-communicable diseases related to Western lifestyle, such as cancers and heart attacks induced by smoking and obesity.

POPULATION AGING AND DECLINE also present severe challenges to the global economy. One reason is that population growth is a major source of economic growth. More people create more demand for the products capitalists sell, and more supply of the labor capitalists buy. Economists may be able to construct models of how economies *could* grow amidst a shrinking population, but in the real world it has never happened.

New businesses flock to areas where the population is increasing, such as the Sun Belt, and avoid or leave areas where population is falling. Across the Great Plains of the United States, for example, where fewer people now live than in the 1920s, thousands of small towns are caught in a vicious cycle of depopulation, as younger workers and local business flee in search of economic opportunity, leaving behind shuttered storefronts, empty schools, and understaffed nursing homes. Drought and falling commodity prices may in this instance have set the cycle in motion, but once depopulation begins, new investment soon vanishes. Indeed, capitalism has never flourished except when accompanied by population growth, and is now languishing in those parts of the world (Japan, Europe, the Great Plains of the United States), where population has become stagnant.

A nation's gross domestic product (GDP) is literally the sum of its labor force times average output per worker. Thus, a decline in the number of workers implies a decline in an economy's growth potential.

When the size of the workforce is falling, economic growth occurs, if at all, only through compensating increases in productivity. The European Commission, for example, projects that Europe's potential economic growth rate over the next 50 years will fall by 40 percent due to the shrinking size of the European work force. Italy expects its working-age populations to plunge by 41 percent by 2050, meaning that output per worker will have to increase by at least that amount just to keep Italy's rate of economic growth from falling below zero. With a shrinking labor supply, Europe's future economic growth will depend entirely on getting more out of each remaining worker (many of them unskilled, recently arrived immigrants) even as it has to tax workers at higher and higher rates to pay for old age pensions and health care.

Meanwhile, abundant evidence also suggests that these very population trends work to depress the rate of technological and organizational innovation. Cross-country comparisons imply, for example, that after the proportion of elders increases in a society beyond a certain point, the level of entrepreneurship and inventiveness decreases. In 2002, Babson College and the London School of Business released their latest index of entrepreneurial activity by country. It shows that there is a distinct correlation between countries with a high ratio of workers-to-retirees and countries with a high degree of entrepreneurship, and that conversely, in countries in which a large share of the population is retired, the amount of new business formation is low. So, for example, among the most entrepreneurial countries on earth are India and China, where (at least for now) there are roughly five people of working age for every person of retirement age. Meanwhile, Japan and France are among the least entrepreneurial countries on earth and have among the lowest ratio of workers-to-retirees.

There are many possible reasons for this correlation. One, of course, may be that aging workers and investors tend to be less flexible and more risk averse. Both common sense and a vast literature in finance and psychology support the claim that as we approach retirement age, we become more reluctant to take risks with our careers and nest eggs. It is not surprising, therefore, that aging countries such as Japan, Italy, and France are marked by exceptionally low rates of job turnover, and by exceptionally conservative use of capital.

Because prudence requires that older investors take less risks with their investments, we can also expect that as populations age, investor preference will shift toward safe bonds and bank deposits and away from speculative stocks and venture funds. As populations age further, we can expect an ever-higher share of citizens to be cashing out their investments and spending down their savings. Neither of these trends is consistent with a future marked by high levels of high-risk investment in new technology. Instead, many observers believe that population aging will eventually cause steep and destabilizing drops in stock and real estate prices.

Also to be considered are the huge public deficits projected to be run by major industrialized countries over the next several decades. Because of the mounting costs of pensions and health care, government-financed research and development expenditures as well as educational spending will likely be under increasing budgetary pressure. Moreover, massive government borrowing could easily crowd out financial capital that would otherwise be available to the private sector for investment in new technology. Even after assuming a rebound in fertility rate levels, a massive increase in the percentage of women in the labor force, and large cuts in future pension benefits, the European Commission recently calculated that population aging in Europe will lead to an increase in public spending of between 3 and 7 percentage points of GDP in most member states by 2050. To finance the cost of aging, Germany would have to increase its public indebtedness by as much as 384 percent while the French national debt would rise to more than three times the country's entire annual economic output. Population aging gives Japan an even gloomier long-term financial outlook.

Theoretically, a highly efficient, global financial market could lend financial resources from rich, old countries that are short on labor, to young, poor countries that are short on capital, and make the whole world better off. But for this to happen, old countries would have to contain their deficits, while also investing their savings in places that are themselves either on the threshold of hyper-aging (China, India, Mexico) or highly destabilized by religious fanaticism, disease, and war (most of the Middle East, Sub-Saharan Africa, Indonesia), or both.

Moreover, who exactly, under this scenario would buy the products produced by these investments? Japan, Korea, and the other recently industrialized countries relied on massive exports to the United States and Europe to develop. But if the population of Europe and Japan is falling away, while the only population growth in the United States comes from old people, where will the demand come from to support development in places like the Middle East and sub-Saharan Africa?

Population aging is also likely to depress economic activity by creating huge legacy costs for employers. This is particularly true in the United States, where health and pension benefits are largely provided by the private sector. General Motors (GM) now has 2.5 retirees on its pension rolls for every active worker, and an unfunded pension debt of $19.2 billion. Honoring its legacy costs to retirees now adds $1,800 to the cost of every vehicle GM makes, according to a 2003 estimate by Morgan Stanley. Just between 2001 and 2002, the U.S. government's projected short-term liability for bailing out failing private pension plans increased from $11 billion to $35 billion, with huge defaults expected from the steel industry.

An aging workforce may also be less able or inclined to take advantage of new technology. This seems to be part of what is behind Japan's declining rates of productivity growth in the 1990s. Before that decade, the aging of Japan's highly educated work force was a weak, but positive force in increasing the nation's productivity, according to studies. Older workers "learned by doing," developed specialized knowledge and craft skills, as well as the famous company spirit that made Japan an unrivaled manufacturing power. But by the 1990s, the continued aging of Japan's workforce contributed to Japan's declining competitiveness.

No longer did the Japanese firms with the oldest workforces show the strongest rates of productivity growth; instead they showed the weakest. Japan was able to use information technology to compensate for its vanishing supply of low-skilled, younger workers, but did not succeed in using information technology to boost the productivity of its highly skilled older workers. Yoshiaki Nakamura of the University of Tokyo and other economists have found that during the 1990s, Japanese firms reached the limits of what productivity increases could be achieved by deepening the skills and experience of Japan's manufacturing workers, who were essentially hardworking, but aging craftsmen. Aging went from having a mildly positive to a negative effect on productivity growth that technology could not overcome.

Population aging works against innovation in another way as well. As growth in population dwindles, so does the need to increase the supply of just about everything, save health care. That means there is less incentive to find ways of making a gallon of gas go farther, or of increasing the capacity of existing infrastructure. Population growth is the mother of necessity. Without it, why bother to innovate when you could be contentedly enjoying an ample supply of affordable houses, open roads, and comparatively abundant natural resources? An aging society may have an urgent need to gain more output from each remaining worker, but without growing markets, individual firms have little incentive to learn how to do more with less—and with a dwindling supply of human capital, they have fewer ideas to draw on.

IMMIGRATION IS AT BEST only a partial solution. To be sure, the United States and other developed nations derive many benefits from their imported human capital. Yet immigration does less than one might think to ease the challenges of population aging. One reason is that most immigrants arrive not as babies, but with a third or so of their lives already behind them, and then go on to become elderly themselves. In the short term, immigrants can help to increase the ratio of workers to retirees, but in the long term they add much less youth to the population than would newborn children.

Indeed, according to a study by the United Nations Population Division, in order to maintain the current ratio of workers to retirees in the United States over time, it would be necessary to absorb an average of 10.8 million immigrants annually through 2050. At that point, the U.S. population would be 1.1 billion, 73 percent of whom would be immigrants who had arrived in this country since 1995 or their descendents. Just housing such a flow would require the equivalent of building another New York City every 10 months.

Meanwhile, it is unclear how long the United States and other developed nations can sustain even current rates of immigration. One reason, of course, is the heightened security concerns about terrorism. Another is the prospect of a cultural backlash against immigrants, the chances of which increase as native birthrates decline. In the 1920s, when widespread apprehension about declining native fertility found voice in books like Lothrop Stoddard's, *The Rising Tide of Color Against White World-Supremacy*, the American political system responded by shutting off immigration. Germany, Sweden, and France did the same in the 1970s as the reality of population decline among the native born started to set in.

Another constraint on immigration to the United States involves supply. Birth rates, having already fallen well below replacement levels in Europe and Asia, are now plummeting throughout Latin America as well, creating the prospect that America's last major source of imported manpower will offer a declining pool of applicants. The fall in Mexican fertility rates has been so dramatic that the country is now aging at a far more rapid pace than the United States, and is destined to do so for at least the next two generations. According to UN projections, the median age of Americans will increase by four and a half years during the first half of the twenty-first century, reaching 39.7 years by 2050. By contrast, during the same period Mexico's median age will increase 20 years, leaving half the population over age 42. Put another way, during the course of a year, the U.S. population as a whole ages by little more than one month, while the Mexican population ages by nearly five months. Notes Enrique Quintana, co-author of a book on Mexico's aging population, "Picture a scenario in which almost 23 million people are over the age of 60, most of them have few descendents and many of them scant savings, no job, no retirement coverage scheme. The results can hardly be described as anything but catastrophic."

Long before Mexico reaches this point, the supply of Mexicans available to work in the United States could easily evaporate, as the example of Puerto Rico shows. When most Americans think of Puerto Rico, they think of a sunny, over-crowded island that sends millions of immigrants to the West Side of New York or to Florida. Yet with a fertility rate well below replacement level and a median age of 31.8 years, Puerto Rico no longer provides a net flow of immigrants to the mainland, despite an open border and a lower standard of living.

Sub-Saharan Africa still produces many potential immigrants to the United States, as does the Middle East and parts of South Asia. But to attract immigrants from these regions, the U.S. must compete with Europe, which is closer geographically and has a more acute need for imported labor. Europe also offers higher wages for unskilled work, more generous social benefits, as well as large, already established populations of immigrants from these areas.

Moreover, it is by no means clear how many potential immigrants these regions will produce in the future. Birthrates are falling in sub-Saharan Africa as well, even as war and disease leave mortality rates extraordinarily high. UN projections for the continent as a whole show fertility declining to 2.4 children per woman by mid-century, which may well be below replacement levels if mortality does not dramatically improve. Although the course of the HIV/AIDS epidemic through Sub-Saharan Africa remains uncertain, the Central Intelligence Agency projects that AIDS and related diseases could kill as many as a quarter of the region's inhabitants by 2010.

GLOBAL AGING IS A SLOW moving phenomenon. The long-term deficits and unfunded liabilities it creates are more akin to termites in the basement than to a wolf at the door. Yet it is also true that any solutions to the challenges presented by global aging will take decades to achieve, and must therefore be initiated in short order.

For example, the single greatest requirement of an aging society is sustained improvement in productivity. Yet the productive potential of workers 30 or 40 years from now depends critically on the health and education of today's children. We cannot expect, for example, that today's 10-year-olds will to grow up to be far more productive workers than today's 50-year-olds ever were, or that they will be able to work for a far greater share of their lives, unless we quickly address problems like the rising incidence of childhood obesity and childhood poverty.

Sustaining future productivity growth also requires many other short-term trade offs. In general, for example, protecting jobs in declining industries entails a long-term loss of productive potential. So does running up large public deficits to underwrite current consumption. Similarly, the longer the United States waits to reform its Social Security and Medicare systems, the more the deficits in those systems will crowd out more productive uses of the nation's resources.

Fortunately, for the United States at least, the cost of aging may be offset in part by an ability to reduce its enormous military budget without any compromise of national security. China, for example, may emerge as a formidable economic competitor, but its ability to expand its territory will diminish as its supply of youth dwindles and the cost of its elders soars. By 2030 more than 23 percent of China's population will be 60 or over—a higher share than seen in Japan today. Just as Japan now lacks the human resources to invade any of its neighbors, or even to maintain a large standing army, China in the next generation will likely turn away from militarism. Instead, it will become even more preoccupied with pampering its few children and with a quest for meaning and community as more and more individuals find themselves aging without the support and comfort of large kinship networks.

Similarly, the "youth bulges" in the Middle East will likely prove to be transient phenomena that do not require an ongoing military response. Just as population aging in the West during the 1980s was accompanied by the disappearance of youthful indigenous terrorist groups like the Red Brigades or the Weather Underground, falling birth rates in the Middle East could well produce societies far less prone to radicalism and political violence. Scanning the future, one can imagine population aging leading to political and economic turmoil of the kind recently seen in Argentina, as citizens revolt against cuts in benefits and other austerity programs. But revolts led by outraged pensioners and laid-off middle-aged workers over changes in domestic policy, while perhaps capable of producing failed states, are not nihilistic by nature.

Yet while global aging will likely diminish straightforward military threats to the United States, the phenomenon creates new and more baffling challenges. Clearly, there is no law of nature that ensures human beings will reproduce themselves. It is in precisely those areas of the world where life is most safe and prosperous that children are scarcest. When the economic and social incentives to procreate and raise families are weak or negative, as they increasingly are in most nations, and when people know how to achieve sexual gratification without producing children, avoiding extreme population aging and decline may require enormously increased incentives to parents, or else a radical shift in values away from individualism. If free and liberal societies do not discover equalitarian means to raise their fertility rates to replacement levels, then the future belongs to societies that use more coercive measures, such as reduced freedom for women, or eugenics programs. Global aging puts much more at stake than simply the sustainability of today's health and pension plans.

In his 1968 bestseller, *The Population Bomb*, Paul R. Ehrlich warned: "The battle to feed all of humanity is over. In the 1970s the world will undergo famines—hundreds of millions of people are going to starve to death in spite of any crash programs embarked upon now." Fortunately, Ehrlich's prediction proved wrong. But having averted the specter of over-population, the world now faces the unexpected challenge of population aging and decline. We are in many ways blessed to have this problem instead of its opposite, but a problem it still is.

30

Democracy in the Islamic World

Noah Feldman

If we want democracy in the Middle East, we will have to accept the fact that it will come with an Islamic face.

IN A REMARKABLE SPEECH at the National Endowment for Democracy in November 2003, President Bush acknowledged 60 years of American error and announced a policy of encouraging democracy, not dictatorship, in the Muslim world. Whether this long overdue message is followed by an actual policy change or simply results from the short-term need to explain the Iraq war in the absence of weapons of mass destruction (WMD) remains to be seen. But in any event, Bush neglected to mention a crucial fact that looms over every discussion of democratization in the Muslim world: if freed to make their own democratic choices, many Muslim peoples will choose Islam, not secularism.

The fact that Muslims in many countries have a strong preference for Islamic parties is evidenced by the results of elections, free and quasi-free, in which Islamic-oriented parties have consistently scored significant victories. The paradigm case took place in Algeria in 1989 and 1990. There, the first free elections in decades yielded substantial majorities for Islamic parties before the military government thought better of its democratic experiment, rescinded the election results, and by banning the Islamic parties thrust Algeria into a decade-long civil war. More recently, the Turkish Justice and Development Party came to power with a decisive plurality in the autumn 2002 elections, and the Moroccan moderate Islamic party of the same name won a disproportionately large share of the seats in an election—held around the same time—in which they were limited to running in only two-thirds of the contested districts. In Pakistan, the more radical Mutahhida Majlis-i Amal (MMA) achieved the best results ever by an Islamist party in the country's history, emerging as the third-largest party in a parliament whose power is in any case limited by the extraordinary authority of President Pervez Musharraf. Islamic parties also performed well in recent elections in Jordan and in the cautiously liberalizing Gulf emirates.

The reasons for the success of Islamic politics are not difficult to discern: disillusionment with existing regimes, especially characteristic of the Arab states, pervades the Muslim world more broadly. With secular nationalism and socialism discredited, political Islam has grown in appeal wherever it has not been tried. Islamists enjoy organizational advantages in countries where normal democratic politics are outlawed or highly restricted. Islamic parties speak the language of justice, the paramount political value to most Muslims—that is why so many Islamic parties have the word in their names—and are perceived as relatively free of corruption, especially where they have not yet had the opportunity to govern. Except in Iran, where corruption and the abject failure of clerical rule have discredited religion, Islamic politicians can convincingly present themselves as pure and untainted by scandal.

But perhaps most important, Islam itself remains a rich and vital force, informing the lives of 1.2 billion persons in the realm of faith, a realm not automatically segregated from politics either for Muslims or others. It should surprise no one that such a resilient source of values affects political life in countries where it is the predominant or overwhelming faith. In places like Turkey, Indonesia, and Malaysia, secular forces in the society counterbalance rising Islamic politics; but in Arab dictatorships, where secularist politics are associated with autocracy, increased political freedom will most likely lead, at least in the short run, to new victories for political Islam.

The intriguing fact about political Islam in the last decade is that it has moved away from the rhetoric of revolutionary violence that characterized its approach during the 1980s, and has increasingly embraced the language, and to a degree the ideology, of constitutional democracy. Seeking the votes of the public in competitive elections, Islamic politicians are saying that democracy and Islam are compatible, indeed supplementary. As in Iraq, where Ayatollah Ali Sistani has emerged as the leading spokesman for an Iraq that would be both democratic and expressive of Islamic values, theorists elsewhere in the Muslim world—whose theories underwrite moderate Islamic politics—today argue for what they call Islamic democracy. If political freedom in the Muslim world is likely to empower Islamic parties and politicians, then the viability of the project to democratize Muslim countries may well turn on the question of whether Islam and democracy can be reconciled or are simply a contradiction in terms.

In its ambitions, attractions, and dangers, the Afghan draft constitution of November 2003, which enshrines Islamic values even as it guarantees basic liberties, can be understood as a metaphor for the prospects of Islamic democracy more generally. If the United States is to promote democracy in Muslim lands, we need to ask the crucial question implicit in the Afghan draft: Can Islam and democracy be fused without compromising on human rights and equality? If not, then democratization in places like Iraq and Afghanistan will be a pyrrhic victory for freedom. But if a synthesis of Islam and democracy can satisfy believing Muslims, while protecting liberty and the rights of women and non-Muslims, then Islamic democracy may be the best hope for improvement in countries where Islamic politics prevails. Indeed, perhaps only Islamic democracy can give democratic values and institutions staying power in political cultures to which they are essentially newcomers.

Make no mistake: drafted by Afghans who consider Islam the glue that holds together their country's ethnic diversity, the Afghan constitution is pervasively Islamic. Its first three articles declare Afghanistan an Islamic Republic, make Islam the official religion, and provide that "no law can be contrary to the sacred religion of Islam and the values of this constitution." The Supreme Court, which has the power to interpret the constitution, is to be composed of judges trained either in law or in Islamic jurisprudence. The flag features a prayer niche and pulpit, and is emblazoned, for good measure, with not one but two Islamic credos: "There is no God but Allah and Mohammed is his Prophet," and "Allah Akbar"—"God is Great." The government is charged with developing a unified curriculum "based on the provisions of the sacred religion of Islam, national culture, and in accordance with academic principles," and the provision requiring the state to ensure the physical and psychological well-being of the family calls, in the same breath, for "elimination of traditions contrary to the principles of the sacred religion of Islam."

Yet the draft constitution is also thoroughly democratic, promising government "based on the people's will and democracy," as the preamble says, and guaranteeing its citizens fundamental rights. One essential provision guarantees that the state shall abide by the UN Charter, international treaties, international conventions that Afghanistan has signed, and the Universal Declaration of Human Rights. Because Afghanistan has, as of March 2003, acceded to the Convention on the Elimination of All Forms of Discrimination against Women (a treaty which the U.S. Senate, by contrast, has never ratified), the draft constitution guarantees women far-ranging rights against discrimination. The drafters' strategy here is certainly to avoid a pitched ratification battle with extremists, incorporating progressive rights by reference instead of by direct decree. In Afghanistan, and anywhere else where radical Islamists continue to oppose democratic constitutionalism, this prudent approach may be unavoidable; but of course it would also be possible and probably preferable to make basic rights, including women's rights, more explicit.

The draft also requires the president to appoint women to half of the seats in the upper legislative house that are under his control, ensuring women at least 16.5 percent of the total membership. Today, 83 years after women got the vote in the United States, a record 14 of 100 U.S. Senators are women, and it would be hard to imagine constitutional quotas for women legislators. Yet Morocco and Pakistan have adopted similar set-asides for women in their parliaments, following a model pioneered in Western Europe. And, so far it has not attracted major opposition in those countries.

Observers of the Afghan constitutional process worried that religious liberty might not be adequately protected, and the United States reportedly brought pressure on the Afghan drafters to ensure that this would not be the case. Perhaps as a result, the same provision that makes Islam the official religion simultaneously recognizes the right of non-Muslims "to perform their religious ceremonies within the limits of the provisions of law." This carefully chosen language might arguably leave room to restrict proselytization, as, for example, does the law in India and Israel; but the constitution also guarantees expression as an inviolable right, and the Universal Declaration of Human Rights, embraced by the draft, guarantees the right to change one's religion as well as the freedom of conscience.

There can be little doubt that, if the draft is ratified by the Loya Jirga and actually implemented despite Afghanistan's shaky political situation, tensions in the constitutional structure would have to be resolved later by the Supreme Court. According to the draft, for instance, political parties must not be organized around a program contrary to Islam or the constitution. That would exclude an anti-democratic Taliban party; but would it also exclude a party of secularists who wanted to remove Islam from the constitution? What if the legislature enacts laws that make it a crime to blaspheme Islam or the Prophet? Such laws would appear to violate the freedom of speech—but would the Supreme Court be prepared to say so? What about laws requiring women to dress modestly: unconstitutional as a violation of women's rights, or constitutional as in accord with the teachings of Islam? The Afghan draft constitution gives guidance on all these questions, but a Supreme Court dominated by illiberal religious scholars might interpret the text one way, while the cases might come out differently if a majority of the Court were trained in a secular legal tradition. The constitutional strategy of deferring such contentious problems until institutions are in place to resolve them has its risks, of course. But in practical terms, it may be far preferable to trying to resolve tensions at the ratification stage, when the nascent republic is at its most fragile.

Some will say that we should avoid democracy promotion in the Middle East lest we open the door to elections that might be, in the memorable words of former Assistant Secretary of State Edward Djerejian, "one man, one vote, one time." These same skeptics will point to the Afghan constitution and emphasize its potential to marginalize democracy and render Afghanistan purely Islamic. But this conservative approach, which calls for preserving the undemocratic status quo at the expense of Muslim freedom, neglects to acknowledge that the alternative to trying Islamic democracy may be much worse. In

Afghanistan, the alternative to the vision of the new constitution is not idealized secular democracy: it is a return to the Taliban. In other Muslim countries, the alternative to trying democracy is autocracy, whether secular dictatorship or religious monarchy.

In Iraq, for example, now that Saddam is gone, the only alternative to democracy is anarchy and civil war. Some ex-Baathists among the Sunni Arabs might prefer these options, in the mistaken hope that they could reestablish something like the old autocratic régime. That certainly seems to be what is motivating the present insurgency. But Iraq's Kurds and Shi'a Arabs, who together make up nearly 80 percent of the population, want to produce a functioning constitutional order; and if the Kurds' *idee fixe* is federalism and greater autonomy, the Shi'is seem as of the present writing committed to giving Islam a key role in the federal constitution. The Shi'i majority can be expected to demand provisions not entirely unlike those in the Afghan draft as the price of constitutional democracy. Those who call for the United States to impose secularization in places like Afghanistan and Iraq are therefore simply unrealistic. For a constitution to work in practice, it must garner the support of the citizens whose will it represents. Nothing could make a constitution illegitimate more quickly than imposing secularist red lines in a well-meaning show of neo-imperialism.

In Afghanistan and Iraq, however, all these questions may become academic if the United States and the West do not help create the material and political conditions for the success of Islamic democracy. After driving out the Taliban, the U.S.-led coalition has done little to bring Afghanistan under the control of a centralized government. Nor has the UN presence in Kabul made much difference to the de facto control of the country by the regional warlords who made up the former Northern Alliance. Unless the West takes further steps to help give an elected Afghan government actual sovereignty, the Afghan constitution will matter more as a symbol than as an actual charter of governance. Similarly, if the United States and its coalitional partners don't do more to establish security and a working economy in Iraq, then real democracy will have little chance there.

Of course Iraq and Afghanistan are distinctive in that the United States removed existing régimes and continues to play the role of military occupier, directly in Iraq, and mediated through the United Nations in Afghanistan. The leverage of exercising de facto sovereignty cannot, and probably should not, be replicated elsewhere. Inevitably, then, American influence over democratization and its constitutional expression in other Muslim states will be significantly less direct. Circumstances differ greatly among Muslim countries, both with respect to internal political economy and the government's relations with the United States. A free vote in today's Saudi Arabia would replace the royal family—which, whatever its considerable demerits, has been a reliable American ally—with Islamists whose radicalism might preclude real democracy, and who might use oil profits to sponsor terrorism officially, not just accidentally; Saudi Arabia therefore needs liberalization before elections.

By contrast, a country like Egypt needs to be encouraged to make elections more meaningful and to allow a wider array of political actors to participate. Economic assistance provides leverage against Egypt, while only America's security alliance can influence the Saudis. Syria is susceptible to American pressure to the extent it shares a long border with Iraq, where the presence of American troops constitutes an implicit threat to it. Conditions in the majority Muslim republics of Central Asia are different still, inflected both by local al-Qaeda offshoots and by America's different security posture in Afghanistan.

One-size-fits-all approaches to democracy in the Muslim world are bound to fail. Statecraft calls for nuance, not just generalities, and it would be foolish to assume that instant democratization would serve U.S. interests—or those of Muslims themselves—in the same way everywhere. But our overarching, unifying goal must be to support the belief of the majority of the world's Muslims that Islam and democracy are perfectly compatible. To lose the debate over the compatibility of Islam and democracy would be to lose the opportunity to win over Muslim states to the side of democratic liberty, equality, and justice. If we insist that only secular government can be truly democratic, we are bound inevitably to alienate many of those we are most eager to convince. This will be especially true in Iraq, where the constitutional process must publicly convince both Iraqis and the rest of the world that the Coalition intends to let Iraqis govern themselves. Worse yet, denying the possibility of Islamic democracy may bolster the case of Islamist radicals who, for their own reasons, claim that Islam cannot accommodate democracy.

The draft Afghan constitution suggests one possible picture of how Islam and democracy can coexist in the same political vision, not without risk or tension, but with the possibility of success. There are no guarantees in constitution writing, in nation-building, or indeed in history itself, and it is too soon to predict that the idea of Islamic democracy will in fact succeed in taking hold in practice, either in Afghanistan or elsewhere in the Muslim world. In light of the alternatives, however, we should stick to the course on which the United States, at least rhetorically, has already embarked. We should press hard for democracy in the Muslim world with our eyes open: not because we naively expect a victory for secularism, but because, in the end, freedom only makes sense as a value extended equally to all, to make of it what they will.

31

Nation-Building 101

Francis Fukuyama

The chief threats to us and to world order come from weak, collapsed, or failed states. Learning how to fix such states—and building necessary political support at home—will be a defining issue for America in the century ahead.

"I don't think our troops ought to be used for what's called nation-building. I think our troops ought to be used to fight and win war."
—George W. Bush, October 11, 2000

"We meet here during a crucial period in the history of our nation, and of the civilized world. Part of that history was written by others; *the rest will be written by us* . . . Rebuilding Iraq will require a sustained commitment from many nations, including our own: we will remain in Iraq as long as necessary, and not a day more." (italics added)
—George W. Bush, February 26, 2003

THE TRANSFORMATION OF GEORGE W. BUSH from a presidential candidate opposed to nation-building into a President committed to writing the history of an entire troubled part of the world is one of the most dramatic illustrations we have of how the September 11 terrorist attacks changed American politics. Under Bush's presidency the United States has taken responsibility for the stability and political development of two Muslim countries—Afghanistan and Iraq. A lot now rides on our ability not just to win wars but to help create self-sustaining democratic political institutions and robust market-oriented economies, and not only in these two countries but throughout the Middle East.

The fact is that the chief threats to us and to world order come today from weak, collapsed, or failed states. Weak or absent government institutions in developing countries form the thread linking terrorism, refugees, AIDS, and global poverty. Before 9/11 the United States felt it could safely ignore chaos in a far-off place like Afghanistan; but the intersection of religious terrorism and weapons of mass destruction has meant that formerly peripheral areas are now of central concern.

Conservatives never approved of the so-called "humanitarian interventions" undertaken during the 1990s, including those in Somalia, Haiti, Bosnia, Kosovo, and East Timor. Liberals, for their part, remain unconvinced by the Bush Administration's rationale for its invasion of Iraq. But whether for reasons of human rights or of security, the United States has done a lot of intervening over the past fifteen years, and has taken on roughly one new nation-building commitment every other year since the end of the Cold War. We have been in denial about it, but we are in this business for the long haul. We'd better get used to it, and learn how to do it—because there will almost certainly be a next time.

Critics of nation-building point out that outsiders can never build nations, if that means creating or repairing all the cultural, social, and historical ties that bind people together as a nation. What we are really talking about is statebuilding—that is, creating or strengthening such government institutions as armies, police forces, judiciaries, central banks, tax-collection agencies, health and education systems, and the like.

This process has two very separate phases, both of them critical. The first involves stabilizing the country, offering humanitarian assistance and disaster relief, rebuilding the infrastructure, and jump-starting the economy. The second phase begins after stability has been achieved, and consists of creating self-sustaining political and economic institutions that will ultimately permit competent democratic governance and economic growth.

The first of these phases is well understood, and although difficult, it lies within the capability of both the United States and the broader international community. (The United States Agency for International Development has a very spotty record in promoting longterm economic growth but is actually pretty good at delivering humanitarian assistance.) The second phase, the transition to self-sustaining devel-opment, is far more challenging; and it is even more important in the long run. The key word is "self-sustaining": unless outside powers are able to leave behind stable, legitimate, relatively uncorrupt indigenous state institutions, they have no hope of a graceful exit.

What long-term lessons can we draw from the American experi-ence so far in the reconstruction of Iraq? The Bush Administration has been heavily criticized for its failure to plan adequately for the postwar period; but we must remember that nation-building is inherently diffi-cult. If an unexpected problem arises, that does not necessarily mean there was a planning failure, because it is not possible to anticipate every contingency.

Administration officials argue that they did considerable planning for which they don't get credit, because it had to do with contingencies that never arose. Chemical and biological weapons, and also oil-field sabotage and fires, were much discussed before the war. But the Iraqis evidently had no such weapons; and, largely because the country was occupied so fast (the result of a war plan that emphasized lightness and speed over numbers and redundancy), the oil fields were not sabotaged. Before the war some 60 percent of the Iraqi population lived on food donated by the UN World Food Programme, and the Administration worked quietly with that agency to ensure that food would flow to the whole Iraqi population during the war. Extensive plans were made to deal with a major humanitarian or refugee crisis like the one that fol-lowed the Gulf War of 1991—but none emerged.

For what, then, can the Administration justly be held accountable? By far the most important oversight was its failure to develop contin-gency plans against the possibility that the Iraqi state would almost completely collapse. The Administration hoped to decapitate the coun-try's Baathist leadership and allow new leaders to take over quickly. Instead there was a severe breakdown of order, as the army melted away, the police stopped patrolling the streets, and government min-istries stopped functioning. The consequences of this disorder were significant: the government's physical infrastructure disappeared, as ministries were stripped of doors, toilets, and wiring and then torched; the search for weapons of mass destruction was compromised by the looting of weapons sites; and many Iraqis' first impression of their "liberation" was one of crime and chaos.

There were precedents for what happened in Iraq—most obviously the aftermath of the U.S. intervention in Panama in 1989, when days of looting and disorder resulted in billions of dollars' worth of damage. Could the Bush Administration, with better foresight, have hedged against the possibility of large-scale chaos in Iraq?

Perhaps. One consequence of the decision to invade the country with a very small force—about 150,000 strong—was that after major combat operations there were simply not enough soldiers to spread around the country. Flooding the zone with forces would have helped. But combat troops are notoriously unprepared to deal with civil disturbances and police functions, and often make things worse through the heavy-handed use of force. The United States does not maintain a national police force for use in such situations; the only option would have been to bring in follow-on peacekeeping or constabulary forces such as Italian *carabinieri*, Canadian peacekeepers, or the Spanish Guardia Civil.

But before we assume that a multilateral approach would have prevented looting in Iraq, we should recall that earlier multilateral missions, to deploy police forces in Haiti, Somalia, Bosnia, and Kosovo, were poorly organized and understaffed, and in most cases arrived too late to perform their functions when they were most needed. It is not likely that a slow-moving international police force would have made much difference. The Italians did eventually send the *carabinieri* to Iraq, but they arrived long after the looting had subsided.

America's involvement in nation-building over the past fifteen years has yielded some significant knowledge about organizing for the task, as a recent study by the RAND Corporation demonstrates. But the Bush Administration failed to draw on this institutional knowledge. Its most serious planning mistakes were to set up its postwar-reconstruction organization at the last minute, to endow it with insufficient authority, and to put it under the overall control of the Pentagon, which did not have the capacity to do the job properly. The result was an organization that, instead of hitting the ground running after the end of major combat, wasted precious weeks and months building its own capabilities.

Sometime in August of 2002 President Bush signed the executive order that put in train final military planning for the war, and U.S. forces began deploying to the Persian Gulf toward the end of the year. But not until January 20 of last year was Jay Garner, a retired lieutenant general, appointed to coordinate the new Office of Reconstruction and Humanitarian Assistance. He had less than two months to pull together the planning efforts of various U.S. agencies before the ORHA was relocated to Kuwait, on March 17, at the start of the war. The ORHA went from a staff of six and a phoneless office in the Pentagon in late January to an organization with a staff of 700 just three months later—an impressive feat of institutional creation by any standard. Nevertheless, since the State Department, USAID, the CIA, and the Army War College had prepared extensive plans for the postwar period, the question remains why the Administration did not seek to integrate their recommendations into a coordinated process as soon as the war planning began.

There was, moreover, a serious problem of authority. Garner, who had led humanitarian relief efforts in Kurdistan after the Gulf War, was a former three-star general, and thus not in a position to give orders to the four-star CENTCOM Commander Tommy Franks. Garner was succeeded in mid-May by Ambassador L. Paul Bremer, a very senior foreign service officer and counterterrorism expert who now heads the Coalition Provisional Authority, the successor to the ORHA. Bremer was far more visible and well known back in Washington—an insider who could command much more authority than Garner could.

The unfortunate public perception is that Garner was replaced for having presided over a chaotic and disorganized reconstruction effort. In fact he did an amazing job under the circumstances. It had been the Bush Administration's plan all along to replace Garner with a more distinguished and visible administrator; so why wasn't Bremer, or someone of his stature, in place before the beginning of the war?

The Administration has argued that it could not have begun coordinated postwar planning in the fall of 2002, because it was still seeking the approval of the international community for the war. This argument is disingenuous: the President clearly signaled that he would proceed with or without the approval of the international community, and did not wait for the United Nations before deploying military forces to the Gulf—a deployment that, like Von Moltke's railroad schedules in July of 1914, could not easily be reversed. In reality, the late planning and weak command were rooted in a series of interagency battles that took place in the fall of 2002.

The first phase of nation-building—postconflict reconstruction—is extremely difficult to implement, because the necessary capabilities are widely spread out among a host of government and civilian agencies. Earlier nation-building exercises suffered from poor coordination, both within the U.S. government and within the broader international community. In Bosnia, for example, the Dayton Accords gave military authority to NATO, whereas civil authority was divided among the Office of the High Representative, the Organization for Security and Cooperation in Europe, the United Nations High Commissioner for Refugees, the World Bank, the International Monetary Fund, and the International Criminal Tribunal for the former Yugoslavia. Some functions, including the creation of an international police force, fell through the cracks. Within the U.S. government the military clashed with civilian agencies over its role in noncombat missions such as demobilization and policing.

The U.S. officials involved learned some important lessons during the 1990s, which the Clinton Administration codified in Presidential Decision Directive 56, in May of 1997. PDD 56 established an inter-agency framework for coordinating the U.S. response to post-conflict emergencies, and was used during the reconstruction of Kosovo following the 1999 NATO intervention there. Owing in part to the better U.S. coordination, the nation-building effort in Kosovo was much better organized on an international level than the one in Bosnia, with greater unity of command and considerably quieter interagency squabbles.

At the beginning of the Bush Administration, efforts were made to replace PDD 56 with a new directive that would have put the White House's National Security Council staff in charge of coordinating any nation-building activities. By all accounts this was a sensible idea, but the President never signed the draft, apparently because of persistent objections from the Defense Department. Then came September 11, the Afghan war, and the ensuing reconstruction effort. The Bush

Administration still had no agreed-upon policy framework for nation-building, and many officials regarded the reconstruction effort in Afghanistan as a fiasco.

This was the background against which the Pentagon put forth, shortly after passage of UN Security Council Resolution 1441, in November of 2002, its "big idea" that all postwar planning should be centralized under its own control. The delay in the appointment of a reconstruction coordinator was due to the big fight that ensued from the big idea.

Secretary of Defense Donald Rumsfeld had some serious reasons for wanting to retain control over the reconstruction effort. Previous nation-building exercises had always had two chains of command, one dealing with military security and the other—through the local ambassador and the State Department—with civil affairs. In Rumsfeld's view, this split authority tied down U.S. forces, because the civilian chain of command could never agree on an exit strategy and was constantly calling on the military to do things for which it was not prepared, such as police work. This problem, according to Rumsfeld, was particularly acute in Bosnia, where U.S. forces were still deployed seven years after the signing of the Dayton Accords, and it had emerged in Afghanistan after the United States ousted the Taliban.

Meanwhile, the Pentagon had been fighting for months with the State Department and the intelligence community over the role of Ahmed Chalabi and the Iraqi National Congress. At the extremes were those in the Pentagon who believed that the democratization of Iraq could be delegated entirely to Chalabi, and those in the State Department and the intelligence community who thought him unfit for any role in postwar Iraq.

By late December of 2002 Rumsfeld, the consummate bureaucratic infighter, had prevailed. President Bush agreed to give control to the Pentagon because the idea of a unified command appealed to him. But this strategy had distinct disadvantages: the Pentagon, which lacked the institutional knowledge or capacity to do many of the things that need to be done in reconstruction, did not turn to the right places. The Defense Department does not have any particular expertise in writing constitutions or in producing attractive TV programs to compete with al-Jazeera and al-Arabiya for the hearts and minds of Arab viewers. It does not have good relations with the international NGOs that provide humanitarian services; nor does it have a way of coordinating activities with the UN and other multilateral institutions.

Once it became clear that the reconstruction of Iraq was going to be far costlier and longer than expected, there were immediate calls in Congress for international help. But although such help would be welcomed by American taxpayers, the international community is no better coordinated for nation-building than the U.S. government.

To begin with, no central authority exists within the international community to lead nation-building efforts. Much as other countries might like to give this responsibility to the United Nations, that is not a practical solution. The UN does not have the expertise or the resources, human and otherwise, to run nation-building programs authoritatively. For these it depends on the heavyweight funders—namely, the United States, the European Union, and, to a lesser extent, Japan.

Moreover, no one has solved the more serious problem of how to implement the second phase of nation-building—the transition to self-sustaining indigenous institutions. As the human-rights expert Michael Ignatieff memorably put it, whereas the mantra of the international community is "capacity building," the reality is often "capacity sucking-out," as well-endowed international agencies, contractors, and NGOs arrive with their cell phones, laptops, and First World salaries. In a recent article in the *Journal of Democracy*, Gerald Knaus and Felix Martin argue that Bosnia seven years after the Dayton Accords has become a "European Raj," in which the High Representative acts as a viceroy presiding over a colonial dependency that is without either democracy or selfgovernment. Neither there nor in Kosovo is an exit strategy evident, because the departure of the international community would leave both places with the intractable political problems that led to intervention in the first place.

None of this means that the United States should exclude the international community from future nation-building exercises. Multilateralism means the difference between the $70 billion contributed by foreign powers to pay for the Gulf War and the $13 billion they have pledged for reconstruction this time around. The international community can provide constabulary forces, water engineers, land-mine-removal experts, and other resources that the United States often cannot field quickly. What is needed is a standing U.S. government office to cooperate with this community, with an eye to the long lead times that are inevitable.

The Bush Administration's experience in Iraq does not teach new lessons about nation-building but, rather, reinforces some old ones that have been forgotten. The first is that nation-building is a difficult, long-term enterprise with high costs in manpower, lives, and resources. The places where it has been most successful—Germany, Japan, and the Philippines—are ones where U.S. forces have remained for generations. We should not get involved to begin with if we are not willing to pay those high costs.

That being said, we are now fully committed in Afghanistan and Iraq, and are likely to take on other nation-building commitments in the future, simply because the failed-state problem is one that we cannot safely ignore. It therefore behooves us to draw some lessons from our recent experience.

The problems that the Administration faced in Iraq were not so much the results of specific misjudgments as the predictable by-products of the Administration's poorly thought-out institutional structure. Fixing that structure would involve at least four things.

First, the United States needs to create a central authority, backed by a permanent staff, to manage ongoing and future nation-building activities. One possibility, recommended by the Commission on Post-conflict Reconstruction of the Center for Strategic and International Studies, is to appoint a director of reconstruction. The director could be located in any of a number of places in the government, though the White House would be the most logical, given the delicate interagency relationships involved. (Recognizing that it had been a mistake to grant the Pentagon primacy over the reconstruction of Iraq, the White House staff moved to take back that authority in October of 2003.) The director's office would serve as a fund of institutional memory, so that we would not have to perpetually run around teaching ourselves what we already knew.

Second, this coordinating office must be endowed with sufficient authority to bring the government's warring agencies under control when a crisis emerges. That means a civilian equivalent of the CENT-COM commander should be appointed to take charge of postwar civil planning, coincident with and on a par with military planning.

Third, any standing organization devoted to nation-building should maintain ties with similar agencies in other countries. Although the international community has—through efforts in Somalia, Bosnia, and East Timor—gotten better at nation-building, it, too, lacks the means for preserving institutional memory, and could use American help.

Finally, the reconstruction effort must remain under clear civilian control as it moves from the first stage, stabilizing the region, to the second stage, creating self-sustaining institutions that will ultimately allow the United States a graceful exit. Decisions about how rapidly to turn over authority to local actors, what the sequence for political reform should be, and when and how to reduce aid levels and presence in a country cannot be left to the Department of Defense, which will always be biased in favor of a quick exit.

This bias will be of particular importance as the reconstruction of Iraq progresses. Donald Rumsfeld has articulated a strategy of nation-building "lite," involving a rapid transition to local control and a tough-love policy that leaves locals to find their own way toward good government and democracy. This is a dubious approach, at least if one cares about the final outcome. The new Iraqi government will be administratively weak and not regarded by its citizens as fully legitimate. It will be plagued by corruption and mismanagement, and riven by internal disagreements—witness the fight between the Iraqi Governing Council's Shia and non-Shia members over how to draft a new constitution. Nation-building requires a lot more than training police and military forces to take over from the United States: unless such forces are embedded in a strong framework of political parties, a judiciary, a civilian administration, and a rule of law, they will become mere pawns in the internal struggle for power. Nation-building "lite" risks being used as an intellectual justification for getting out, regardless of the mess we leave behind.

A standing U.S. government office to manage nation-building will be a hard sell politically, because we are still unreconciled to the idea that we are in the nation-building business for the long haul. However, international relations is no longer just a game played between great powers but one in which what happens inside smaller countries can have a huge effect on the rest of the world. Our "empire" may be a transitional one grounded in democracy and human rights, but our interests dictate that we learn how better to teach other people to govern themselves.

CONCLUSION

32

Dysfunctional Duopoly

Ted Halstead

An intellectual audit of the Democrats and the Republicans.

THIS YEAR MARKS the 150th anniversary of the rivalry between the Democratic and Republican Parties. Ever since 1854, when the implosion of the Whigs paved the way for the birth of the Republican Party (twenty-six years after the emergence of the Democrats), this rivalry has dominated and even defined American politics. Although the reign of these two parties has endured for well over half the life of our republic, it would be a mistake to assume that either party has remained consistent—or even recognizable.

Quick—which party stands for small government, states' rights, and laissez-faire economics? Which favors an activist federal government, public infrastructure projects, and expanded civil rights? Today the answers would be Republican and Democratic, respectively. Yet each party was founded on precisely the principles now associated with the other. And consider that the South, originally a stronghold of the Democrats, is now the anchor of the Republicans. But the most dramatic inversion in partisan identity is this: the Republicans in recent years have emerged as revolutionaries, while the Democrats have relegated themselves to defending tradition and the status quo.

The 150th anniversary of their rivalry provides an occasion for an intellectual audit of these two ever changing parties.

LET'S BEGIN WITH THE REPUBLICANS, who under President George W. Bush have become the party of big ideas. There is no denying the range and boldness of their initiatives, from privatizing Social Security to institutionalizing a doctrine of preventive warfare; from eliminating taxes on capital gains and dividends to pulling out of numerous international treaties; from encouraging school choice to remaking the Middle East. This boldness is in itself an anomaly for a party that in past decades has tended to revere inherited norms and institutions, but it is just one of the signs that this is not the Republican Party of George W.'s father. Indeed, its identity seems to have no clear lineage.

The modern Republican tradition is usually thought to have originated with the firebrand rhetoric of Barry Goldwater, which ultimately paved the way for the two-term presidency of Ronald Reagan. The Reagan revolution was built on three unifying principles: anti-communism, social conservatism, and limited government. The sudden end of the Cold War left the Republicans with only two of these principles around which to organize. But most Americans let it be known that they were not particularly interested in fighting domestic culture wars, much less in turning back the clock on newfound personal freedoms. The Republican Party's anti-government agenda, meanwhile, culminated in the Gingrich revolution of 1994, which sought to downsize all sorts of federal programs. To Newt Gingrich's surprise, the majority of Americans didn't really want a dramatic cutback in government programs and perceived his agenda as extremist.

George W. Bush is the first Republican President to recognize that the constituency for the Goldwater-Reagan-Gingrich anti-government crusade is dwindling—inspiring him to try to reposition his party. Although Bush calls his new and improved governing philosophy "compassionate conservatism," a more accurate description might be "big-spending conservatism."

Unlike Reagan, who shrank nondefense spending considerably and vetoed a number of spending bills in his first three years, Bush has so far increased total federal spending by a dizzying 20.4 percent and has yet to veto a single spending bill. The contrast is all the more dramatic when Bush is compared with Bill Clinton, who declared the end of big government, who in his first three years increased total government spending by only 3.5 percent, and who actually reduced discretionary spending by 8.8 percent. Clinton's Republican successor is quietly reversing course with a vengeance, leading the libertarian Cato Institute to accuse Bush of "governing like a Frenchman."

The President's reason for engineering this reversal, apparently, is to overcome the budgetary obstacles to parts of his agenda. For example, he seeks to privatize public services and enhance individual choice —school choice, retirement choice (through private Social Security accounts), and medical choice (through private health insurance instead of government-run programs). But moving from one-size-fits-all government programs to more-flexible privatized ones may require more public outlay, not less, than simply preserving the status quo. As the price for bringing competition into Medicare, for instance, Bush enacted a prescription-drug benefit that represents the largest expansion in entitlements since Lyndon Johnson's Great Society. And moving to private Social Security accounts would entail funding two entirely separate systems during the transition period.

Fighting the war on terrorism, too, is expensive. But rather than adjusting his agenda accordingly, Bush has pushed through three huge tax cuts in as many years. In the process he has fatally undermined the coherence of his overall program. Fusing vast new spending with deep tax cuts, Bush is locking into place long-term structural deficits whose costs to both our nation and the Republican Party would be difficult to overstate.

To understand why the Republican majority in Congress is playing along with the President, it helps to think of today's Republican Party as a theocracy; call it the Party of the Church. Under Bush the party is guided by a core ideology that it pursues with a near religious fervor, regardless of countervailing facts, changing circumstances, or even opposition among the conservative ranks. The President and his inner circle not only set the canon but demand—and usually get—strict compliance from Republican legislators in both houses of Congress. The two central tenets of Bush's orthodoxy are tax cuts and regime change in Iraq. He has staked the success of his presidency on them.

In the Party of the Church the theologians' role is played by hundreds of conservative scholars in think tanks, at publications, and on radio talk shows. That the academy is missing from this list is not an accident: conservative scholars could not find comfortable perches within university settings. But being banished from the academy served the Republican theologians remarkably well, because it enabled them to cultivate a style of argument and writing far better suited to reaching—and converting—both the public and politicians. The infrastructure of conservative thought is as well financed as it is complex; it includes seminaries in which to train conservative young scholars (the Heritage Foundation even has special dormitories for its interns), and what might be thought of as separate "orders," each upholding a slightly different school of thought—from the libertarians to the social conservatives to the neoconservatives. This sprawling idea machine produces not only policy innovations but also the language ("welfare queens," "the death tax") with which to sell the party's agenda.

Not surprisingly, the Party of the Church is highly moralistic. President Bush tends to frame issues in terms of ethical absolutes: good and evil, right and wrong. Moralism may or may not make for good politics, but it rarely makes for good policy, because it substitutes wishful and parochial thinking for careful analysis. Its ascendancy reflects a broader shift in the Republican Party—a shift away from an identity that was secular, pragmatic, and northeastern toward one that, like the President himself, is more evangelical and southern. Nowhere is this more evident than in foreign policy, where Bush—reviving what the historian Walter Russell Mead calls the Jacksonian tradition—is turning his back on both the realpolitik of Richard Nixon and the conservative internationalism of Reagan and his own father, making preemption rather than containment the central organizing principle and favoring unilateral action over multilateral diplomacy. In doing so Bush has discarded hundreds of years of international law and decades of American tradition. The most immediate cost is that the United States has alienated much of the world in the name of making it safe.

WHEN IT COMES TO economic orthodoxy, the Party of the Church is no more consistent with traditional Republican principles. Although the Republicans claim to be devoted to free markets, most of the big economic interests identified with the party are surprisingly dependent on federal subsidies, protectionism, or both. The most obvious examples are southern growers of cotton, sugar, oranges, and peanuts, and midwestern producers of grain. The Administration is so committed to shielding these interests from global competition that it elected to let the Cancún round of trade negotiations collapse—dealing a significant blow to the prospects for expanded free trade—rather than pressure Congress to reduce U.S. agricultural subsidies. In similar fashion, the Bush Administration supports lavish federal subsidies for a wide range of extractive industries (including oil, gas, and coal) and for cattle ranching.

No assessment of the modern Republican Party would be complete without a discussion of the elaborate mythology of supply-side economics, whose logic has been strained to the breaking point under Bush's watch. The basic supply-side argument is that tax cuts increase the incentive to work, save, and invest, which boosts economic growth. During the Reagan years such logic was used to argue that slashing tax rates would actually increase tax revenues, by producing additional growth—but this has long since been dismissed by mainstream economists and shown false by the record of history. The party also uses supply-side economics to justify tax cuts that are disproportionately skewed in favor of the well-to-do, on the grounds that they are the most likely to save and invest. This argument has always been suspect, and it is even less credible in the aftermath of the technology bubble; the economic woes of the past few years have been due not to lack of investment but, rather, to an excess of capacity.

By sticking with the old supply-side formula—cut taxes as often as possible, especially for the wealthy—Bush has delivered a particularly costly and inefficient stimulus package to help the nation out of its economic downturn. And the Administration seems to recognize as much, given that it has hedged its bets by marrying large supply-side tax cuts with equally large demand-side spending increases, yielding an odd hybrid that might be called "supply-side Keynesianism." This contradictory policy suggests that not even Republicans still believe in the magic of their standard fix. Yet they are not about to abandon the myth. It is far too sacrosanct and convenient an article of faith in the Republican canon.

A major risk in combining moralism and policy, evidently, is that dogma often trumps intellectual honesty. This is particularly clear in the case of official claims that the Administration's overall economic agenda is aimed at helping middle-class families. A more candid articulation of its domestic-policy vision appeared in a June 2003 *Washington Post* op-ed article by Grover Norquist, one of the most influential of conservative strategists. "The new Republican policy is an annual tax cut," Norquist wrote; he predicted that Bush would proceed step by step to abolish estate and capital-gains taxes altogether, to exempt all savings from taxation, and to move the nation to a flat tax on wages only. Implicit in this vision is not only a grand contradiction—cutting taxes while raising spending is unsustainable—but also a significant shift in the burden of taxation from the wealthy to the working class and the poor. Apparently the contemporary Republican Party does remain faithful to at least one old conservative belief, which Clinton Rossiter, in his book *Conservatism in America*, described nearly fifty years ago as "the inevitability and necessity of social classes."

FOR ITS PART, the Democratic Party suffers from a different sort of incoherence: plagued by constant squabbling among the interest groups that make up its base, it cannot agree on a clear message or purpose. The sheer breadth of the Democratic coalition is remarkable: it includes organized labor, teachers' and other public employees' unions, environmentalists, racial minorities (especially African-Americans), Hollywood, trial lawyers, the gray lobby, the gay lobby, civil libertarians, pro-choice activists, and a good bit of Wall Street. Although this breadth might seem to be an asset for the Democrats, all these groups are veto-wielding factions when it comes to their respective chunks of the policy turf. This can be downright paralyzing.

If the Republicans are now the Party of the Church, then the Democrats are the Party of the Chieftains. They treat an election almost like a parade: groups that otherwise have little in common come together every year or two, only to return to their niches afterward. The multiplicity of purpose is all the more evident when the party is out of office. During his eight-year presidency Clinton relied on his political skill and charisma—and the benefits of a growing economy—to keep most Democratic factions happy and essentially reading from the same playbook.

When Bush took office, however, the deep tensions among the Democrats resurfaced. For instance, take the relationship between Wall

Street and Main Street. Under the New Deal, when U.S. industry was little challenged by competition from abroad, workers and owners of capital managed to reach common ground on a number of issues, from workers' rights to basic benefits. But the subsequent globalization of manufacturing and services led to the collapse of this alliance. Thus whereas Wall Street and some high-tech firms favor financial liberalization, copyright protection, balanced budgets, and a strong dollar (to make imported goods less expensive), working-class Americans want curbs on job flight, tougher international labor standards, strengthened safety nets, and a weaker dollar (to boost exports of the goods they manufacture). The fiercer the global competition, the fiercer the tension between these traditional Democratic camps. The party is just as torn on social issues: Hollywood, members of minorities, and civil libertarians favor identity politics, social liberalism, and political correctness, whereas this agenda tends to offend the sensibilities of working-class white men.

In the run-up to this year's primaries, the tensions among the Democratic Chieftains have culminated in an all-out struggle for their party's soul, with one camp claiming to represent the "Democratic wing" and another claiming to represent the "electable wing." Although the feuding is over style as well as substance, at least three issues clearly divide left and center: the left is resolutely against the war in Iraq, whereas the center defends it (though averring that it should have been conducted in a more multilateral fashion); the left wants to repeal all Bush's tax cuts, whereas the center favors repealing only some; and the left is wary of unregulated free trade, whereas the center embraces free trade and globalization. In many ways this is a battle over the Clinton legacy. Clintonian centrists fear that the party's new image on welfare, crime, free trade, foreign policy, and fiscal policy—which they worked so hard to establish—will be undermined by a nominee from the party's left.

Fiscal responsibility is another major source of tension within the Democratic Party. Ever since Clinton salvaged the party's credibility in this area, Democrats have tried to build on that new reputation. But those efforts produced two serious problems for the party, one short-term and one longer-term. Over the past three years, while the economy was weak, it may have been a mistake for the Democrats to hew to a policy of fiscal rectitude—especially when it prevented them from thinking creatively about a temporary stimulus package. Maintaining fiscal discipline over the longer term, however, is truly important. Yet it is unclear whether the Democrats will be able to do so given all the programs the various Chieftains are demanding. The race for the Democratic presidential nomination has thrown this conflict into sharp relief. All the contenders cite fiscal prudence as grounds for repealing some or all of Bush's tax cuts—but all then propose to spend the money thus recouped on everything from expanding health insurance to improving schools. From a budgetary perspective there is no difference between decreasing public revenue through tax cuts and increasing public spending through new programs. The Democrats could argue that theirs is a more compassionate form of fiscal irresponsibility (it's better to have health insurance for children than tax cuts for the rich), but they can't argue that they're being any more fiscally responsible than George Bush.

Regardless of who emerges as the Democratic nominee or which camp he hails from, the bulk of his agenda may be disturbingly predictable and backward-looking. Given the power of the Chieftains, it is almost a certainty that the Democratic candidate in 2004 will be against school choice (to appease teachers' unions) and Social Security reform (the gray lobby), and in favor of affirmative action (minorities) and employer-based health care (organized labor). In these and other ways he will be a defender of the status quo. As Al Sharpton recently put it, approvingly, the Democrats are now the true conservatives.

IN ITS LEGITIMATE DESIRE to preserve the achievements of the New Deal and the Great Society, the Democratic Party has become trapped in the past, routinely defending antiquated industrial-era programs even when these no longer serve their original ends. George Santayana once defined fanaticism as redoubling your efforts when you have forgotten your aim. Democrats are no fanatics, but they are increasingly guilty of confusing ends and means. Consider employer-based health insurance. The link between health insurance and employment was an accident of history, devised in a bygone era when spending one's working lifetime with a single company was the norm. Now that most Americans change employers every couple of years, does it make sense to rely on a system that forces one to change insurers—or, worse, risk losing coverage— every time? And when it comes to protecting Social Security, the Democrats are waging a battle against immutable demographic forces: a program that originated when working-age Americans far outnumbered retirees cannot remain essentially unchanged in a rapidly aging society.

Underlying this abdication of new thinking is a still more troubling liability: the Party of the Chieftains does not trust the American people to make responsible choices for themselves. Although the Democrats are known as the "pro-choice" party, the kinds of choice they are most eager to defend are in the private realm—reproduction and lifestyle. When it comes to the public sphere (where your child goes to school, or how to invest your Social Security contributions), the Democrats tend to oppose expanding individual choice, largely because some of the leading Chieftains fear that it would weaken their own influence. The Chieftains' reluctance also derives in part from a fear that public programs with more options would undermine equity; but it's possible to devise creative new programs to enhance flexibility and fairness at the same time. Regardless of their reasons, in resisting the expansion of individual choice, a sine qua non of any successful information-age politics, the Democrats have positioned themselves on the wrong side of history.

This inability to advance creative policy solutions hints at yet another problem for the Democrats: the Party of the Chieftains is so busy playing defense that it has forgotten how to play offense. When the Republicans were in the minority during the early Clinton years, they introduced one bold proposal after another—never expecting that these would pass in the short run, but hoping to galvanize the party and set precedents for the future. To a considerable degree this worked. In contrast, the Democrats have spent the past three years turning timidity into an art form, allowing President Bush to set the terms of the debate and confining themselves to criticizing his agenda rather than venturing one of their own. This is the case even in the foreign policy arena: other than vague calls for multilateralism and diplomacy, it's unclear how a Democratic grand strategy would differ from the President's.

In short, the Democrats have failed utterly to replenish the intellectual capital on which any party's success ultimately hinges. Whereas the Republicans can turn to large, multi-issue think tanks for guidance and inspiration, the Democrats have mainly single-issue groups—environmentalists, civil-rights activists, women's-rights activists—with neither the capacity nor the incentive to forge a greater whole. The flimsiness and Balkanization of the Democratic intellectual infrastructure owes much to the proclivities of progressive philanthropies, which are far more likely to invest in grassroots demonstration programs than in the war of ideas, and which tend to award grants that are strictly limited to particular subject areas, thereby discouraging cross-pollination. Lacking other options, most liberal scholars therefore gravitate to the academy—which actually inhibits them from shaping the public debate. As academic disciplines become ever more specialized, professors are encouraged to publish in esoteric journals—whose only audience is other professors—rather than in the popular press. Whereas conservative scholars have influence far out of proportion to their numbers, liberal scholars have numbers far out of proportion to their influence.

Not only is the Party of the Chieftains at a loss for new ideas, but it lacks a language for defending its core values. In part this is because the Chieftains like to describe their respective constituencies as victims in order to secure concessions from a party that tends to root for the underdog. Republicans, in contrast, are likely to address citizens as if they were all just around the corner from becoming millionaires. This creates a perception that the Republicans are the party of winners and the Democrats the party of losers.

During the Great Depression, when it was painfully obvious that citizens were vulnerable to forces beyond their control, it was easier for a Democratic leader such as FDR to craft a message of collective well-being—that all Americans would be better off if each American were given a helping hand by the government. Nowadays American culture increasingly emphasizes the opposite message: that individuals are to blame for their own problems. Yet the profound dislocations caused by globalization and technological change make the need for an overarching vision of a better society just as urgent as it was in FDR's time.

"THE SUCCESS OF A PARTY," Woodrow Wilson claimed, "means little except when the nation is using that party for a large and definite purpose." By this standard both the Party of the Church and the Party of the Chieftains are failures. The Republicans are handicapped by an ideology holding that it is somehow possible to pursue big-spending conservatism at home and an interventionist military program abroad while cutting taxes repeatedly. The Democrats, meanwhile, are paralyzed by the micro-agendas of numerous feuding factions. Both parties wear straitjackets of their own design.

The American people deserve better—and they know it, to judge by the legions of self-described "independents." Fortunately, our major parties are mere vessels; the principles, agendas, and coalitions they contain can vary dramatically from decade to decade. It is just a matter of time, history suggests, until both parties are reinvented. Let us hope they will improve.

Contributors

Geneive Abdo is an Adjunct Fellow at the New America Foundation and a staff writer at *The Chicago Tribune.*

Ricardo Bayon is a Fellow at the New America Foundation.

Katherine Boo is a Senior Fellow at the New America Foundation and a staff writer at *The New Yorker.*

Ray Boshara is director of the Asset Building Program at the New America Foundation.

Shannon Brownlee is a Senior Fellow at the New America Foundation.

Michael Calabrese is vice-president, director of the Spectrum Policy Program, and co-director of the Retirement Security Program at the New America Foundation.

James Fallows is chairman of the New America Foundation's Board of Directors, a national correspondent for *The Atlantic Monthly,* and the author of numerous books.

Noah Feldman is a Fellow at the New America Foundation, an assistant professor at New York University School of Law, the author of *After Jihad: America and the Struggle for Islamic Democracy,* and he was the senior adviser for constitutional law to the Coalition Provisional Authority in Iraq.

David Friedman is a Senior Fellow at the New America Foundation and a contributing editor at the *Los Angeles Times*.

Francis Fukuyama is the Bernard L. Schwartz Professor of International Political Economy at the Paul H. Nitze School of Advanced International Studies, Johns Hopkins University, a member of the New America Foundation's Board of Directors, and author of numerous books, including *State-Building: Governance and World Order in the 21st* Century.

Jacob Hacker is a Fellow at the New America Foundation, the Peter Strauss Family Assistant Professor at Yale University, and the author of two books, including *The Divided Welfare State: The Battle over Public and Private Social Benefits in the United States*.

Ted Halstead is founding president and CEO of the New America Foundation and co-author with Michael Lind of *The Radical Center: The Future of American Politics*.

Karen Kornbluh is director of the Work & Family Program at the New America Foundation.

Michael Lind is the Whitehead Senior Fellow and director of the American Strategy Program at the New America Foundation, as well as the author of numerous books, including *What Lincoln Thought: The Values and Convictions of America's Greatest President*.

Phillip Longman is a Senior Fellow at the New America Foundation and the author of three books, including *The Empty Cradle: Freedom and Fertility in an Aging World*.

Maya MacGuineas is director of the Fiscal Policy Program and co-director of the Retirement Security Program at the New America Foundation.

Matthew Miller, a Fellow at the Center for American Progress, is a syndicated columnist and a consultant, and the author of *The Two Percent Solution: Fixing America's Problems in Ways Liberals and Conservatives Can Love*.

James Pinkerton is a Fellow at the New America Foundation and a columnist at *Newsday.*

Jedediah Purdy is a Fellow at the New America Foundation and the author of two books, most recently *Being America: Liberty, Commerce, and Violence in an American World.*

Jonathan Rauch is a correspondent for *The Atlantic Monthly,* a senior writer at *National Journal,* and the author of numerous books, including *Government's End: Why Washington Stopped Working.*

Gregory Rodriguez is a Senior Fellow at the New America Foundation and the author of a forthcoming book on the coming of post-minority America.

Laurie Rubiner is director of the Universal Health Insurance Program at the New America Foundation.

Sherle Schwenninger is director of the Fellowship Program and co-director of the Global Economic Policy Program at the New America Foundation, as well as a Senior Fellow at the World Policy Institute.

J.H. Snider is a Fellow and co-director of the Spectrum Policy Program at the New America Foundation.

Paul Starobin is a contributing editor for *The Atlantic Monthly* and a staff correspondent for *National Journal.*

Margaret Talbot is a Senior Fellow at the New America Foundation and a staff writer at *The New Yorker.*

Jennifer Washburn is a Fellow at the New America Foundation and author of a forthcoming book on the commercialization of higher education.

Acknowledgments

IN WRITING AND COMPILING this manuscript, my greatest debt is to its brilliant contributors, most of whom I have the honor of working with on a day to day basis in their capacity as Fellows, staff, or Board members of the New America Foundation. Their camaraderie, originality of thought, and profound commitment to improving our country is a constant source of inspiration for me.

Two of my colleagues at New America deserve special recognition for their indispensable roles in bringing this book to life. Sherle Schwenninger proved himself to be an outstanding ally in shaping and editing several of the pieces. Indeed, many of the authors, including myself, owe him a huge intellectual debt. I am also particularly grateful to John Mangin for the diligent assistance, editorial skill, and critical insight he provided.

This book grew out of two strategic partnerships that New America forged in recent years—one with *The Atlantic Monthly* and one with Perseus Books—each of which have been extremely important to our ongoing institutional success.

I am greatly indebted to David Bradley, chairman and owner of Atlantic Media, who first envisioned the State of the Union collaboration between New America and *The Atlantic*, and under whose ownership *The Atlantic*, a great magazine for nearly 150 years, has achieved new heights. I owe no less a debt to Frank Pearl, chairman of Perseus Books, whose support and imagination has made the New America/ Basic Books Imprint a reality. These two men have done as much as anyone to save a place for serious and high-minded writing in the increasingly frivolous world of magazine and book publishing.

I am grateful to the remarkable staff of *The Atlantic Monthly*, especially managing editor Cullen Murphy, a marvel who has guided *The Atlantic* for twenty years now, and whose keen editorial vision is reflected throughout these pages, and senior editor Scott Stossel, whose skill with the red pen is unsurpassed. Working alongside Cullen and Scott has been one of the great joys of the State of the Union project.

Next I would like to thank Liz MacGuire, publisher of Basic Books, Joann Miller, our editor there, and editorial assistant Ellen Garrison. Their guidance and encouragement at every stage of the process has helped to make this a far better book.

Since the publication of *The Real State of the Union* coincides with the fifth anniversary of the New America Foundation, I would also like to take this opportunity to express my profound gratitude to the foundations and individual donors who believed in New America in the early years. None of New America's success over the past five years would have been possible without their generous support.

On the foundation side, these include: the Annie E. Casey Foundation, the Arca Foundation, Atlantic Philanthropies, the California Physicians' Service Foundation, Casey Family Programs, the Charles and Helen Schwab Foundation, the Charles Stewart Mott Foundation, the David and Lucile Packard Foundation, the Florence and John Schumann Foundation, the Ford Foundation, the James Irvine Foundation, the John D. and Catherine T. MacArthur Foundation, the John Merck Fund, Joy Family Foundation, the Joyce Foundation, the Markle Foundation, the Nathan Cummings Foundation, the Open Society Institute, Pew Charitable Trusts, Rockefeller Brothers Fund, the Rockefeller Foundation, the Smith Richardson Foundation, the Surdna Foundation, the Wallace Global Fund, the William and Flora Hewlett Foundation, and the Turner Foundation. On the individual donor side, they include: Gregory & Anne Avis, Eric A. Benhamou, Scott M. Delman, Peter Derby, Tommy Jacks, Norman & Lyn Lear, Lenny T. Mendonca, Constance Milstein, Steven Rattner & Maureen White, Eric Schmidt, and John C. Whitehead, among others.

TH

Index